Manufacturing
WORKS

The Vital Link Between Production and Prosperity

Fred Zimmerman AND Dave Beal

Dearborn™
Trade Publishing
A **Kaplan Professional** Company

Senior Acquisitions Editor: Jean Iversen
Senior Managing Editor: Jack Kiburz
Interior Design: Lucy Jenkins
Cover Design: Scott Rattray, Rattray Design
Typesetting: the dotted i

02 03 04 10 9 8 7 6 5 4 3 2 1

Library of Congress Cataloging-in-Publication Data

Zimmerman, Fred, 1935-
    Manufacturing works : the vital link between production and prosperity
/ Fred Zimmerman and Dave Beal.
        p.   cm.
    Includes bibliographical references and index.
    ISBN 0-7931-5198-8
    1. Industrial productivity—United States.   2. Industrial productivity—
Developing countries.   3. United States—Economic conditions—1981-2001.
4. Developing countries—Economic conditions.   5. Manufacturing industries—
United States.   6. Manufacturing industries—Developing countries.
7. Comparative economics.   I. Beal, Dave, 1939-   II. Title.
HC110.I52 Z56 2002
338.4'767—dc21

                                                                    2002000194

DEDICATION

To our wives, Joanell and Caroline.

To our children, Fred, Carita, Christina, Brigitte, Hans, Nancy, Robert, James, Gregory, Susan, and Jeffrey.

To our grandchildren and foster children. And to all of the people in manufacturing, and to those who believe in them.

Contents

Prologue   ix
Acknowledgments   xiii

PART ONE Production Means Prosperity

1. Unsung Achievements   3
   Prosperity Is Not without Pain   7
   Foreign Trade—Fueled by Success   8
   Getting Out Manufacturing's Story   10
   U.S. Manufacturing: Still Good—But not Alone   11

2. Where the Money Is   17
   The Rewards of Adding Value   22
   Productivity and Output   24
   Foreign Producers Follow Money and Opportunity   28

3. Indiana: Jitters in Comeback Land   31
   Seeding the Rebound   34
   The Battle Over Steel   37
   Contrarian Approach Helps Region   41
   Sources of Anxiety Remain   42

PART TWO Changing Geography and What It Means

4. The Relocation of Industry   49
   Relocation: A Combination of Attracting and Repelling Forces   56
   Repelling Forces   57
   Attracting Forces   60
   The Important Variable—The Company Itself   62

5. Counties Gaining Momentum   64
   Hinterland Highspots   64

Freeway Flyers   68
Metro Movers   70
Gradual Growers   73
Special Cases   76
Manufacturing in Search of Good Places   79

6. Counties Losing Momentum   82
   Sliding Goliaths   85
   Midrange Sliders   88
   Smaller Sliders   91

7. Big-City Blues—Philadelphia and Beyond   95
   A City's Glorious History   96
   Urban Industrial Decline—A Multitude of Whys   105
   Troubles in Other Core Cities   106
   Could Industry Come Back?   108

8. Manufacturing and Community Prosperity   111
   Jobs versus Poverty   111
   Manufacturing and Taxes   114
   Manufacturing and Income Disparity   115

PART THREE Coping in a World Economy

9. A Deeper Look at the Trade Deficit   119
   Balance Slipping in Key Industries   120
   Larger Deficits in Key Industries   122
   Deficits with Whom?   125
   China and the Pacific Rim   127
   Contrasting Experiences   128
   A Tale of Two Neighbors   130
   How the Dollar Counts   133

10. Globalization and the Transfer of Skills   136
    The Big Problem with the Trade Deficit   138
    Suppliers Are Key Building Blocks   140
    Shrinking and Shifting Economies of Scale   143
    Has Outsourcing Gone Too Far?   144

11. The Shifting Defense-Industrial Base   150

12. Investment: Booster Shot from Abroad   158

PART FOUR A Sector Still at Risk

13. Factories: An Unspoken Word   169
    Runaway NIMBYism? 170
    Even Desirable Growth Is Hard to Sell 172
    Engineering—Out of Favor Here, In Favor Overseas 173
    Snubbed 175
    Aging Industrial Professionals 176
    Factories—Good Places to Work 177

14. The Darker Side of Merger Mania   178
    Today's Mergers—Bigger and More Disparate Than Ever 182
    Two Kinds of Mergers 184
    The Search for a Managerial Model 188

15. Wanted: Better Leaders   191
    The Need for a Noble Purpose 192
    Managers People Can Read 194
    The Importance of Stewardship 197

PART FIVE Staying on the Edge

16. Wall Street: Return to Sanity?   201
    The Cost of the National Crap Shoot 206
    Is Going Private the Answer? 208

17. Driving Innovation: Manufacturing and Research   211
    Constructing Research Triangle Park 212
    Teflon and Green Clean 222

18. Partnerships That Work   225

19. Raising the Odds for a Better Tomorrow   232
    Sudden Changes Can Jolt Counties 233
    A Warning on Competitiveness 235
    Many Bright Spots 236
    Identifying the Small Knobs 237
    An America without Manufacturing 241

    Appendix A—Methodology for Choosing the
       County Groups   247
    Counties Gaining Momentum 247
    Counties Losing Momentum 248
    Census Bureau Shift from the SIC System to the NAICS Methodology 249

Appendix B—Detailed Statistics on Sample Counties   250
Appendix C—Manufacturing Organizations   261
Bibliography   267
Index   283
About the Authors   297

Prologue

America was in a sharp recession in 1990–1991. Journalists, politicians, professors, and consultants blamed American manufacturers. They said cheap foreign labor, automation, and consolidation were flattening U.S. producers.

They argued that Japan Inc. and Germany Resurgent had done it right and the United States had done it wrong. Thus, they said, America was in for sustained hard times.

In those dark and doubtful days, this book took root. In the years that followed, it turned out that American manufacturing didn't just shrivel up and go away. The scope of production, from the tractors made at John Deere's factories to Dick Conrow's tool-and-die shop in northern Indiana, was too vast and too essential to disappear.

In fact, our research, factory visits, and interviews taught us that American manufacturing has grown more productive in recent years. For sure, keeping the factories going has not been easy. The country's manufacturers are burdened with a daunting array of vulnerabilities, sometimes self-inflicted by their own managements. Managers face difficult challenges from producers abroad, and they have to comply with regulations not always enforced elsewhere. Yet, American workers still make things, many things, that are the best in the world. At the end of the day, making things—from instruments to engine blocks—remains embedded in our national work culture and is essential to our prosperity.

Curiously, we found that U.S. manufacturers did not get much credit for the good times of the 1990s. Mere mention of the word *manufacturing* frequently stirs images of layoffs, shuttered plants, unskilled workers, dirty floors, and faded glory. This vision, enhanced by the technology stock bubble of the late 1990s and the rapid growth of service jobs in recent years, held promise for greater opportunity in nonindustrial sectors. Frequently, though, such service work is done by manufacturers or through their complex networks of service providers. The rush to endorse the new economy, often diminishing the role of our industrial sector, became much less persuasive as the country fell into an economic recession in 2001.

BEHIND THE DATA

Manufacturing is subtly, almost invisibly, woven deeply into the U.S. economy. At auto dealerships, employees rebuild cars and parts. At banks and insurance companies, print shop workers turn out brochures and financial statements. At distribution centers, lift-truck operators rumble through the aisles picking and stacking goods. Watching them go about their work may well give the sense of being in a factory. Yet, the federal government views these jobs as outside the manufacturing sector. We use the government's job classifications for the purpose of this book, even though these occasionally change. These classifications say that employers must be engaged principally in the production of tangible products.

Seeking to get at the stories behind our data, we talked with managers, workers, and others holding stakes in the manufacturing sector. We went to the principal regions of the country and viewed firsthand manufacturing on other continents. In counties away from a state's major metropolitan areas, we found many factories doing well. In the larger cities, we saw the distress of layoffs and shutdowns. Where manufacturers were succeeding, so were their communities. Where they were faring less well, cities and towns were often slipping. Everywhere, we saw close links between production and prosperity.

We have organized our material into five parts. The first part is an overview of the U.S. industrial scene. Part Two examines the striking contrasts we found between counties. Part Three explores our trade deficit and other aspects of today's global economy. In Part Four, we look at the negatives facing U.S. manufacturers. We conclude in Part Five by considering the positives.

Throughout our project, we unearthed substantial data to support the fact that manufacturing is one of the biggest forces behind the U.S.

economy's successes in recent years. Roughly 17 million Americans work for manufacturers, slightly fewer than a generation ago. The service and retail workforces have grown at the same time that industrial productivity has risen, so that only one of every seven jobs is in manufacturing today versus one in three in 1960. Yet, American manufacturers still generate rising output, drive exports, pay good wages and benefits, spark most of the country's innovation, and provide immigrants with their first jobs. They still set the pace for making the American economy more productive.

America's challenge is to maintain a competitive economy, sensitive to demand and capital markets. Then, if the country supports its factories with education, transportation, utilities, and public services, U.S. manufacturers will be better equipped to respond to customers' needs and thus to survive and prosper in their communities. This is the way it was with the emergence of American agriculture and railroads more than a century ago. It's true of tool-and-die makers and instrument makers today, even though these craftsmen may be using computers as well as acetylene torches and precision machines.

The need for prosperity has been apparent through history. And, manufacturing still matters, if we care enough to consider its importance. That is the overriding reason for this book.

Acknowledgments

 The contributors to this book include academics, journalists, professionals, people we met on our travels through factories, and the beloved members of our own families. It would be impossible for us to mention them all just as it would be beyond the scope of Ford, 3M, or Deere to recognize all the people who contribute so meaningfully to the creation and production of the goods those companies make. But we would like to single out a few people as particularly helpful.

Bob Werner, of the University of St. Thomas Geography Department, offered much help to us in formatting complex geographic material. David Hall, the Pulliam Professor of Journalism at DePauw University, gave us many useful suggestions for personalizing the data, focusing our ideas, and writing concisely. Professors John Adams and Ed Schuh, of the University of Minnesota's Humphrey Institute, provided needed advice on how we could better address the myriad of research imperatives that surfaced as we analyzed 30 years of data from thousands of governments and companies. Chris Worthington, Senior Editor for Business and Technology at the St. Paul Pioneer Press, cleared the way for us to publish in that newspaper a special report on manufacturing that helped develop our ideas for a broad audience. Art Rolnick, of the Federal Reserve Bank of Minneapolis, provided both welcome humor and access to some of the most useful research. Stock market historian Steve Leuthold supplied financial data and explanations illuminating securities market trends. Graham Toft, an economic development specialist in Indiana, helped us ferret out important considerations not always present in the data.

We are also indebted to our many friends who cheerfully escorted us through their factories and provided us with valuable insights into the inner workings of an industrial economy. They include Red Heitkamp of Remmele Engineering, Keith Busse of Steel Dynamics, Tony Johnson of Dura Automotive, Gary Gately of Porter-Cable, Dick Peterson of Ford, Dane Miller of Biomet, Dick Conrow of C&A Tool, Bill Kuban of Kurt Manufacturing, Fred Berdaas of Bermo, and Bob Olson of Winnebago. It would not have been possible for us to write this book without them.

We benefited from the wisdom of people living in the communities we described and analyzed. Especially helpful were Frank Maguire in Philadelphia, Lincoln Schrock in Fort Wayne, Bob Cook in Tennessee, Shelia Dunigan in North Carolina, and Frank Riley in Connecticut. Riley took the time to write several letters updating us on the status of U.S. industry and the state of its technology. These were precious contributions.

Our employers, the University of St. Thomas and the Pioneer Press, also helped—perhaps more than they initially intended. Both remained supportive as our project grew in scope and depth and came to span nearly a decade. Special thanks are due to Dr. Ron Bennett, Chair of the Engineering Department at the University of St. Thomas, Reverend Dennis Dease, President, and Quentin Hietpas, Vice President of External Affairs, for their enthusiastic moral support and their creative ideas for external funding.

We received grants from the Bauervic Foundation in Michigan and the McKnight Foundation in Minnesota, which were critical in providing us with significantly more time and resources to pursue our project.

Several librarians helped us greatly—especially Eric Kallas, of the University of St. Thomas Library system, and Steve Plumb, of the Hill Reference Library.

And we are indebted to Jean Iversen, our editor at Dearborn, for her competence and resourcefulness in helping us to improve our manuscript.

Finally, our families deserve special mention. Neither family is small. One author has six children, the other five. During the course of our effort, we engaged in countless late-night conversations and debates about this book. We also worked through 14 graduations, 4 weddings, and the birth of 4 grandchildren. Our spouses began to wonder if we would ever finish, but they remained consistently cheerful and encouraging. Both Joanell and Caroline did heavy duty in shouldering family responsibilities, tasks we should have taken on more often. They also provided valuable critiques, which often influenced what we emphasized in the manuscript. They were wonderful, and remain so every minute of every day.

Production Means Prosperity

This book advocates a simple premise: manufacturing provides a vital link to prosperity. But not everyone believes that. In fact, the manufacturing sector has become the invisible economy to many of us. Other parts of the economy have commanded more attention—for example, finance and services, and subsectors such as software and Internet-related companies. Yet, manufacturing remains enormously important. The industrial sector is special because of its size, its ability to generate value, its role in meeting people's wants and needs, and the dignity of the work it provides for millions of Americans.

Part One embarks on that journey by scrutinizing the data and by getting out to the front lines to talk with the people who make manufacturing work:

Chapter 1 defines and describes the often-unheralded accomplishments of manufacturing and considers why there is such confusion about this sector.

Chapter 2 analyzes which parts of manufacturing contribute the most to prosperity.

Chapter 3 reaches beyond the data to tell the story of northeastern Indiana, a region whose recent comeback and current concerns say so much about the state of American manufacturing today.

CHAPTER 1

Unsung Achievements

 Mansour Mohamed had a bright idea. Couldn't machines be designed to knit and weave textile fibers into three-dimensional composite materials stronger than steel and lighter than aluminum? Couldn't the materials then be used to fashion a kaleidoscopic array of products, from I-beams to protective vests, from artificial limbs to bridge materials to parts for cars, buses, trains, and planes?

Mohamed pursued his dream, initially with uneven results. He and his school, North Carolina State University, landed $100,000 in federal money to build a prototype of his looms. They got the machine patented. However, Mohamed couldn't convince manufacturers to license the technology, so he started his own company to make the machines. Raising money was an uphill battle. Investors were riveting their attention on Internet, software, and telecommunications startups. Helping a weaving specialist for a textile industry startup seemed, well, old-fashioned. For two years, he was the only employee.

Then an unlikely alliance took shape. Mohamed needed a partner, someone with more managerial experience in manufacturing. He turned to an acquaintance, Brad Lienhart, who agreed to run the company. Both men had engineering degrees, but in other ways they could not have been more different. Mohamed was born in Egypt. He emigrated to the United States in 1980, then, as a textile engineering professor, watched American industry from the outside. Lienhart was raised on a farm in central Illinois, where he sold farm equipment parts when he was seven years old and drove a $10,000 combine three years later. He spent 28 years rising into the inner circle of top executives at Dow Chemical, then retired, at age 50 in 1994, with a mission of starting a company.

But did he really want to launch a *manufacturer,* in the heyday of the so-called dot-com age? Exactly.

It's far too early to say how much success the company, known as 3Tex, will achieve in the long run. However, by late 2000, 3Tex had grown to 45 employees. The company opened a plant in the shadows of shuttered textile factories in Rutherfordton, an economically depressed community in western North Carolina. It raised more than $10 million in three rounds of financing, and built up a customer list that included Ford and Johnson & Johnson. Don't be surprised, advises Lienhart. Over the last century, he explains, the United States has gone from an agrarian society to the industrial era to the information age. Now, he contends, that latter era probably has peaked. Lienhart argues that a better way to view the nation's economic evolution is to recognize that we never fully left those earlier times; rather, we laid one era atop another, like the chapters of a book. "Material technology is the future," he declares. By that, he means composites, ceramics, nanotechnology products, micro devices, biochemistry, and pharmaceuticals.

What about the *new economy,* a term that stamps this era as a time of immense productivity gains believed to be spurred on by emergence of digital technology? Heavy use of the term suggests that all prior time must be designated as an *old economy* era. "That irritates the heck out of me," says Lienhart. "Companies that make products and make a profit—I don't buy the concept that's old."

The new economy mantra led to frequent stereotyping of businesses as "old economy companies" or "new economy companies." Many manufacturers were arbitrarily tossed into the former category. That tended to stigmatize them as investors piled into Internet-related opportunities. Facile labels—new economy, service economy, information economy—play well in the media. Often, users employ these terms as euphemisms for a transformation from a manufacturing-dependent system to a higher-performance economy where manufacturing is assumed to be fading into the history books.

"Manufacturing firms do not equate to old economy firms," Bob McTeer, president of the Federal Reserve Bank of Dallas and a leading observer of the new economy concept, told the board of the National Association of Manufacturers (NAM) in October of 2000. "Your productivity growth has led the nation's. You've been applying high tech to production for a long time. You know the game . . . whatever widgets look like years from now, we'll still want them."

That, in a nutshell, is the basis for this book. Look around the room you are sitting in; the rooms nearby; the vehicle in the garage; the buildings down the road; your schools, airports, stadiums, and shopping centers. At every turn, you will see tangible products, more of them and more varieties, than ever before. If there is a new economy, certainly it must include them.

| *Manufacturing firms do not equate to old economy firms.*

We think the enthusiasm espoused by many new economy advocates has too often given rise to a widespread sense that digital technology trumps hard work and makes the mastery of trades and skills less necessary. The term itself became so beguiling that it led many managers of "new economy companies" to a false sense of superiority. Good management is hard work, whether you are managing a garbage dump or a wireless provider. And, as venture capitalist Andy Kessler pointed out soon after the dot-com bubble burst, manufacturers are an essential part of the digital age. In fact, Kessler argues, some of the companies that make the "picks and shovels" used to build the Internet will have an edge over the long haul, because they offer something Internet service companies lack—physical products with intellectual property that can be defined and protected.

Ironically, at the very time the infatuation with the Internet became most intense, American manufacturing was setting the pace for the American economy. We think this performance is remarkable, given the stress this sector has been under and the degree to which it is misunderstood.

| *Some of the companies that make the "picks and shovels" used to build the Internet will have an edge over the long haul, because they offer something Internet service companies lack—physical products with intellectual property that can be defined and protected.*

Measuring this misunderstanding is an elusive task, but one indication of the concern has come from the NAM. In 1995, the association embarked on a broad outreach program to boost Americans' understanding of manufacturing. Five years later, the NAM concluded it needed to do more. Its chairman, W.R. Timken Jr., led the association's officials on a 30-city barnstorming tour designed to convince opinion leaders in the media, the investment community, and other influential fields, of the merits of manufacturing.

It should not be surprising that both the media and financial firms need a refresher course in manufacturing. The control centers for the nation's media and investment communities are in New York City, where some of the deepest plunges in manufacturing activity have occurred. It was not much of a leap for publishers, editors, reporters, producers, television anchors, investment bankers, portfolio managers, traders, and securities analysts to conclude that manufacturing is heading into the history books. After all, their perceptions of manufacturing were shaped by what they saw every day—abandoned factories, vacant brownfields, few modern plants. There is far more manufacturing activity elsewhere, but they had little direct contact with it. Yet, in areas far from the nation's epicenters of finance and publishing, manufacturing was growing, prospering, and adding life to communities.

The role of manufacturing in the 1990s was immense. Consider production. The manufacturing sector grew by 47 percent from 1992 to 2000, according to the U.S. Department of Commerce's estimate of gross domestic product by industry. Durable goods production—for example, autos, airplanes, and data processing equipment—rose 73 percent over this period. *Fortune* magazine cites figures from the United Nations Industrial Development Organization that show the value of American-made goods in 1998 was 50 percent higher than Japan's total, and greater than the combined output of France, Germany, and the United Kingdom. "No major industrial nation matched the U.S. rise in manufacturing output since the early 1990s," the magazine said.

Productivity gains drove the rising output, and hence the economy. From 1992 to 1999, productivity—output per hour worked—rose 31.6 percent in the manufacturing sector. That was more than twice the 13.4 percent gain for the entire nonfarm business economy. Productivity gains in the services sector, which accounts for the biggest share of the labor market, lagged far behind.

Then, when the economic slowdown became apparent in the fall of 2000, this sector made its importance known in a different way. As producers eliminated hundreds of thousands of jobs, unemployment rates and jobless insurance claims rose. Eventually, the ripple effect moved on to slash or even eliminate the surpluses of the federal government and many states. The Federal Reserve's index of manufacturing production fell from 152.8 in September of 2000 to 147.9 in March of 2001. Six months later, the index had fallen to 141.1. Thus, the condition of the manufacturing sector served as an advance indicator of the new century's first recession. Manufacturing's importance is bidirectional.

PROSPERITY IS NOT WITHOUT PAIN

The productivity increases of the 1990s did not come without controversy or pain. At Frigidaire's sprawling St. Cloud, Minnesota, freezer plant, workers complained. They went on strike for three weeks late in 2000, charging that the management had boosted output by employing "speed-up" tactics—trimming break time and reducing designated times for plant cleanups. Elsewhere, companies had shut down many low-productivity plants. Often, the workers who lose their jobs encounter difficulties in matching the pay and benefits they were forced to give up. And technological advances, while they may create new jobs elsewhere, have often reduced jobs in manufacturing even when output is increasing.

Manufacturing employment has changed relatively little since 1970, ranging from between 17 million and 21 million workers. Improved management and better equipment have enabled roughly the same number of workers as there were 30 years ago to produce more than twice as much. While the labor force has grown immensely over the past generation, manufacturers' share of the workforce has fallen to less than 15 percent from more than twice that share at midcentury. Most of the employment increases have come in the service industries, thereby helping to popularize terms such as the "service economy." The manufacturing sector itself has contributed directly to the rise in service jobs by outsourcing to service providers countless nonproduction jobs in fields such as plant security, food services, and public relations.

Thus, manufacturing sent forth mixed signals to the rest of society during the 1990s. On the one hand, it was growing slowly in employment. On the other, it was one of the few segments of the U.S. economy, along with mining, wholesale trade, and agriculture, to dramatically improve its efficiency. In some ways, it appeared less glamorous than a few of the service industries it helped to create, but more basic in business fundamentals.

FOREIGN TRADE—FUELED BY SUCCESS

The strong performance of U.S. industry in the late 1980s and 1990s helped to encourage world confidence in the United States. Investments from abroad flowed into the United States in hopes of participating in the substantial gains being registered on Wall Street. As these capital flows continued, the value of the U.S. dollar increased—particularly during the Asian financial crisis of 1997. This sudden upsurge in the value of the dollar worked to reduce the prices of goods imported by the United States from abroad, and some enterprising foreign producers took advantage of the situation by shipping more to this country.

The rise of manufacturers abroad has stiffened competition for American producers. The nation's growing trade deficit, which reflects this stepped-up rivalry, is reason for concern. In some cases, entire industries have vanished after their suppliers moved abroad. Still, the United States continues to hold a bigger share of all the goods that move across borders than any other land. Moreover, U.S.-made goods account for four-fifths of all U.S. exports, far exceeding the agricultural products and various services that we send overseas. As for global investment, American manufacturers invest seven times as much at home as abroad. Conversely, foreign manufacturers continue to make massive investments in the United States. In some cases, foreign-backed plants in the United States have grown to become significant exporters—and much more American in tone.

U.S.-made goods account for four-fifths of all U.S. exports.

Innovation is another often overlooked measure of manufacturing's continuing importance. National Science Foundation figures show that roughly two-thirds of all private investment in research comes from manufacturers. Visits to America's research parks provide the most visible evidence of this activity. The largest of these parks—Research

Triangle in North Carolina, Stanford near Silicon Valley, Cummings in Huntsville, Alabama—are packed with manufacturers' research and development (R&D) centers and pilot production operations.

Another sign of this sector's importance is the size of its payroll. Manufacturing workers took home 22.6 percent of the nation's overall payroll in 1997, far more than their share of all the jobs. Their employers also support many more jobs in government, trade, services, and other parts of the economy. In our geographical study of manufacturing-intense counties, we found the overall payroll growing rapidly, from 38 percent to 60 percent between 1988 and 1997, in the counties where manufacturing performed well. Conversely, the payroll grew minimally in counties that did less well in manufacturing.

Manufacturing plays another role that goes beyond the value of the payroll. Historically, factories have provided younger people, workers with limited formal education, and new arrivals with career starting points. Today, the conventional wisdom is that factory jobs for new immigrants have virtually disappeared as technological change and the movement of low-wage jobs to developing countries have wiped out repetitive assembly work. Many of these jobs remain, though, particularly in coastal areas that have had a historic role as receiving points for immigrants. A study by the Massachusetts Institute for a New Commonwealth and the Citizens Bank concluded that were it not for the influx of immigrants, many fewer people would be working in New England factories in 2000.

Bronwyn Lance, a senior fellow at the Alexis de Tocqueville Institution, says that by the late 1990s, immigrants had come to hold dominant shares of the jobs in many blue-collar niches of the New England workforce, particularly those critical to production and output in manufacturing. "They were nearly twice as likely to be employed in skilled production crafts as native-born workers, and three to five times as likely to be employed as fabricators, assemblers, and machine operators, the very occupations that keep factories running," writes Lance, who has studied the economic impact of immigration.

Long-established manufacturers have also held prominent roles in charitable giving. While Bill and Melinda Gates and other donors with immense new wealth steal the headlines, most of the nation's largest foundations—Lilly, Kellogg, McKnight, and others—grew from fortunes created by manufacturers.

"Manufacturing is still a huge part of the economy," concludes Stephen Hardis, the retired CEO of Eaton Corp. in Cleveland. "I think that, in many ways, is the untold story of the 1980s and 1990s. People aren't telling that story."

GETTING OUT MANUFACTURING'S STORY

It's a complicated story to tell. To get at it, we looked at how production-intense counties were performing, then used the data to identify significant trends, similarities, and contrasts in certain counties, regions, and states. We gathered information from job and payroll changes over time and location, plant visits, and company data. One shortcoming of job and payroll statistics is that they do not directly address productivity gains. A county could suffer a 10 percent loss of manufacturing jobs over time, yet show a 20 percent gain in manufacturing productivity during that same period. In such a case, the county could have contributed substantially more than its share to the nation's increase in production. Paradoxically, industrial success can be the driving force behind job losses, because a restructured manufacturer can gain efficiencies that enable the company to do more with fewer workers. As writer William Nothdurft put it in an essay for the Northwest Area Foundation, ". . . the community may be declining even if the industrial sector it depends on isn't."

Also limiting our data are jolts that can alter the economic landscape of a county almost overnight. Our classifications of counties are based on a study of the past quarter century, rather than an attempt to foresee the future. Conditions change rapidly in today's tumultuous economy, particularly in smaller counties heavily dependent on a single employer or industry. What seemed to be good fortune can suddenly turn into misfortune. For example, some counties that prospered from booming defense manufacturing in the 1980s suffered in the 1990s, when post–Cold War military cutbacks forced such employers to cut their payrolls sharply. From 1990 to 1995, the United States lost nearly a million defense manufacturing jobs. The 2001 terrorist attacks could again affect the fortunes of defense contractors and the communities in which they operate.

Nonetheless, we feel our county-by-county analysis of manufacturing job and payroll data is helpful. It provides a useful springboard from which to draw a road map of trends in this sector, and to sketch out the portrait of manufacturing's striking diversity of people, products, and plants.

Many surprises awaited us. In North Dakota, we found that Cass County (Fargo) gained more manufacturing jobs, on net, than all of California between 1988 and 1997. In the Midwest, we saw impressive rebounds but also learned that much of this region continues to be heavily dependent on the auto industry. In Philadelphia, we found steep manufacturing declines that symbolize the devastation inflicted on the inner cities of the Northeast and Midwest by factory shutdowns. In Tennessee, we saw firsthand evidence of the close relationships that make manufacturing work well in so many different situations.

Across the country, we found abundant evidence of the changes wrought by globalization. Examining such shifts half a century ago would have been mostly a one-way exercise. Never was a country more fabulous than America in 1949, the British historian Robert Payne wrote after visiting the United States. "Half the wealth of the world, more than half the productivity, nearly two-thirds of the world's machines are concentrated in American hands; the rest of the world lives in the shadow of American industry, and with each day the shadow looms larger, more portentous. . . ." Indeed, the United States had been fortunate. U.S. manufacturers had emerged unscathed from World War II after war damage had disrupted countless factories in the rest of the industrialized world.

U.S. MANUFACTURING: STILL GOOD—BUT NOT ALONE

Gradually, these nations rebuilt their industrial bases. Today, as so many of us know from the products we buy, their industries have often wrested competitive advantages from their American rivals. Some critical U.S. industries have slipped precipitously. One is the machine tool industry, which came out of the war as the world leader after producing the machines so necessary to the Allies' military effort. Today, the U.S. machine tool industry has fallen to third place in production, far behind No. 1 Japan and No. 2 Germany, and not far ahead of No. 4 Italy. America's world-leading trade deficit in machine tools tops the deficits of the next four countries combined. One-time world-beating machine tool builders from the United States—Cincinnati Milicron, Kearney & Trecker, Warner & Swasey, Giddings and Lewis, and others—have ceased operation or been acquired, often by producers from abroad. America has only 2 of the world's 25 largest machine tool builders, Unova and Ingersoll Milling; Japan has 12, Germany 8.

The trade deficit has become the topic of endless wrangling, with most economists and corporations backing free trade and arguing that the deficits aren't much to worry about. Labor unions and manufacturers in steel, textiles, and other industries heavily affected by imports counter that they need protection from unfair trade practices. The merits of either side are not an issue for this book, but we do think there should be more recognition of the dynamic that unfolds when a domestic industry's suppliers leave the United States to operate abroad. All too often, the record shows that the industries themselves soon follow suit.

Americans should recognize that their country has no curb on engineering and management talent so important to manufacturing operations. Engineering schools in the United States are packed with students from abroad. Most return to their native lands after they have earned their often-subsidized degrees. In Singapore, Mexico, India, China, and many other lands, curriculums in math, science, and other disciplines have been improving rapidly.

The growing strength of many overseas manufacturers has given them the resources to invest more in the United States, a trend that has led to construction of numerous plants. The pacesetters for this investment have been Japanese and German auto and truck manufacturers. Since 1982, they have built, expanded, or announced plans for assembly plants in nine states—Illinois, Indiana, Ohio, Kentucky, Tennessee, Alabama, South Carolina, Mississippi, and California. This activity has been most visible in Ohio, where Honda now employs more than 13,000 workers at two assembly plants, an engine factory, and various support facilities. The company has, at times, exported close to a sixth of its Ohio production.

American manufacturers have been facing immense challenges in coping with the foreign competition. One of their most common responses has been mergers and acquisitions, the largest thus far being the 1998 sale of Chrysler to Germany's Daimler-Benz. They have also turned more to cost-cutting, often through downsizing and outsourcing to contract manufacturers. The increased competition has often led to overcapacity and price-cutting. U.S. producers have expanded abroad, seeking more direct access to foreign markets and lower labor costs through significant investments of their own. However, the net flow of investment has been into, rather than out of, the United States. From 1994 to 1998, American manufacturers invested $147 billion abroad while foreign producers invested $209 billion in U.S. manufacturing.

From 1994 to 1998, American manufacturers invested $147 billion abroad while foreign producers invested $209 billion in U.S. manufacturing.

Other pressures have also been pounding away at U.S. manufacturers. One is the stock market, which has become more unforgiving by punishing companies that miss "quarterly earnings expectations" for whatever reasons. The market has become so fascinated with quarter-to-quarter achievements that many publicly held manufacturers engaged in the thoughtful development of workable long-term strategies are often not seen as attractive.

Add to this the preoccupation with acquisitions, divestitures, and mergers. The market's often favorable reaction to acquisitive strategies has boosted the rationale for more mergers, many of which fail to live up to their promise. "This trend is the biggest single impediment to U.S. survival in the global marketplace," contends Frank Riley, a longtime top executive at Bodine Co. and a former president of the Society of Manufacturing Engineers, who has seen many reputable producers fall prey to poorly executed acquisitions. Riley, still active as the head of a Connecticut-based builder of automation equipment, remains optimistic about the future of U.S. manufacturing but he laments the damage done by poorly implemented acquisitions.

Another obstacle for manufacturers is the "not in my backyard" opposition to the location of factories and their suppliers. As community groups have become more pervasive in blocking such projects, their opposition has effectively shut down efforts to build factories, refineries, and power generating stations at many sites across the country.

Sometimes, manufacturers damage themselves with their own actions. For example, according to Riley, manufacturers' purchasing and financing practices often make them less competitive. In one such practice, he says, directors of some U.S. manufacturing companies require approvals for capital equipment spending of as little as $1,000, yet they allow massive advertising campaigns and other noncapital spending projects to move ahead without board approval. "The process of requesting approval to buy capital equipment has become such a nightmare as to make even planning in the largest companies impossible," Riley declares. In another such practice, he says the average payback period expected for buying factory automation equipment is one year. Quips Riley: "If you know any banks paying 100 percent interest, please let us know and I would like to invest my money there."

In some cases, poor decisions and mismanagement have hurt. It's hard to say whether these factors have been more or less prevalent in manufacturing than in other parts of the economy. Clearly, though, manufacturers are not immune to such afflictions. The integrated steel companies were widely criticized for failing to invest in new equipment until minimills and foreign competitors forced them into action. Everyone knows the sad story of how "Chainsaw Al" Dunlap, who slashed jobs wherever he went, dismembered Sunbeam Corp. (see Chapter 15), but the manner in which so much of the investment community encouraged and even endorsed Dunlap's illusory leadership for so long is less widely known.

Consider a Harris Poll survey, taken in 1998 for the American Association of Engineering Societies and the Institute of Electrical and Electronics Engineers (IEEE). The survey found that a broad slice of the U.S. public thinks of engineering as "the stealth profession." Forty-five percent of Americans believe they are "not very well informed" and another 16 percent "not at all well informed" about engineering and engineers. Concluded IEEE-USA President John R. Reinert: "The poll manifests both a subjective and objective American ignorance about the work of engineers." The Harris survey places much of the blame for this condition on the media.

In the industrial Midwest, the poor image of manufacturing has hurt recruiters. "Most people believe manufacturing is on a steep decline across the United States," Susan Maine, managing director of the Pittsburgh-based Advanced Manufacturing Network, said in a 1998 press release. "This is a real problem in industrial cities like Pittsburgh, Detroit, Cleveland, and Chicago. People in our region believe all the steel mills and factories are closed, when in fact manufacturing still contributes more to our region's economy than any other employment sector. Local manufacturers are having a very difficult time finding interested and qualified workers. Part of the problem is that parents and educators are clinging to old views of manufacturing, and are not themselves aware of the career opportunities available in today's modern factory."

Maine's group showed high school students a list of 18 popular career choices. When asked what field they would like to work in, only 1 percent of the students picked manufacturing, which tied with religion for last place in the survey. They ranked sports and entertainment first.

Another source of confusion is the tendency to exclude vast portions of manufacturing from the high-tech category. A Federal Reserve Bank of Chicago study published in late 2000 points out that Michigan and the Midwest place much differently in rankings of "technology intensive" states and regions depending on how the rankings are done. The American Electronics Association ranked the Midwest eighth among the country's nine regions and Michigan seventeenth among the 50 states in high-tech workers per 1,000 jobs in 1998. However, the Michigan Economic Development Corporation ranked the Midwest third and Michigan fourth in that same year. What accounted for these differences? The Michigan agency's study counts the auto and aerospace industries, including their R&D operations, as high-tech, while the Association's study does not. "At first blush, we might not think of motor vehicles as high-tech goods," write bank economists Richard Kaglie and William Testa. "But modern vehicles are equipped with a range of high-tech devices, such as on-board computers that monitor the function of the engine, sensors that detect when one wheel is slipping and transferring power to another, and global positioning systems that provide driving directions."

More confusion arises from the trend to contract out manufacturing, which makes it appear that many producers want to get out of production. The more they opt to farm out various functions, the harder it becomes to figure out who's doing what.

Then there was that International Monetary Fund report in 1997. The study concluded that "contrary to popular perceptions, deindustrialization is not a negative phenomenon but is the natural consequence of the industrial dynamism in an already developed economy." Don't fight it, fund officials advised. Celebrate it.

Maybe we should not celebrate so quickly. If deindustrialization means shedding high-value industries, the effects may not be so beneficial. People and nations around the world want those industries, for good reason, and they are working hard to get them.

CHAPTER 2

Where the Money Is

 All industries may be created equal, but some quickly emerge as more profitable to their employees and their communities.

For example, consider the contrasts in wage levels that set the manufacturing sector apart from retail trade. In 1999, the nation's manufacturing workers received average pay of $37,485. That same year, retailing workers made barely half as much, $19,448. Customers are willing to pay more for the products of some industries and this differential is often passed on to employees, shareholders, and the general community.

This is evident not just in the United States, but all over the world. In the later decades of the 20th Century, more and more countries came to appreciate the benefits to their communities of pursuing higher-valued manufacturing endeavors. This realization has led them to vigorously pursue these lucrative industries.

A look at the federal government's employment and payroll data for manufacturing provides the most meaningful starting point from which to build a better understanding of these differences. Statisticians have divided the U.S. manufacturing economy into 21 major industries. From the perspective of wealth creation, these industries are by no means equal. Just 4 of the 21—machinery, transportation equipment, computers, and fabricated metal products—account for nearly half (46.7 %) of the nation's industrial payroll. Another 3—chemicals, plastic products, and food—account for another 19 percent.

Figure 2.1 illustrates these differences by showing the shares of jobs, payroll, and average pay for each of the 21 industries in 1999, the most recent year this data was available.

18   Production Means Prosperity

FIGURE 2.1   Manufacturing Employment and Payroll by Major Industry

NORTH AMERICAN INDUSTRY CLASSIFICATION CODE #	DESCRIPTION OF MANUFACTURING INDUSTRIES	MFG. EMPLOY-MENT 1999	PAYROLL 1999 ($ 000)	AVERAGE PAYROLL PER EMPLOYEE 1999	% OF U.S. MFG. PAYROLL 1999	% OF U.S. MFG. EMPLOYEES 1999
324	Petroleum	109,104	$6,058,224	$55,527	0.97%	0.65%
334	Computer & Electronic Products	1,615,177	83,841,985	51,909	13.40	9.69
325	Chemical Mfg.	886,354	44,738,273	50,474	7.15	5.32
336	Transportation Equipment Mfg.	1,906,216	90,608,982	47,533	14.49	11.44
322	Paper	559,020	23,226,723	41,549	3.71	3.36
331	Primary Metal Mfg.	597,623	24,765,637	41,440	3.96	3.59
312	Beverage & Tobacco Product Mfg.	172,349	6,991,562	40,566	1.12	1.03
333	Machinery Mfg.	1,398,226	55,874,118	39,960	8.93	8.39
327	Nonmetallic Mineral Product Mfg.	510,316	18,272,582	35,806	2.92	3.06
335	Electrical Equip. & Component	586,421	20,599,635	35,128	3.29	3.52
332	Fabricated Metal Product Mfg.	1,788,484	61,603,757	34,445	9.85	10.74
323	Printing	833,649	27,940,066	33,575	4.47	5.00
339	Miscellaneous Mfg.	734,242	24,353,888	33,168	3.89	4.41
326	Plastics & Rubber Products Mfg.	1,046,935	33,350,608	31,855	5.33	6.28
311	Food Mfg.	1,464,354	41,857,959	28,585	6.69	8.79
321	Wood Product Mfg.	595,176	16,372,899	27,509	2.62	3.57
337	Furniture & Related Product Mfg.	623,153	17,127,833	27,486	2.74	3.74
313	Textile Mills	362,286	9,694,368	26,759	1.55	2.17
314	Textile Product Mills	221,971	5,313,455	23,938	0.85	1.33
316	Leather & Allied Product Mfg.	73,966	1,737,933	23,496	0.28	0.44
315	Apparel Mfg.	574,908	11,205,644	19,491	1.79	3.45
	Total U.S. Manufacturing	16,659,930	$625,536,131	$37,547	100.00%	100.00%

SOURCE: Bureau of Census, U.S. Department of Commerce, 2001

The contribution that each of these major industries makes to the prosperity of the nation varies broadly. Average payroll per employee in 1999 ranged from $19,491 in the apparel industry to $55,527 in petroleum and coal. The economic impact of some industries is huge relative to others. The petroleum and coal industry is relatively small in terms of jobs—just .65 percent of the U.S. total. Yet, this industry accounts for a much greater share of the pay—nearly 1 percent. The leather industry is even smaller by the measure of jobs—less than one-half of 1 percent of overall manufacturing employment—but, in this case, the wages are not so high. Leather workers account for about one-quarter of 1 percent of the overall U.S. manufacturing payroll. Food manufacturing is a big employer, with 8.79 percent of U.S. manufacturing jobs, but accounts for only 6.69 percent of payroll, because average pay is lower than in some other major industries. The transportation equipment industry is large in both respects, accounting for 11.44 percent of employment and 14.49 percent of payroll. The condition of the industries that account for greater shares of payroll becomes a matter of more than passing interest. They count for more in determining tax receipts, budget surpluses, and, more broadly, the strength of the overall U.S. economy.

Unfortunately, some of the industries with the biggest payrolls have been losing jobs. These trends are best understood by examining the shifts in the years before the U.S. Department of Commerce changed its industrial classification system in 1998, a change that we will describe in more detail later. From 1988 to 1997, mostly a robust economic period, Figure 2.2 shows manufacturing employment declined in 13 of the 20 major industries. It fell by 274,076 in transportation equipment and 188,910 in instruments. It grew by 145,321 in the rubber and plastics industries and 30,352 in machinery. Overall, however, manufacturing employment decreased by 628,995 from 1988 to 1997, with 64 percent of this decline occurring in the higher-paying durable goods industries such as primary metals, transportation equipment, and instruments.

Fringe benefits also vary greatly by industry. In 1994, voluntary fringe benefits (those not required by law) varied from roughly $1,500 per worker annually to more than $10,000 even within the 20 manufacturing industries (Figure 2.3). The industries that add more value

FIGURE 2.2   Employment Changes by Major Industry 1988 to 1997

STANDARD INDUSTRY CLASSIFICATION CODE #	DESCRIPTION OF MANUFACTURING INDUSTRIES	EMPLOY-MENT 1988	EMPLOY-MENT 1997	EMPLOYMENT CHANGE 1988–1997	AVERAGE SIC PAY 1997
20	Food & Kindred Products	1,438,668	1,539,682	1,010,144	$27,963
21	Tobacco Products	46,619	34,166	(12,453)	46,672
22	Textile Mill Products	682,674	553,198	(129,476)	24,642
23	Apparel Products	1,070,973	835,219	(235,754)	18,528
24	Lumber and Wood Products	712,498	745,254	32,756	24,964
25	Furniture and Fixtures	519,911	514,504	(5,407)	25,817
26	Paper and Allied Products	625,238	621,072	(4,166)	38,606
27	Printing and Publishing	1,524,887	1,501,714	(23,173)	32,869
28	Chemicals and Allied Products	831,621	832,546	925	46,900
29	Petroleum and Coal Products	118,263	107,829	(10,434)	52,766
30	Rubber & Miscellaneous Plastic Products	869,856	1,015,177	145,321	29,626
31	Leather and Leather Products	129,561	83,387	(46,174)	21,378
32	Stone, Clay, & Glass Products	518,820	500,828	(17,992)	32,971
33	Primary Metal Industries	725,201	686,161	(39,040)	39,420
34	Fabricated Metal Products	1,491,640	1,537,591	45,951	33,624
35	Industrial Machinery & Equipment	1,924,409	1,954,761	30,352	38,934
36	Electrical & Electronic Equipment	1,595,832	1,528,348	(67,484)	38,660
37	Transportation Equipment	1,847,865	1,573,789	(274,076)	44,639
38	Instruments & Related Products	1,002,522	813,612	(188,910)	44,540
39	Miscellaneous Manufacturing	386,761	399,391	12,630	27,347
	Total U.S. Manufacturing	19,261,691	18,632,696	(628,995)	$36,958

SOURCE: Bureau of Census, U.S. Department of Commerce, 2001

FIGURE 2.3   Voluntary Fringe Benefits per Worker

Tobacco Products
Transportation Equipment
Primary Metal Industries
Petroleum & Coal Products
Chemicals & Allied Products
Instruments & Related Products
Paper & Allied Products
Industrial Machinery & Equipment
Electronic & Other Electric Equip.
Fabricated Metal Products
All Manufacturing
Stone, Clay, & Glass Products
Rubber & Misc. Plastics Products
Food & Kindred Products
Printing & Publishing
Misc. Manufacturing Industries
Furniture & Fixtures
Textile Mill Products
Lumber & Wood Products
Leather & Leather Products
Apparel & Other Textile Products

$0 $5,000 $10,000 $15,000

SOURCE: U.S. Department of Labor, 1996

provide higher levels of benefits. The stronger these industries are, the less the pressure on taxpayers to provide benefits such as health insurance. In recent years, discussions of the availability of health insurance have taken the form of a social question. While it is, in fact, a social question, it is also a question of which industries expand or contract.

Profits vary greatly by industry (Figure 2.4). In general, profitability was high in the late 1990s, but especially high in a few key industries. The makeup of U.S. manufacturing profits has changed over the years. Several industries that were important contributors to the nation's profits in the past are now finding it difficult to make substantial contributions. Primary metals, motor vehicles, and petroleum all contribute much smaller shares of U.S. manufacturing profits than they did 40 years ago. The food industry has increased its share of profits. The important electronic industry had high profits during the mid-1990s but eroded in recent years.

Profits represent a source of prosperity for society in general—not just for shareholders. Profitable industries hire people, pay dividends, expand their facilities, and contribute cash earned through exports.

FIGURE 2.4   Percent of U.S. Manufacturing Profits by Major Industry
1959, 1968, 1994, and 1999

INDUSTRY	1959	1968	1994	1999
Primary Metals	8.68%	4.56%	1.50%	1.43%
Fabricated Metal Products	4.15	5.52	7.81	10.08
Industrial Machinery & Equipment	8.30	10.07	5.44	12.56
Electronic & Electric Equipment	6.42	6.95	16.12	6.77
Motor Vehicles & Equipment	11.32	13.19	5.23	3.80
Other Durable Products	13.21	13.43	14.47	16.19
Total Durable Products	51.70	53.72	50.57	50.77
Food & Kindred Products	9.43	7.67	13.97	12.06
Chemicals & Allied Products	13.21	12.71	15.90	16.46
Petroleum & Coal Products	9.81	8.87	−0.07	2.97
Other Nondurable Products	16.23	17.03	19.70	17.73
Total Nondurable Products	48.30	46.28	49.43	49.23
Total U.S. Manufacturing	100.00%	100.00%	100.00%	100.00%

SOURCE: Council of Economic Advisors, Economic Report of the President, 2001, Table B-92

Marginally profitable industries cut back, purchase fewer services, and close facilities—particularly during slower economic periods. This is evident in the declining fortunes of cities where major industrial employers have ceased being competitive and profitable.

Profits can erode quickly when times become difficult. As an example, International Harvester, at one time the fourth largest company in the United States, suffered severe losses during the 1980 to 1983 recession after experiencing its best year ever in 1979. As revenue declined from $8 billion to $3.5 billion, employment at that company declined from 103,000 employees to 17,000 in just six years.

THE REWARDS OF ADDING VALUE

In making the products society needs, manufacturing adds value to raw materials to create finished products. The short-hand accounting definition of the term *value-added* is revenue minus the cost of materials and purchased services. Though the term is used sparingly in the

United States, it is the basis for taxation systems of most of western Europe and is common in other parts of the world.

Much variation exists in the mixes of investments, methods, wages, profits, and social purpose that go into production processes to produce value. Ultimately, though, the public, through market action, renders some products more valuable than others. The world is willing to pay workers more for the creation of a jetliner or a precision instrument than for informal apparel or advertising inserts.

The greater the value that gets added to a product, the higher the wages. Figure 2.5 shows this relationship for 123 manufacturing industries, subsectors of major industries more finely defined by a three-digit Standard Industry Classification (SIC) code. Note that annual wages are much higher in those industries where the value-added per employee is higher. The higher wages, in turn, contribute to the prosperity of both the employees and their communities.

This important relationship between value-added and community prosperity is a subtlety that escapes some public officials and policy makers. Prosperity is not entirely a matter of social justice, though questions of social justice do arise. Prosperity is inevitably linked to the performance of value-producing activities aimed at providing high-

FIGURE 2.5   Value-Added and Annual Pay

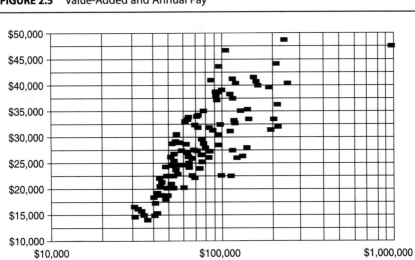

SOURCE: U.S. Census of Manufacturers, 1987 and 1992 3 digit industries

quality and cost-effective goods and services to people who are willing to pay for them. In the communities where companies with these attributes exist, prosperity usually reigns. When these attributes are not present, communities often suffer gradual declines in the living standards of their citizens.

The retention of competitive expertise is not easy, however. It involves investment, cooperation, fairness, far-sightedness, and innovation. Above all, it involves the constant improvement of productivity.

PRODUCTIVITY AND OUTPUT

Productivity improvements, if they can be achieved, can provide valuable spillover benefits to citizens of a modern industrial economy. According to the "rule of 70," if productivity increases at a 1 percent annual rate over a long stretch, it will take 70 years to double living standards; at 2 percent, just 35 years. Calculating productivity rates, though, can be an extremely difficult process. If more can be produced with same or fewer inputs, goods and services become available at reasonable cost or even reduced cost. Calculating productivity rates, though, requires both insight and caution.

In the late 1990s, advocates of the idea that Internet-driven technologies were ushering in a golden era—the so-called new economy—cited U.S. productivity figures as the strongest evidence of their belief. Indeed, the reported surges in this critical measure of the economy were impressive. Productivity had risen at an average annual rate of 2.7 percent from 1950 to 1972. From 1973 to 1995, though, the rate of growth fell off to just 1.1 percent. Then the reports brightened. By the spring of 1999, as new economy euphoria came to dominate the stock market, the federal government was reporting that productivity gains had skipped up to a 2.1 percent average for the 13 previous quarters dating back to 1996.

Among economists, doubters were in the minority then. One of the foremost of them was Robert Gordon, an economist at Northwestern University. Gordon argued that one subsector—computer hardware manufacturing—accounted for nearly all of the productivity surge in the U.S. economy from 1994 to 1998. Later, he moderated that estimate, finding that durable goods manufacturers other than the com-

puter makers also accounted for a substantial share of the nation's reported productivity growth in late 1990s. Then, as the findings of more
studies emerged and the government revised productivity numbers
downward, other skeptics joined Gordon.

The Economist magazine noted that the federal government's mid-
summer 2001 revisions cut average productivity growth in 1999 and
2000—"the very period when most American economists started to
believe in the new economy"—to 2.6 percent from 3.4 percent.
Government statisticians also trimmed average productivity growth
over the previous five years to 2.5 percent from 2.8 percent. The publication also argued that a fifth of the 2.5 percent surge was temporary,
because it came from an extraordinary spurt in information technology investment. "The miracle of the late 1990s was not quite so miraculous," The Economist concluded. Among the others who had grown
more skeptical was economist Paul Krugman. In his New York Times
column, Krugman questioned the claims of optimists (including
Federal Reserve Chairman Alan Greenspan) that a productivity revolution driven by information technology has decades to run. "Since
the 1960s, futurists have consistently overestimated the future rate of
technological progress and economic growth," Krugman observed.
Just go to the video store and rent 2001: A Space Odyssey, he suggested,
or read Herman Kahn's The Year 2000.

Arriving at the final productivity numbers is a tricky process fraught
with controversy. For one thing, the government estimates productivity in the computer industry by constructing a "hedonic price index"—
a highly arbitrary exercise—that attempts to measure how much the
cost of computing power has fallen. Critics charge that this process
overstates productivity gains. They also say the government failed to
recognize that the initial productivity figures for 1999 were high because of the Y2K-related spending on information technology. Yet
another factor in boosting the productivity numbers, contracting
out—outsourcing—grew rapidly. Many companies outsourced everything from janitorial help to cafeteria services during the 1990s. Such
moves lessened the hours worked at these firms, but did not affect the
quantity of the goods they produced. Therefore, output per labor hour
increased.

Productivity usually rises in times of economic expansion and
weakens when times are slow. When companies are busy, more gets

done. The buoyant U.S. economy in the late 1990s should have been expected to show productivity improvements. As the economy slows, these gains will partially disappear.

Measurements and estimates of U.S. productivity have been made and published almost continuously since the *Hand and Machine Labor Report* in 1898. No statistics are flawless, and productivity statistics are no exception. The intricacy of measuring certain transactions makes the task especially difficult. So does the burden of gathering lengthy reports from a vast array of employers, agencies, and industries. Productivity coverage throughout the economy is by no means uniform. Estimates are reported for industries covering about 54 percent of U.S. employment, but the degree of coverage varies greatly by sector. Mining and manufacturing are nearly fully covered. Services, which is expanding, is only 16 percent covered; finance, insurance and real estate, 19 percent; wholesale trade, 2 percent. Medical services are not covered at all.

Perhaps the most valuable measure in the productivity statistics is unit labor costs—a key determinant of our long-term competitive position. Comparing the fourth quarter of 1999 to the third quarter, productivity grew more rapidly than compensation (4.8 percent vs 3.6 percent), so unit labor costs *decreased* 1.2 percent. That seemed impressive, but the year-to-year comparison was not quite so impressive. Comparing the fourth quarters of 1998 and 1999, output per hour grew by 3.3 percent and compensation by 4.5 percent, so unit labor costs *increased* by 1.2 percent.

Another cautionary note: Variations in manufacturing productivity gains within industries are huge. Nucor is far more efficient than Bethlehem or LTV at making steel. Andersen Windows, Ford, and other companies outproduce competitors, sometimes larger, in the same industry. Thus, there is no "typical" U.S. productivity level for manufacturers.

Despite all of these shortcomings and caveats, there is widespread agreement that manufacturing productivity gains remain far above those for the rest of the economy. A study by the Joel Popkin and Co. consulting firm for the Association for Manufacturing Technology found that output in the durable goods sector of manufacturing grew at roughly twice the rate of the overall economy from 1992 to 1997. The Popkin firm also estimated that multifactor productivity grew at an average annual rate of 1.1 percent from 1959 to 1996. The overall non-farm economy grew notably more slowly over the same period, 0.8 percent, by this measure—the most fundamental yardstick that considers factors beyond capital and labor.

Agriculture, mining, and wholesale trade are also quite productive. The biggest drag on overall productivity in the United States is in the service sector, which for decades has registered low rates of productivity improvement. Thus, the more service-oriented the U.S. economy becomes, the more vulnerable it will be to stagnating overall productivity unless the services become markedly more efficient, an attribute that has thus far not been achieved. Figure 2.6 shows how these segments have increased their output per person from 1977 to 1997. Finance, insurance, and real estate (referred to by the government as F.I.R.E.) and retail trade managed only slight increases.

Thus, the more service-oriented the U.S. economy becomes, the more vulnerable it will be to stagnating overall productivity unless the services become markedly more efficient.

FIGURE 2.6   Percent Increase of Real Gross Domestic Product per Employee 1977 to 1997

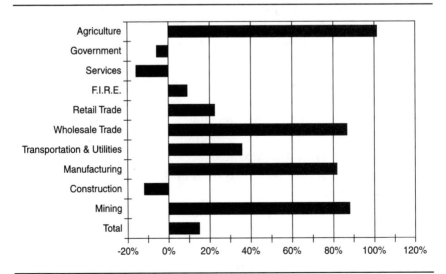

SOURCE: U.S. Bureau of Economic Analysis, 1999 and University of St. Thomas

FOREIGN PRODUCERS FOLLOW
MONEY AND OPPORTUNITY

Our international competitors have been getting more productive, sometimes at a more rapid clip than the United States. Given the fact that there are roughly six times as many science and engineering graduates being turned out in Southeast Asia as in the United States, we cannot assume that productivity gains in the United States will outstrip those of aggressive competitors in other countries. Many of the world's most respected technical advancements now take place outside of the United States. Month after month of record-setting trade deficits give testimony to the emerging technical prowess of our competitors during a time when their unit labor costs are decreasing.

Managers and policy makers in rapidly industrializing countries such as Taiwan, Korea, Singapore, Brazil, Spain, and China understand that high value-added manufacturing is where the money is. The wages are higher in high value-added industries and the profits are usually higher. As producers get better and enter more high-value industries in these countries, they are launching programmatic assaults on these industries not just in the United States but also in Japan, Europe, and, to some degree, other emerging nations.

Consider computer components. In the early 1960s, Asian companies became significant producers of computer parts because the stringing of core memories was labor-intensive and labor in Asia was cheap. Now technologies have made core memories obsolete and many computer products are no longer labor-intensive. Today, formidable Asian companies dominate the production of such key components as disk drives, displays, electronic components, cabinetry, and memory modules. Optics provides another example. Germany and the United States dominated the development and production of optical instruments. Then the Japanese became involved, followed by other participants. Now, most precision optical instruments are manufactured in Asia.

There are other equally important industries under assault from intense international competition. In aircraft, Boeing's preeminence as an international supplier of the world's best commercial airliners disguises the tumult that has been tearing through that industry. McDonnell Douglas, once a leading producer, succumbed to competition and was acquired by Boeing. Years earlier, Lockheed left the business. Airbus Industries, the heavily subsidized European consortium, now controls roughly half of the commercial airliner market. New competitors have arisen, but they are based in Brazil and Canada rather than the United States. It may be only a matter of time before companies in other emerging lands join the fray, partly because it will be easier for them to participate than it was for us initially. That's because there is a global market for key aircraft components, some of which are no longer made in the United States. A careful perusal of the bill of materials for the U.S.-built Boeing 777 jetliner would turn up a long list of key components manufactured abroad—instruments, optics, sensors, actuators, gears, bearings, and many other parts. The supply network, once the domain of the leading U.S. manufacturers, is now available to anyone who wants to buy parts. The specifications, prices, order forms, and support resources are usually available for free, often on the Internet.

The automobile industry, long the font of so much of America's industrial expertise, faces well-documented competitive pressures. Less visible are three changes that may have a profound impact in the way the industry unfolds: new manufacturing technologies allow greater efficiencies to take place on a smaller scale; the number and variety of vehicles available to the public has proliferated; the expansion of production capacity, both by vehicle assemblers and component suppliers, has generally outrun demand.

Automobile manufacturing is still very capital-intensive. That probably won't change in the near future, but the capital is buying different capabilities. In former years, capital spending would buy bigger scale and lower cost per unit. Now, the capital is providing greater flexibility as well as lower cost, and the systems and machinery necessary to accomplish these capabilities are readily available worldwide at reasonable costs. Tariffs, exchange rate fluctuations, business cycles, and other variables are constantly redrawing the map of where vehicles get made, but the long-term trend is to the world beyond our shores. In the late 1950s, U.S.-based producers still made more than half of the world's motor vehicles. In 1999, manufacturers around the world produced 56.3 million autos and trucks; manufacturers in the United States turned out 13.1 million, or 23.2 percent of them.

Despite the decline, this country remains a very major player in the world automotive industry. Its profit performance is even more impressive, because many of the foreign producers have rarely achieved the profitability levels of the U.S. producers, despite being heavily subsidized by either banks or governments. Yet, automobile manufacturing expertise is proliferating. Volkswagen, Ford, GM, Honda, Renault, DaimlerChrysler, and Toyota all have vast global networks of well-equipped plants. Korean manufacturers have the capacity to produce two million vehicles a year. Southeast Asia is rapidly becoming a major production area as is South America. As more major plants get built, in more countries, they spawn and invigorate manufacturing expertise that becomes applicable in other industries.

It is often stated that U.S. productivity, overall, is the highest in the world and, thus, there is little to be concerned about regarding the nation's ability to compete effectively in world markets. What long-term threat could there be to a plant in Mexico, this logic holds, because educational standards are lower there and productivity lags far behind the levels achieved in the United States? The facts suggest that such a viewpoint is not realistic. Though the number of people earning college degrees abroad is often a smaller percentage of the population than in the United States, the degrees granted overseas are frequently in more technical subjects and the standards met by those who complete programs are often quite high. The Society of Manufacturing Engineers recently selected Nonyang University in Singapore as the recipient of its annual "Lead Award"—the top manufacturing engineering school in the world. With many science and engineering graduates pouring forth from institutions in Asia, Europe, and South America, we are likely to see geographically widespread productivity improvements in the years ahead. Such growing expertise has become a huge, growing asset that is helping multinational manufacturers in these lands become more competitive. So if the equipment is the same as in the United States, the people are sometimes more qualified, and the processes are conceived and carried out by many of the same multinationals drawing from the same body of expertise, it seems clear that manufacturing in these lands is destined to become more competitive.

CHAPTER 3

Indiana: Jitters in Comeback Land

A visit to C&A Tool in downtown Churubusco, a small Indiana town near Fort Wayne, is guaranteed to jar your senses. From the outside, the place resembles a 19th Century European industrial village where craftsmen from various trades gather together to share skills and know-how. Founder Dick Conrow calls one building the *Schliefhaus* and another the *Fraeshaus*, German for grinding shop and milling shop, respectively. Yet, once you get a close look at what happens inside, C&A Tool quickly takes on a state-of-the-art, 21st Century aura.

Conrow started the company, a tool-and-die shop and specialized manufacturer, in his garage in 1969. C&A makes everything from high-tech parts for defense manufacturers to fuel pumps and chicken feeders. Highly skilled grinders achieve tolerances of 40 millionths of an inch in shaping parts. The company's new headquarters, opened in 1999 on a 46-acre site overlooking a small lake at the edge of town, looks like an industrial-sized Swiss chalet. Meanwhile, C&A still maintains a dominant presence downtown, where its 13 buildings blend in with the designs of others nearby.

"Our first building was built right between the public library and a doctors' and dentists' office," says Conrow. "The community was quite concerned. I told them, 'Just give me time. We'll be asking you to clean up your facilities,' which is basically what they had to do. We're supposed to be in manufacturing, but we got into urban renewal."

Conrow is, as a sportscaster might say of an outspoken football star, a piece of work. He scorns academia, Wall Street, and much of American manufacturing. Ownership has become faceless, he declares, thanks to the unending run of mergers, buyouts, and acquisitions. C&A has never made an acquisition; on the other hand, Conrow has rejected dozens of potential acquirers who sought to buy the company. *Modern Machine Shop,* a trade publication that rarely profiles companies more than once, has profiled C&A three times since 1990. First came "The Radicals of Churubusco," then "The Radicals Revisited," finally "A Radically Different Production Plant."

Conrow is a big believer in northeast Indiana, where manufacturing has made a remarkable comeback. The region rebounded, he says, because its people never strayed from basic skills and a strong work ethic. "There are a lot of things here you take for granted that you are hard-pressed to find anywhere else," he says.

Many other factors also powered the recovery, which saw the region's unemployment rate fall to 3 percent in mid-2000. By fall of 2001, it had climbed back up to 5 percent as manufacturers trimmed their payrolls. Nonetheless, that was still far below its 13 percent level of the early 1980s. Manufacturers, drawn to strategic locations near Interstates 69 and 80-90, flocked to the region like teenagers to a rock concert. Rebounding suppliers, drawn by relatively low costs of doing business and large pools of qualified workers, led the way. Often-warring interest groups pulled together to create a regional development program. Governments offered subsidies, which lubricated developers' efforts to bring more jobs to the region. And entrepreneurs, notably Conrow and Keith Busse at Steel Dynamics Inc., showed how startups can make it in seemingly mature manufacturing fields. So powerful was the recovery that over the two decades ended in 1998, the region gained jobs at a greater rate than the United States as a whole. The manufacturing sector drove the rebound in northeastern Indiana, with its jobs growing 35 percent to nearly 111,000 over this stretch. Today, about a third of the region's jobs remain in manufacturing, more than twice the national average.

As the new century dawned, though, uneasiness remained. The regional economy still rose and fell with the auto industry. Wage levels lagged behind those of the nation overall. Business leaders fretted that high-tech startups and venture capital were in short supply. Organized labor protested that the region was losing waves of factory jobs to Mexico. In some years, plant shutdowns or cutbacks cost the area more jobs than were added at new or expanded plants.

These recent downturns brought back memories of a deeply depressed period in 1982, when the lights almost flickered out. Plant closings and cutbacks darkened life in Fort Wayne, which for more than a century had been one of the country's most vibrant manufacturing centers. The nine-county area became a microcosm for all that ailed industrial America, much as its later successes and eventually the new uncertainties of the 2001 downturn would also reflect the entire manufacturing sector's mood across the land. International Harvester sent shivers through Fort Wayne when it decided to shut down its heavy-duty truck assembly plant on the city's east side. The announcement capped a three-year tanking that ushered in the worst times the area had seen since the Great Depression. The region lost roughly 30,000 jobs—3 of every 20. Harvester's Fort Wayne Works, whose 10,500 workers in 1979 had made it one of the cathedrals of American manufacturing, fell silent. Late that year, workers throughout the company, repelled by concessions that management demanded, walked off the job. By the time their bitter, 170-day strike had ended, Harvester's financial statements were in shreds and the economy was in a tailspin. By 1982, only 2,000 workers remained. Beyond Harvester, the recession was battering the region's many auto suppliers, heavily dependent on Detroit's struggling Big Three automakers.

Fort Wayne and the rest of Allen County, home to about three-fifths of the region's population, lost 13,000 manufacturing jobs from 1979 to 1982. Since then, they have gained back 7,000, and the remaining eight counties have picked up another 34,000. The city is prospering as a service center for factory employees who work in new industrial parks in and around the many small towns nearby. More than 2,000 employees work at manufacturing research centers in the region.

Fort Wayne had treasured its long history of innovation. Entrepreneurs recorded their earliest achievements in the Civil War era. A foundry, started then in the city, emerged as the world's largest producer of railroad wheels. Fifty miles north, the Auburn Cord Duesenberg Co. became a notable automaker. One of the seven companies that merged to form General Electric grew up in Fort Wayne. The city became the magnetic wiring capital of the world. It staked claims as the birthplace of the washing machine, baking powder, juke boxes, television, hand-held calculators, the refrigerator, streetlights, gas pumps, stereophonic sound, even night baseball. The Detroit Pistons professional basketball team, originally the Fort Wayne Pistons, got its nickname from one of Fort Wayne's best-known products. When the Harvester debacle hit, though, past glories provided little solace.

SEEDING THE REBOUND

Harvester went into 1982 saturated with excess truck-making capacity. Most of the production was in Fort Wayne and in Springfield, Ohio. After company officials let it be known that one of the plants had to go, the two cities battled for the one that would stay. Both cities put together incentive packages aimed at winning over Harvester. Fort Wayne offered $31 million, a number eventually matched by Springfield. The Ohio city's newer plant, built in 1965, gave it the edge over Fort Wayne's factory, built in 1922. Yet, Fort Wayne fought on gamely, even staging an all-day Harvester rally complete with Dixieland and rock bands. Rally-goers sent the powers-that-be at Harvester up to 100,000 pleas, wrapped in sandbags, to keep the factory going. "With both towns promising about the same amount of cash up front, the age of the plants made the difference, as expected all along," Barbara Marsh concluded in her 1985 book, *A Corporate Tragedy: The Agony of International Harvester Company.*

The loss of the International Harvester factory scarred the lives of many families in Fort Wayne. Sociology professors Pat Ashton and Peter Iadicola found in 1985 that the shutdown cost ex-Harvester employees $21 million in income, seriously depleting their assets, and burdened many of them with depression, anger, and anxiety.

But the Harvester debacle had one redeeming outcome: It gave rise to a new spirit of cooperation in the region. Public officials and business leaders promptly joined forces to establish Indiana Northeast Development. Lincoln Schrock, a former aide to Fort Wayne's mayor, has headed the regional development agency from the start. At the outset, Schrock proposed and won support for an annual development conference designed to help manufacturers close deals to locate in the region. In an unusual twist, Schrock keeps the guest list confidential so companies searching for a site will not be hounded by communities or vendors they aren't interested in. Since the conference began in 1982, Schrock says attending companies, mostly manufacturers, have gone on to do more than 75 expansions or relocations in northeast Indiana.

Many of the companies sending representatives to the early conferences were Michigan-based auto suppliers concerned about their high costs. Such costs, particularly for workers' compensation and unemployment insurance and in some cases wages, were lower in Indiana. Some industrial sites near I-69 and the Indiana Toll Road were even better located for shipping goods than the suppliers' existing plants in Michigan. Vestil Manufacturing, a truck equipment maker in Albion, Michigan, began the exodus in 1983 when it moved 40 miles south to Angola. Soon, many other Michigan auto suppliers followed, sometimes moving south no more than 20 miles. Schrock has kept score. He says 79 Michigan companies either expanded in or relocated entirely to northeast Indiana from 1983 to 1998. This influx brought 10,776 jobs, and a total investment of $905 million, to the region.

Easily, the biggest breakthrough came in 1984. "I was sitting at my desk one morning when I got a call from a real estate agent who said somebody was looking for a 1,000-acre industrial site," recalls John Stafford, then economic development director for Allen County. "When I got back up off the floor, I was fine. It was apparent from day one that these people were dead serious."

Stafford and the Norfolk Southern Railroad began searching for such a site in Allen County. The railroad, which benefited from having more shippers along its north-south right-of-way through Indiana, had been working confidentially on behalf of the company seeking the site. Five months later, Stafford learned that the anonymous site-seeker was General Motors Corp., which was moving rapidly to build a new pickup truck plant. GM chose a location at an I-69 interchange in Allen County, just southwest of Fort Wayne. It was the largest single project ever for the county, and a magic moment for northeast Indiana. Most of the plant's 3,000 workers came from the company's Janesville plant in Wisconsin, which GM had planned to shut down. The company spent $500 million to build the Fort Wayne plant, plus another $322 million on three later expansions. By 1999, GM's annual payroll there had grown to $158 million, the plant was the county's largest taxpayer, and the company's investment was approaching $1 billion.

Communities often wave immense incentive packages in front of companies planning to build plants. In this instance, local and state officials provided $70 million for the project—$40 million in infrastructure outlays, $25 million in tax abatements, and $5 million for training grants. County officials argued that this amount, while substantial, was modest compared with the incentives packages of the $160 million that Illinois had given Chrysler and the $120 million that Michigan had given Mazda for new factories. A cost-benefit analysis done by Allen County in 1999 estimated that the governments gained $2.15 in income, property, and sales taxes from 1987 to 1999 for every $1 they spent on GM-related infrastructure costs and incentives. The study added that the plant led the economic turnaround for the region, providing a psychological boost for the citizenry, and enhanced outsiders' views of the county as a good place to do business.

GM had been quietly considering sites in Michigan, but never went public with its plans and thereby avoided an open bidding war for the plant. The company couldn't afford the delays inherent in such a skirmish, and local development officials, fearful that a battle could erupt, negotiated the deal behind closed doors. Thomas Guthrie, director of the Community Research Institute in Fort Wayne, says the belief was widespread that GM wanted to "send Michigan a message" that the state needed to reduce its costs of doing business. The message hit home. The *Wall Street Journal* reported that in July of 1986, Michigan Governor John Engler sent 1,000 letters to Fort Wayne businesses talking up 21 tax cuts the state had made. The letters cited comparisons showing state and local taxes that were lower overall in Jackson, Michigan, than in Fort Wayne. (Edward O. Roberts Jr., of the Indiana Manufacturers Association, fired back, saying Engler had failed to mention unemployment insurance, which cost four times as much in Michigan as in Indiana.)

The GM plant opened in 1986. By the end of that year, the Fort Wayne area was back. It had added some 30,000 jobs since 1983, thus rebuilding its job base to its 1979 high of 177,000 workers. "Congratulations: Take a bow, Fort Wayne. You did it!" boomed a headline in *Impact*, the Community Research Institute's newsletter. The publication pointedly recalled that in 1979, "doomsayers predicted that the area economy would never recover" from the double-barreled disaster of the Harvester shutdown and the severe recession.

Spillover Benefits from Surrounding Manufacturing

The location and nature of the jobs was different. Overall, Allen County's manufacturing job base was substantially below what it had been in 1979. Instead, the county was evolving into more of a service center for the region's outlying counties. Meanwhile, manufacturing employment was growing rapidly in the four counties north of Fort Wayne, all with an interstate or near one.

For the most part, these jobs went to workers at new factories that rose in rapidly expanding industrial parks along the I-69 corridor from Fort Wayne north to the Michigan state line. One of the biggest gainers was the Town of Hamilton in Steuben County, the state's northeastern-most county. From the 1960s until 1982, the town had only two small factories. From 1982 until 1999, Hamilton added $11.8 million in its industrial tax base. That gain helped boost the total tax base to $20.3 million in 1999 from just $2.4 million in 1981. The higher base generated more tax revenue, which in turn led to improved government services and better schools. "It's allowed us to expand our street department and our police department," says Robert Howard, administrative assistant for the town. "We've been able to have better equipment and service for our residents. The Hamilton Community Schools probably could not exist without the industrial tax base."

THE BATTLE OVER STEEL

The region's comeback was also marked by a second blockbusting industrial investment—Keith Busse's 1995 startup, Steel Dynamics Inc. (SDI). By 2000, this company, which enhanced the efficiency of a new steel-casting process, had sunk more than $900 million into a new steel manufacturing cluster near Fort Wayne.

Steel is omnipresent. It's in the cars and trucks we drive, the bridges we cross, our skyscrapers and stadiums, the machines that make our machines, everywhere. We use products made of steel every day, whether they be silverware, garden tools, or the parts buried deep inside our computers, television sets, and kitchen appliances. The steel industry also produces many more jobs in other sectors for every job created or maintained in primary steelmaking. Indeed, so coveted is this industry that every country wants its own steel mills. That has led to overcapacity, fierce global competition, complaints about unfair trade, razor-thin profit margins, and intensifying pressure to produce steel more efficiently.

Throughout the first two-thirds of the 20th Century, America's steel industry grew and prospered by building fully integrated steel plants that handled every step of a steelmaking process developed in the previous century. Workers at these gargantuan mills mix iron ore and coking coal to create liquid pig iron, which they then turn into liquid steel. They shape the liquid steel into ingots or slabs, which are cooled, reheated, and converted into sheet steel. Shortly after World War II, American producers made more steel than all the rest of the world combined. When foreign steelmakers found more efficient ways of making steel, it became clear that America's big integrated producers had failed to invest in more productive equipment and to adopt innovative management practices. Over the decade ended in 1987, the industry's domestic workforce plunged to 235,000 from 600,000 as shutdowns and bankruptcies became widespread. However, by then, the U.S. steel industry was well into a renaissance, led by the new minimills. These plants, usually located away from the traditional steel-producing areas, employ a far more efficient process than the integrated producers. They feed scrap steel—stripped from junked cars, demolished buildings, and discarded parts—into electric arc furnaces and then cast the steel into sheets. The minimills quickly took away markets for bar steel and roof joists from the integrated mills. Still, the established producers maintained a lock on Fortune 500–sized customers in industries such as autos and appliances. To win away that business, the minimills needed a way to produce thin, high-quality sheets of steel. The job of finding the way fell to Keith Busse, the Fort Wayne native who founded SDI.

In 1972, Busse had joined Nucor Corp., the company destined to become the leader of the minimills. Sixteen years later, he was leading Nucor's "Crawfordsville Project" at the company's new Indiana mill in the open prairie near Crawfordsville. The mill was the linchpin in Nucor's strategy for going after the integrated producers' blue-chip markets. Time after time over the previous century, innovators had tried and failed to come up with a machine that could make long slabs of steel and then cast them into thin sheets in a single continuous process. Busse and his charges believed they had found the answer in an unproven "Compact Strip Production" machine designed by German inventor Manfred Kolakowski for his company, SMS Schloemann-Siemag A.G. of Dusseldorf. The Crawfordsville startup took longer than expected. Kolakowski's machine worked, but only after a terrifying accident that illustrates the risks steelworkers face every day. One evening, a ladle filled with liquid steel plunged to the ground. The steel made contact with water, triggering a thunderous explosion that sent molten steel, scrap, and cement flying through the air. A vendor, severely burned, died three weeks later. Eventually, the Crawfordsville Project's pioneering effort enabled Nucor to turn out higher-grade steel more efficiently and thus to penetrate markets that had been the exclusive preserves of the big integrated producers. Since then, steel mills all over the world have turned to similar thin-slab casting processes.

Busse built a reputation as an energized, undaunted driver of the "hot metal men" who make their livings by creating and managing the fiery white glow and thunderous claps that transform molten metal into sheets of steel. Author Richard Preston, whose book *American Steel* chronicled the Crawfordsville startup, likened him to a swashbuckling sheriff out of the Wild West. Busse landed in the steel industry's executive suites by happenstance. His family couldn't afford to send him to college. After graduating from high school in 1961, he used money from his own jobs and a $750 loan from his godfather to earn a two-year accounting degree from Fort Wayne's International Business College. He pumped gas at the nearby Montgomery Ward auto center from 4 PM until 9 PM, often unloading truckloads of auto batteries after his regular shift to earn extra money. He recalls that it wasn't unusual for his father, a Fort Wayne firefighter, to arrive home at 6 AM to find his son asleep at the kitchen table slumped over his homework.

In 1963, Busse joined the McGill Bearing Corp. in Valparaiso, Indiana, near Indiana's Lakeshore mills, as a cost accountant. Even today, these huge mills, which rim the tip of Lake Michigan, reign as America's largest steelmaking concentration. At this time, Bethlehem Steel was building a massive integrated mill, the last such plant to go up in the United States, at Burns Harbor on Lake Michigan. "I didn't have anything to do on weekends, so I'd drive up along the lakeshore and get acquainted with the community," Busse says. "I watched a behemoth rise up out of the ground and I've got to tell you, I was awesomely impressed."

Busse moved on to accounting and financial management jobs at Square D and Dresser Industries. Then he went back to school at St.

Francis College to get a bachelor's degree majoring in business and finance and, while working at Nucor, an MBA from Indiana University. When he left Nucor to start SDI, his top two managers, Richard Teets and Mark Millet, came with him. Early in 1994, they unveiled an audacious plan to build a $514 million thin-slab minimill 25 miles northeast of Fort Wayne in Butler. Sensing a fresh opportunity and sharing a passion for steelmaking, more than 30 others from Nucor followed. Six of the nine supervisors in the SDI mill's melting and casting departments came from Crawfordsville. Busse also hired many talented young workers with no steel mill experience, just as Nucor had done at Crawfordsville. Damon Keck, who was put in charge of furnace operations at Butler, arrived just in time for the first casting test there. He had come to the Crawfordsville mill barely out of high school. In his first year there, he made $48,000—more than his father was making. Glenn Pushes was employee No. 5 at Butler. Pushes, a Purdue University graduate, had started his career in 1986 as an engineer at LTV's aging Lakeshore mill in East Chicago. One day, a headhunter called and asked: "Would you be interested in making a move?" Maybe, he replied, if it's to Nucor. Teets promptly tapped him for a mechanical engineering job in Crawfordsville. Pushes's father-in-law, who worked for Acme Steel near the Lakeshore mills, mocked him for choosing the remote and risky "CrawfordsTurkey" project instead of remaining at an established Lakeshore mill. "He said the Big Three steel mills up here are going to crush them," Pushes recalls. "Now he looks at me and thinks I'm smart." Later, at Butler, Pushes found himself in charge of all mechanical engineering for cold and hot mill projects valued at $350 million. Soon, the Butler plant needed only .7 to .8 of a man-hour to produce a ton of galvanized steel that took 4.5 man hours to make when Pushes was at LTV's Lakeshore mill.

Private investors put $370 million into SDI before it went public in the fall of 1996. A few months later, the company had amassed a market value of close to $1 billion. The startup at Butler went more smoothly than at Crawfordsville, because so much had been learned from Crawfordsville. SDI adopted many of Nucor's pay and work practices, and its relatively flat management structure. Mill workers at Butler make average annual wages of $60,000, with more than half their pay typically coming from incentives tied to the efficiency and production levels of their departments. All employees get stock options. Eventually,

Busse won recognition as one of Business Week's top 10 entrepreneurs in 1997 and became one of three national finalists in that year's Ernst & Young emerging entrepreneur competition.

CONTRARIAN APPROACH HELPS REGION

Like Busse, C&A's Dick Conrow is a maverick and an advocate for northeastern Indiana. But in other respects, the two entrepreneurs display striking contrasts. While Busse became a frontrunner in a flagship industry by moving steelmaking technology forward, Conrow made a smaller splash in a smaller field by bringing back the craftsmanship of bygone days. While Busse is upbeat about the prospects for American manufacturing, Conrow is skeptical.

"The businesspeople say people aren't loyal anymore," Conrow comments, quickly adding, "Well, who would you be loyal to, at what particular time of the month? All walks of life, including manufacturing now, are totally infested with academia."

The way Conrow sees it, parents urged baby boomers to go to college and then "being the good children that they were, they did, so that by the 1960s academia started churning out, if you will, the equivalent of 90-day wonders. You found people with 30 years of experience being monitored by schoolchildren who were taught that anybody could manage—you didn't have to know your job. That was true as long as old Homer and Jake were in the backroom making parts. Homer and Jake are gone now, so now we've got a big problem. People can't function anymore without a directive."

Conrow thinks the large manufacturers' acknowledgment that they can't do precision manufacturing has become a huge asset for C&A. His view, which he titles "the manufacturing world according to Dick," goes like this: Foreign machine builders secured a foothold in the United States after domestic producers decided they no longer wanted to make smaller machines such as lathes and grinders. Then, as the U.S. companies lost their basic expertise, the foreign producers gained competence in more sophisticated machinery. Now, Asian lands turn out big numbers of skilled toolmakers, while shortages rise in the United States. The domestic manufacturers, lacking technically astute workers, often turn to C&A with unrealistic requests for quick production of precision parts. "I turn away large blocks of work," says Conrow. "I tell our customers I do not have the energy or the resources to train their engineering departments. It's that bad. They've lost their expertise and they cannot manufacture effectively because of their work habits. It's an admission that they've completely devoided themselves of their manufacturing expertise." Conrow declares that the United States has created a generation of "green-button people"— workers who know how to run or monitor automated machinery but have not mastered the processes controlled by this equipment.

To develop a workforce with deeper skills than those possessed by the "green-button people," C&A grew from within. The company employs 240 workers, fewer than 50 of them with college degrees. Self-directed teams of machine operators decide schedules and job assignments for workers who run scores of grinders, lathes, and milling machines. About 30 tool-and-die makers are "go-to guys" at the heart of the company, constantly offering ideas and sharing solutions with the rest of the workforce. There are no supervisors, no foremen, no time cards. "You almost get the feeling, in Dick Conrow's place, that everybody is a CEO," says Lincoln Schrock.

SOURCES OF ANXIETY REMAIN

Busse and Conrow have given the region a significant lift. Still, their entrepreneurism and other factors fueling its comeback haven't been enough to keep an unsettled mood from rippling through northeast Indiana.

One of the biggest concerns is wage levels. The Community Research Institute has uncovered an unfavorable and widening gap between average pay levels in the region relative to the national average. The Institute found that while wage and salary earnings in northeast Indiana and the United States were equal in 1979, a gap had opened up by 1997. By then, workers in the region were averaging $26,614 in the region versus $29,814 nationally. The Institute's Thomas Guthrie, in a report issued in mid-2000, stated that "the battle to overcome the 1979 to 1982 economic debacle in northeast Indiana has been won. Declare victory while ahead and choose new goals." The primary new goal, Guthrie advised, should be "quality jobs."

Mark Crouch, an Indiana University professor who does training and research for unions, charges some factories that moved from Michigan to northeast Indiana are "runaway plants" that sought Indiana's lower workers' compensation and unemployment compensation costs.

Older workers who still have factory jobs with good pay and benefits want to keep them. One telling example: In 1992, nearly a decade after the Harvester shutdown, about 100 one-time Fort Wayne workers were still making 280-mile round trips to and from the Springfield plant. They had concluded that retaining above-average pay and benefits at Harvester was their best option, despite having to endure five and a half hours on the bus every working day.

Constant upheavals in the job market are another source of concern. Mergers, acquisitions, and other factors typically beyond the control of anyone in northeast Indiana often lead to shutdowns or cutbacks that offset the gains from new and expanded plants. Lincoln Schrock keeps tabs on the region's comings and goings. From 1997 to 1999, he counted 9,548 new industrial jobs versus a loss of 7,052 through plant closings or downsizing. Schrock's conclusion: The region must continually create new jobs just to stay even.

Moves of Indiana manufacturers to Mexico have been a particular concern of organized labor. Tom Lewandowski, president of the Allen County AFL-CIO, works a night shift at General Electric Co. in Fort Wayne. He notes that in 1948 GE, not Harvester, once employed the largest workforce any company ever had in Fort Wayne, 12,000. In the 1990s, GE moved motor and transformer work from Fort Wayne to Mexico, and today the company has fewer than 1,000 workers in the city.

"I'm a fourth generation GE worker in my family," says Lewandowski. "There's no way my son's going to work there."

Lewandowski pans the working schedules at nonunion SDI, where employees work 12-hour, 4-day weeks. In his view, "that makes people live to work, rather than work to live."

The job churning keeps hitting Indiana workers out of the blue. It happened in March of 1998 to David Quinn, who was earning $10.49 an hour plus good benefits making steering wheels for Breed Technologies near Fort Wayne. Quinn lost his job when the company moved it to Mexico. He finally landed higher-paying work at a manufacturer of ovens and cookware, but not before nearly two years of jumping from job to job. Such experiences often stir angry reactions, firing up strong and sustained union opposition to the North American Free Trade Agreement and other trade pacts. Conservative Mark Souder, the region's GOP congressman since 1995, joined Democrats sympathetic to organized labor's concerns when he voted against admitting China into the World Trade Organization.

Union opposition delayed a second SDI mill in Whitley County, northwest of Fort Wayne. Environmental regulators held up a permit for the project, a $315 million structural steel mill, after a plumbers and pipefitters local spearheaded an unusually intense review of plans for the mill. Busse had hoped to be in production by mid-2000, but construction didn't begin until May of 2001. The delays cost the company an estimated $1 million a month.

The region continues to be heavily dependent on the auto industry, which historically has been a notoriously cyclical business. One of the best measures of how the area remains hooked on this industry comes from Lincoln Schrock, whose statistics show that 66 percent of the new companies coming to the region, 67 percent of their jobs, and 85 percent of their investments over the decade ended in 1992 were auto-related. As Lynne McKenna Frazier, business editor of the *Fort Wayne News-Sentinel*, put it in a column looking back at changes since the Harvester strike and shutdown: "Who finds us attractive? It's mostly auto-related companies. Just as 20 years ago, and despite a lot of effort, the Fort Wayne region still lies under the shadow of Detroit."

Concerns that the region is being left behind in the competition for advanced technology jobs led to the creation of the Northeast Indiana Innovation Center in 2000. The Center, a new think tank backed by academic, business, and government leaders in Fort Wayne, is building a $6 million incubator to attract promising startup companies.

A shift in the state's economic development policy further underscores the worries of the region's leaders about lack of diversification. All through the 1980s and 1990s, Indiana was among a handful of states stressing a strong manufacturing sector as a strategic goal. However, in the spring of 1999, the Indiana Economic Development Commission adopted a new plan designed to enhance the state's environment for fast-growth technology companies.

Counters Schrock: "Our strength is in manufacturing. That is what reengineered northeast Indiana after the bottom fell out. Now they're all saying we're over-represented in manufacturing. To me, that's not a problem. Manufacturers are part of the answer, not part of the problem."

Steelmaking has become a very technology-intensive process at SDI, contrary to the industry's reputation on Wall Street as the melted-down core of a bygone era. "Clearly," Keith Busse says of his successes with the SMS Compact Strip Production machine, "our team made a mousetrap that was highly suspect, a futuristic technology, work." Yet, despite SDI's growth—to annual sales of $619 million in just six years and profitability in its first year as a public company—investors often lump SDI in with the rest of the steel industry. "Not every steel company is cast out of the same mold," says Busse. "We're just painted with that broad brush called 'old industry.' I guess that's what bothers me."

As for northeastern Indiana's future, it will depend on many factors—some related to the overall U.S. economy, some associated with the fortunes of individual industries. Because of its geographic location, it will remain highly linked to the motor-vehicle industry. This industry has been good for the region but it is also an industry with immense overcapacity. The steel industry has similar attributes—highly paid but with excess capacity. When the general economy slows, both of these industries and the northeastern Indiana region also contract. Yet, other regions may be less prepared. It may be that this tenacious region's effective combination of high productivity, heavy investment in modern plants, innovation in manufacturing processes, and the spirit of cooperation between governments, unions, and industry will stand as its best guarantee of a strong tomorrow.

PART TWO

Changing Geography and What It Means

Manufacturing jobs bleed slowly rather than hemorrhage. A square block plant of brick and concrete, filled with machine tools, has a long economic life. As forces of changing competition push and pull work elsewhere, however, the work of many factories withers and the blood of taxes and Little League coaches flows from the community. Most important, a community's self-respect bleeds away.

Profitable manufacturers strengthen communities. The wages, benefits, and taxes they generate lead not only to prosperity and opportunity, but also to pride in community identity. Yet, due to many forces, the concentration of production sites has shifted. Companies, confronted by increased competition, gain efficiencies by moving selected processes to other plants. They shift production to get closer to customers or skilled workers. They reappraise their factory locations when their equipment becomes outmoded or they lack the room to expand.

Part Two maps the movements that have occurred in the last quarter of the 20th Century at the county level to see what they tell us about American manufacturing today:

Chapter 4 outlines our methodology and describes the forces that drive the movement of manufacturing.

Chapters 5 and 6 concentrate on the counties gaining and losing industrial momentum.

Chapter 7 moves in for a closer look at how manufacturing losses have wounded core cities, with the focus on Philadelphia.

Chapter 8 defines the links, in all of the counties we studied, between manufacturing and community well-being.

CHAPTER 4

The Relocation
of Industry

 The news spreads quickly whenever a large, aging factory shuts down. Newspapers and television newscasters interview workers at the plant gates. Their poignant stories, repeated many times since the late 1970s, are not pretty. Longtime employees suddenly lose their jobs, which often paid good wages and benefits. Cities lose the tax base that these plants have provided. The community loses the civic participation and steadying influence of both the workers and the company.

Elsewhere, manufacturing jobs are growing. American manufacturing has been on the move, decentralizing and diversifying, often in ways far less visible than the wrenching shutdowns in the nation's older, more built-up industrial areas.

To get at these trends and many more, we built an extensive database to examine changes in wages, employment, establishments, and other measures of manufacturing for each of the country's 3,142 counties for the years 1977 through 1999.

We identified the 704 counties with the highest manufacturing employment levels and then selected the top sixth and bottom sixth in manufacturing job and payroll change. That left us with 232 counties, 116 where manufacturing was expanding and 116 where it was declining.

We next grouped these 232 counties into seven different categories, based on the size of their manufacturing sector and changes in employment and payroll. This gave us a useful perspective from which to weigh the relative performances of manufacturing in each of the counties. Trends in each of these groups fluctuated significantly from national averages. Four of the seven groups, with 116 counties, did better than the nation. Three, also with 116 counties, fared worse. We gave the groups names: Hinterland Highspots, Metro Movers, Freeway Flyers, and Gradual Growers for the expanding counties; Smaller Sliders, Midrange Sliders, and Sliding Goliaths for the contracting counties. Our methodology is explained in Appendix A but the basic characteristics of each of the seven categories are described in Figure 4.1.

Usually, geographical comparisons of manufacturing have concentrated on comparisons of states or metro areas. By going deeper, to the county level, we were able to examine more closely the complex makeover that has swept across the manufacturing sector. Figure 4.2 shows the variations in employment changes for all of the counties in the lower 48 states, over the 1977 to 1997 period. It is not uncommon to see both expanding and contracting counties in the same state.

In bold relief, our data define a Great Scattering. First, the center of gravity in American manufacturing has moved from the East Coast to the rebounding Midwest, the South, and the West. Second, manufacturing has been shifting outward to the fringes of the metropolitan areas, more outlying sites along the interstates, and, in some cases, to rural counties. From 1979 to 1999, the share of manufacturing wages going to workers in the 25 counties with the largest payrolls in this sector fell from 30 percent to 25 percent. During the same period, the portion of these wages going to workers in the 2,642 counties with the

---

FIGURE 4.1   Categories of Sample Counties

CATEGORY	METROPOLITAN AREA	INTERSTATE HIGHWAY	1995 MANUFACTURING EMPLOYMENT	NUMBER OF COUNTIES
Hinterland Highspots	No	No	4,800 or more	15
Metro Movers	Yes	Either	4,800 or more	40
Freeway Flyers	No	Yes	4,800 or more	20
Gradual Growers	Either	Either	4,800 or more	41
Counties Gaining Momentum Total	—	—	—	116
Smaller Sliders	Either	Either	4,800 to 9,999	34
Midrange Sliders	Either	Either	10,000 to 34,999	46
Sliding Goliaths	Either	Either	35,000 or more	36
Counties Losing Momentum Total	—	—	—	116
Total Counties in Sample	—	—	—	232

FIGURE 4.2   Manufacturing Employment Changes by County (Counties with More Than 4,800 Manufacturing Employees in 1995)

Gains in Manufacturing Employment, 1977–1997

Losses in Manufacturing Employment, 1977–1997

smallest payrolls rose from 18 percent to 22 percent (Figure 4.3). During the last two decades of the 20th Century, manufacturing became much more geographically dispersed.

The dispersion is even more dramatic when comparing individual counties. The largest counties in manufacturing payroll in 1979 were not the same as those in 1999. New York slipped 32 positions, from 4th to 36th; St. Louis slipped from 29th to 103rd; Baltimore City slid from 51st to 119th. Meanwhile, Maricopa County, Arizona (Phoenix), rose from 30th to 10th; Kent County, Michigan (Grand Rapids), from 52nd to 17th; and Travis County, Texas (Austin), jumped all the way from 163rd to 19th.

Often, the counties' destinies rose or fell not so much as a result of a particular public policy, but rather because of the quality of management at their largest manufacturing employers. For example, labor-management relations can vary greatly from one plant to another, even within a single company. General Motors and the United Auto Workers had a particularly hard time getting along at GM's plants in Norwood, Ohio, and Framingham, Massachusetts, but relations have been notably better at the company's plant in Lansing, Michigan.

FIGURE 4.3   Manufacturing Payroll by Size of Community

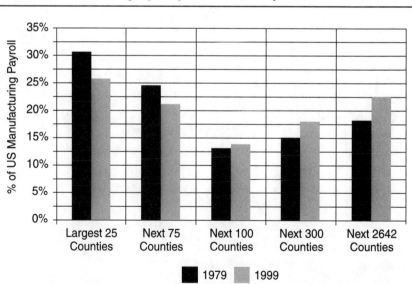

Changes in market tastes can force industrial restructuring that distinctly alters production locations. The late Don Ephlin, vice president of the United Auto Workers, lamented the closing of East and West Coast auto plants, but explained it this way:

It used to be that all Chevrolets were alike and when that was the case, we had six Chevrolet plants scattered across the United States. But when they started to make six different kinds of Chevrolets, it became necessary for economic reasons to produce most of those models near the center of the country.

For this reason and others, the auto industry executed a sweeping locational shift, mostly in the 1980s. Analysts summarized the moves at a 1996 Federal Reserve Bank of Chicago workshop. They found that 24 of the nation's 57 auto assembly plants were in the Northeast and the West in 1979, but that by 1996 these regions had only 14 of 58 plants as production gravitated to the Midwest and the South. Automakers opened 21 plants in the Midwest and the South over this period, but only one in the other two regions. The big winners: the corridors paralleling Interstates 65 and 75, home to 39 auto assembly plants versus only 27 in 1979.

Often, but not always, the states gaining the most in population and political strength are those where manufacturing has by various yardsticks been picking up steam. Texas, several mid-South states, and selected states in the South and the West, all gaining population and congressional seats, also happen to be picking up momentum in manufacturing. The reverse has proven to be true for New York and some other states with minimal population gains and shrinking congressional delegations. Manufacturers seeking lower shipping costs have located plants close to growing numbers of customers in rapidly expanding urban areas such as Atlanta and Dallas.

However, manufacturing is also expanding where population is light. From 1988 to 1997, the states with the most rapidly growing manufacturing payrolls were South Dakota, Nevada, North Dakota, New Mexico, and Idaho with Nebraska, Utah, and Wyoming also ranking in the top ten. Cities are not much of a draw. Counties not part of metropolitan areas, 1,343 in our sample, added 308,000 jobs from 1972 to 1997. Meanwhile, 685 metropolitan counties lost 1,354,000 jobs.

> *From 1988 to 1997, the states with the most rapidly growing*
> *manufacturing payrolls were South Dakota, Nevada, North*
> *Dakota, New Mexico, and Idaho with Nebraska, Utah, and*
> *Wyoming also ranking in the top ten.*

In part, the moves are being driven by a competitive imperative: to become more efficient. A manufacturer saddled with an inefficient three- or four-story, 50-year-old factory in the heart of the city simply cannot hold its own in competition with modern, low-slung plants in less developed areas. In many cases, companies can't find enough land to build in the city, or, if they can find it, face zoning, environmental, or political obstacles. This is particularly apparent in the larger cities of the Northeast and Midwest. There, manufacturing in the core cities of a number of large metropolitan areas has slipped precipitously, but industrial activity has expanded in other counties in the same state. The outlying plants often tend to have newer equipment than did their forerunners in the core cities. Thus, their production processes are more flexible, more mobile.

> *1,343 counties not part of metropolitan areas added 308,000*
> *jobs from 1972 to 1997. Meanwhile, 685 metropolitan counties*
> *lost 1,354,000 jobs.*

The exteriors of the newer plants are indistinguishable—if even they can be seen at all—from structures occupied by, say, insurance companies. Often, they are light assembly plants, seldom identifiable by smokestacks or other unmistakable signs of the industries of an earlier age. In other cases, though, such as with the Nucor plant in Crawfordsville, Indiana, or the Toyota plant in Georgetown, Kentucky, they are huge industrial complexes.

Manufacturing made quite a difference in the economic life of the counties of the seven categories. Figure 4.4 illustrates how much better the four categories of expanding counties did versus the three groups of contracting counties.

Figure 4.5 shows how the country's major regions compare, measured by the number of counties each region landed in the expanding and contracting categories. Although the Midwest, South, and West have fared better in this analysis, special circumstances benefited these

FIGURE 4.4   Summary Statistics of Classified Counties

CATEGORY	1997 MFG. EMPLOYMENT	% INCREASE MFG. EMPLOYMENT 1977–1997	% INCREASE MFG. EMPLOYMENT 1986–1997	% INCREASE MFG. EMPLOYMENT 1995–1997	% INCREASE MFG. PAYROLL 1979–1997	% INCREASE MFG. PAYROLL 1986–1997	% INCREASE MFG. PAYROLL 1995–1997
Hinterland Highspots	119,140	85.9%	54.3%	4.3%	307.7%	139.1%	15.9%
Metro Movers	723,998	152.2	65.1	15.9	445.2	171.7	31.5
Freeway Flyers	169,449	74.3	53.3	6.0	293.2	151.7	18.0
Gradual Growers	651,194	69.1	43.2	7.1	252.3	117.3	18.6
Expanding Counties	1,663,781	99.6	53.9	10.4	333.7	145.2	24.3
Smaller Sliders	209,893	−39.5	−24.2	−9.2	23.8	6.5	−1.3
Midrange Sliders	812,064	−33.2	−22.8	−9.6	54.2	18.6	−3.6
Sliding Goliaths	2,531,768	−41.9	−28.6	−5.3	38.8	14.7	3.4
Contracting Counties	3,553,725	−40.0	−27.1	−6.5	41.0	15.1	1.5
Total Sample	5,217,506	−22.8%	−12.4%	−1.7%	75.2%	35.9%	7.2%

Note: Data was collected on all counties for the years 1977 through 1999. However, the Census Bureau change from SIC codes to NAICS industry codes in 1998 introduces some minor problems in interpreting trends from before 1998 to later periods. The changes do not seriously affect the analysis but the authors feel the years prior to 1998 present a clearer picture of expansion and contraction in manufacturing.

FIGURE 4.5   Counties Receiving Expanding and Contracting Classifications

REGION	EXPANDING	CONTRACTING	NET
New England States (CT, ME, MA, NH, RI, VT)	1	12	−11
Middle Atlantic States (NJ, NY, PA)	0	40	−40
TOTAL NORTHEAST REGION	1	52	−51
East North Central States (IL, IN, MI, OH, WI)	29	22	7
West North Central States (IA, KS, MN, MO, NE, ND, SD)	17	2	15
TOTAL MIDWEST REGION	46	24	22
West South Central States (AR, LA, OK, TX)	14	5	9
East South Central States (AL, KY, MS, TN)	21	9	12
South Atlantic States (DE, DC, FL, GA, MD, NC, SC, VA, WV)	16	22	−6
TOTAL SOUTHERN REGION	51	36	15
Mountain States (AZ, CO, ID, MT, NV, NM, UT, WY)	7	1	6
Pacific States (AK, CA, HI, OR, WA)	11	3	8
TOTAL WESTERN REGION	18	4	14
TOTAL UNITED STATES	116	116	0

Note: Refer to Appendix A for a more detailed discussion of research methodology.

three regions. Auto and truck sales were especially robust during most of the 1990s, and this prosperity greatly aided the Midwest and, to some degree, the South. Computer and aircraft sales were also robust and bolstered the West and a few other areas.

Industry sales, model changes, market shifts, climates, terrain, retirements, acquisitions, mergers, political changes, and luck all influenced which counties expanded and which contracted. In some counties, greater foresight and better planning worked to encourage industrial expansion, while neglect of major repelling forces made expansion more difficult in others.

The differences between regions of the country are quite pronounced, but often not as much as the differences between counties in the same state. Our sample included counties from 43 states and, of these, 17 states (nearly 40 percent) had counties listed in both the expanding and contracting lists.

RELOCATION: A COMBINATION OF ATTRACTING AND REPELLING FORCES

Before looking more closely at each of our groups of counties, we should take note of reasons why manufacturing gradually moves from one location to another. Many factors, based on both realities and perceptions, influence the location of industry. Seldom is any one factor the primary cause of industry relocating. Rather, many forces are often involved, and this mixture rarely repeats itself. Every case is different, depending on the industry, the timing, the age of the plant, and many other variables.

Only infrequently does a manufacturer actually pick up and move an entire plant. Huge investments in machinery, special facilities, logistics, and training occur over the life of a factory, which, on average, lasts about 70 years. The scope of these investments usually offsets the economic advantages of simply pulling up stakes.

Instead, most manufacturing movements take place in small, almost imperceptible increments. Selected processes get moved to satellite plants. More work is contracted out. Mergers lead to partial consolidations. Key employees strike out on their own, perhaps moving to different locations.

REPELLING FORCES

Both attracting forces to the new location and repelling forces from the old location are active when industry expands out of its home location or physically relocates. Our study revealed many repelling forces that influence industrial location. While they are present in all regions, they are particularly evident in large core cities:

1. *Shortage of land.* Expanding and thriving businesses usually need more space, and often more land, for expansion. Cities and built-up suburbs are densely occupied, thus significant amounts of land are seldom available.
2. *High cost of land, particularly if it's polluted.* If land is available in such areas, it can be far more expensive in "brownfield" areas than in virgin, or "greenfield," sites because of the high cost of cleanup. Concern about liability for polluted sites can scare off both buyers and sellers, discouraging redevelopment of such land. Some states and communities have passed legislation to ease this concern, but even in these instances, the cost of buying and preparing industrial land often remains high.
3. *Objections of residents.* Sometimes even the noblest companies meet resistance to expansion from residents. Citizens' objections can lead to prolonged reviews and hearings that drive up costs and scare off the companies.
4. *Inadequate infrastructure.* Modern manufacturing depends heavily on the reliable delivery of energy, communications, and other supplies and services at reasonable cost. Yet, the infrastructure may be aging or ineffective in some communities. Power plants are often old and few new ones are being built. Some electrical transmission systems are overloaded, unreliable, or high-cost. Competent suppliers may have left the region.
5. *Insufficient supply of good labor.* Low unemployment rates limit the labor supply in many regions. Unemployed workers who are available often lack the skills manufacturers need. Sometimes, employers worry that relations with high-risk employees will turn contentious and legalistic.
6. *Building codes that block modernization.* Overly stringent building codes, often in core cities, can discourage expansion and modernization.

7. *High labor costs.* Local union leaders or their rank and file may insist on perpetuating unrealistic work rules, which translate into high costs that erode a company's competitiveness. In some cases, wages well above those paid by competitors encourage managers to look elsewhere.

8. *Incompetent management.* Ultimately, good management is essential for the success of the company, and not every company has it.

9. *Costly or ineffective public services.* Companies sometimes view taxes as inordinately high, especially relative to the quality of schools, police protection, and other services.

10. *Cumbersome regulation.* Regulatory agencies sometimes impose heavy burdens on businesses by holding up approvals on permits or saddling them with many layers of uncoordinated rules.

11. *Mergers and acquisitions.* In some cases, ownership changes, particularly common in recent years, can generate newly rationalized business structures that lead to cutbacks and closings. In other cases, poorly integrated mergers produce similar results.

12. *Poor transportation.* Once-excellent locations with efficient access to primary suppliers and customers via well-established rail networks may today be highly congested areas, surrounded by heavy traffic. In some instances, railroads may have lost their advantages due to the trend to just-in-time shipment of lighter-weight modern products to geographically dispersed locations.

13. *Companies reach the end of their useful lives.* Even well-run companies sometimes decide to cease operations. A retiring owner, facing harsh economic times or lacking an adequate yield on invested assets, might opt for liquidation. Competitors might run the company out of business. In some cases, the property may be more valuable than the business itself. Changing technologies may eliminate the demand for the company's products.

Yet another repelling force merits special mention—litigation, which can expose manufacturers in all parts of the country to huge, unbudgeted expenses. A 1996 *Chicago Tribune* story, which documented the impact of litigation in shutting down one of the nation's most venerable manufacturers of grinding machines, illustrates the problem. That year, a jury awarded $7.3 million to an injured worker in a product liability judgment against Rockford, Illinois–based Mattison Technologies. The worker was injured by a Mattison grinder in 1991, but the company sold the machine in 1948 and it had worked safely until the accident. "I don't see how we can be at fault for a machine we have not seen for 40 years," protested Bill Farris, president of Mattison. The company, which had only $20 million in annual revenue, filed for Chapter 11 bankruptcy reorganization soon after the verdict was returned.

The list of manufacturing companies impaired by capricious product liability judgments is very long. In 1992, an expectant mother was involved in a head-on collision in her car, equipped with an airbag. The bag deployed and both the mother and baby were saved, but the escaping gases allegedly caused some burns on the woman's left hand, which reportedly healed in a few weeks. A jury awarded the plaintiff $3.75 million in punitive damages plus $730 in compensatory damages to every owner of a 1988 to 1990 model Chrysler car registered in Pennsylvania. There are many other examples of such awards.

It is not the purpose of this book to comment on the adequacy of the nation's liability laws or on the many stifled initiatives aimed at reform. Other more qualified people are involved on both sides of this question. Instead, we focus on the ramifications of bizarre awards on the prosperity of the nation, on the availability of employment, and on the long-term competitiveness of American industry. Damage awards are paid by somebody. Though all manufacturers enter business with the realization that they will be held responsible for reasonable product liability, excessively large damage awards limit the money available for researching better methods, developing better products, and expanding manufacturing operations. They can serve as an enormous disincentive to be in business—a powerful repelling force. In some cases, the awards can put the company, and all of its workers, completely out of business.

While none of these repelling forces may be individually sufficient to abruptly cause relocation, they often become meaningful factors in long-term trends. To some degree, they fester. Out of love for the community, loyalty to people, proximity to business associates, or procrastination, company managers may not respond to repelling forces for a long time. Reaction to them often comes only after a cataclysmic event such as a decline in market share, a recession, or the changing of key management. Sooner or later, though, any of the above repelling forces can provide the impetus for change.

The accumulation of repelling forces is somewhat natural. When a plant reaches advanced age, almost everything surrounding it has also changed markedly from the conditions that existed at the time the plant was built. This combination of age, changing conditions, and preferences on the part of contemporary managers can influence the decision to continue in a present location, liquidate the business, or move to a new location. Sometimes, the repelling forces only surface when other attracting forces become evident.

ATTRACTING FORCES

Attracting forces may unfold but often as a second stage after the repelling forces take root. The usual sequence: something about the present location irritates employers and then they become attracted to new locations.

The attracting forces may include the desire to be on an interstate network near the center of a large market. They may include better climates or lower costs—not only labor costs but other costs as well. Following is a list of the attracting forces that influence industrial location:

1. *Shifting locations of major customers or suppliers.* One of the most significant attracting forces is proximity to major customers or suppliers. Some industrial relocation is inevitable, given the shifting locations of emerging industries. Beyond that, end-product companies are trying to reduce their suppliers to a smaller and more trusted number. Sometimes, companies have to move closer to their major customers in order to achieve or maintain their status as preferred suppliers.
2. *Work ethic.* A strong educational system, little competition from capable, high-paying employers, or simply a conviction that people in a particular region are good workers can lead an employer to rate work ethic as a significant advantage.
3. *Quality.* Workers at some plants have strengthened the reputations of their regions by making products widely recognized for their high quality.

4. *Favorable legislative, legal, and tax climates.* Some states have enacted labor legislation or established elements of judiciary systems that are perceived to be fair and even-handed by employers. Some communities stress "business friendly" legal and regulatory climates particularly attractive to manufacturers. Tax levels do matter, though probably not as much as some would suggest.

5. *Industrial swarming.* Sometimes, a single manufacturer or several manufacturers attract a network of suppliers with special technical skills to a region. The strong presence of major manufacturers may give rise to high-technology foundries, machine shops, heat treaters, plating shops, metal stampers, and other supporting industries. The availability of cost-effective services may also provide attraction.

6. *Economic incentives.* Often, manufacturers offer such good wage and benefit packages that they are sought by many communities. This competition has sometimes led governments to offer substantial subsidies to companies locating new plants.

7. *Transportation.* Ready access to the interstate highway system, reasonably priced and effective air transportation, and good rail connections are all attributes appealing to many manufacturers. Some may also be attracted by the close proximity to suppliers and customers.

8. *Ownership changes.* While some ownership changes may be highly leveraged, poorly thought-out ventures with little added value, others may be quite well-developed strategic initiatives. Some ownership changes do result in significant investment at the acquired site.

9. *Attractive wage rates.* Regions with low wage rates are of interest to some employers, particularly when labor costs represent a relatively high percentage of overall costs or when skills crucial to high product quality are easily learned.

10. *The weather.* Weather can become a factor. The milder climates of the mid-South and the Southwest are attractive to some companies.

> *Attracting forces often unfold as a second stage after the repelling forces take root.*

These attracting forces can offer a rosy alternative to the manufacturer wishing to expand, but many locations have these attributes, and not all of them are expanding. Some communities succeed and their industrial base grows, but many do not. So the combination of these repelling and attracting forces, together with the individual situations, are often superimposed on another important variable: the quality of the company itself.

THE IMPORTANT VARIABLE—THE COMPANY ITSELF

Companies vary enormously in their financial strength, innovation, quality, and rapport with workers, suppliers, and home communities. Attracting and repelling factors affect both the good and the not-so-good companies, but the good companies handle these forces differently. Well-regarded companies seem better able to read and prepare for market trends. They focus their investments on important corporate attributes such as higher product quality, better service, expeditious product development, and production efficiency, in order to provide lasting benefits to customers. Not-so-good companies often focus on offices, executive compensation, mergers, acquisitions, public image, the shortcomings of workers, and a variety of topics unrelated to what the customer is buying. The personality and motivation of the larger industrial employers in any community has a great deal to do with the retention and growth of manufacturing.

Later in this book, the authors will present more examples of how corporations vary in their approaches to their missions, markets, and home communities. The United States is blessed with some excellent companies and when they exist, local communities usually prosper. When good companies are not present, economic difficulties for the entire community usually unfold over long periods of time.

Emotionalism as a Locating Force

Although basic considerations of revenue and cost play a role in decisions about industrial location and relocation, these important decisions are not always based entirely on rational appraisals. Emotionalism creeps into decisions about where companies should be, or should not be—particularly if the company is not doing well. In some cases, companies may seek new surroundings largely because management is incapable of running the business properly in any location, but the current location gets the blame. Top officers of poorly performing companies often rationalize their mistakes. Occasionally, managers become introspective and recognize that modifications in their own behavior may be important remedial steps in restoring the health of the firm. Too often, though, executives in charge of troubled companies blame everything else, including the local business climate. This mentality may lead to unnecessary company relocations.

Non-economic factors often influence industrial relocation. Personal factors, including personality clashes between management and unions, between management and city officials, or between management and landlords, affect company expansion, contraction, or relocation decisions. It is by no means certain that rational managers, prudent labor leaders, and statesmanlike public officials will coexist in the same town simultaneously. Often, one incompetence feeds upon another to create cleavages that are not healed. Thus, emotionalism does influence the location of industry.

CHAPTER 5

Counties Gaining Momentum

Counties gain momentum in manufacturing because of a combination of careful planning, frugality, efficiency, educational effectiveness, luck, and the presence of good companies. Yet, beware, because conditions can change quickly. Yesterday's successful county can become tomorrow's lackluster performer or maybe even a trouble spot. From 1977 through 1999, however, the 116 counties singled out in this chapter had vibrant, growing economies, and it is useful and encouraging to examine their successes. These counties operated with the same stock market, the same national economy, the same president, the same Congress, and the same Federal Reserve chairman as the counties that fared less well.

We describe these 116 counties as "gaining momentum." They were the top one-sixth of our sample in manufacturing employment and payroll growth from 1977 to 1999. Our sample included only the larger counties, those with 4,800 or more manufacturing employees in 1995. In some respects, these successful counties were dissimilar: Hinterland Highspots were nonmetropolitan counties but not proximate to the interstates; Freeway Flyers were on interstate highways away from metropolitan areas; Metro Movers were thriving parts of metropolitan areas; and Gradual Growers were simply counties that had less dramatic but very continuous growth.

HINTERLAND HIGHSPOTS

Not part of metropolitan areas, and not blessed with an interstate highway, the Hinterland Highspots often prospered with the presence of a small number of very well-run industrial companies. Often, these companies had specialties such as prosthesis implants, magnetic tape, printer cartridges, technical components, windows, or unique machinery. The counties themselves were not large by population. The most populous Hinterland Highspot counties have about 80,000 residents. They are big enough to be able to supply critical skills and small enough to be nimble and efficient.

Many circumstances have contributed to the successes of the Hinterland Highspots, counties that have prospered in lockstep with the triumphs of their manufacturers. One of their most noticeable traits is an unusually high concentration of manufacturing jobs. Forty-one percent worked in this sector in the Hinterland Highspots in 1995, nearly three times the national average. The portion of total payroll in these counties was even higher with over half of the payroll coming from manufacturing. The principal driver—the presence of first-rate manufacturers making products society needs. (See Figure 5.1.)

Forty-one percent worked in this sector in the Hinterland Highspots in 1995, nearly three times the national average.

FIGURE 5.1   Hinterland Highspots

COUNTY	METRO AREA	MFG. EMPLOYMENT 1977	MFG. EMPLOYMENT 1999	% MFG. EMPLOYMENT CHANGE 1977–1999	% MFG. PAYROLL CHANGE 1979–1999
Benton, OR	None	2,800	8,712	211.1%	474.3%
Sioux, IA	None	1,800	4,711	161.7	325.8
Marion, IA	None	3,100	7,796	151.5	418.2
Barry, MO	None	3,000	6,943	131.4	438.6
Coffee, GA	None	2,800	6,110	118.2	397.3
Franklin, AL	None	2,400	5,188	116.2	328.3
Noble, IN	None	5,500	11,501	109.1	401.0
McLeod, MN	None	4,800	8,990	87.3	296.6
Marshall, AL	None	7,400	13,599	83.8	273.2
Pettis, MO	None	3,200	5,544	73.3	340.1
Winston, AL	None	4,200	6,931	65.0	207.2
Grand Traverse, MI	None	3,700	5,892	59.2	270.5
Kosciusko, IN	None	10,400	14,924	43.5	306.7
Greene, AR	None	4,400	5,991	36.2	247.1
Platte, NE	None	4,600	5,937	29.1	157.9

In north central Indiana, Kosciusko County nurtured a strong ortho-pedic devices industry whose roots stretch back to 1895 when De Puy Inc. began operation. De Puy still has 800 employees at its Warsaw, Indiana, facility. Zimmer, now a division of Bristol-Myers Squibb, was started in 1927 by De Puy's sales manager, J.O. Zimmer, and now employs 1,400. A current fountainhead of the county's considerable prosperity is Biomet, a leading medical-device maker that recorded compounded annual growth rates averaging 30 percent in revenue and 27 percent in earnings per share from 1985 to 2000. Biomet is also based in Warsaw, where many job shops and other suppliers helped to attract the company's founders in 1977. "They chose Warsaw because of the strong support network and the experienced workers here," says Biomet CEO Dane Miller. "The people know how to drill a hole in cobalt-chrome (a basic material in the prosthesis industry)."

Kosciusko County has businesses beyond medical devices. In 1999, Donnelley & Sons had a printing plant employing 1,700 and Dana Corp. employed more than 700 people building motor-vehicle components. The county's healthy combination of well-established businesses has helped move average manufacturing pay to the top quartile of the nation.

Manufacturing can generate and sustain pockets of prosperity in rural regions hurt by declining agricultural employment. Platte County, 90 miles west of Omaha in the heart of the Nebraska prairie, has few native attributes suggesting that it should be a manufacturing center. It is far from major markets and key suppliers, has no four-year col-lege or university, and is 50 miles from the nearest interstate highway. Yet, manufacturers there make medical devices, industrial machinery, electronics, farm equipment, food, auto seats, and surgical supplies. A large Becton-Dickinson factory employs more than 1,000 workers and five other manufacturers each employ more than 500. The county's manufacturing payroll has nearly doubled since the late 1980s. In Sep-tember of 2000, Columbus Mayor Gary Gibelhaus gleefully announced the arrival of yet another plant. Much of Platte County's manufactur-ing grew from Behlen Manufacturing, founded in 1936 by inventor Walter Behlen in his garage. Today Behlen, which started out making steel toe caps for industrial shoes, exports agricultural equipment to 50 countries. Many of Behlen's employees, like Gary Schmale, have ben-efited from extensive training. Schmale has taken numerous on-site courses since joining the company in 1995 as a welder trainee, and he has risen to become a second-shift team leader at Behlen, which now employs more than 1,200 workers.

In Georgia's Coffee County, poultry slaughtering and the production of aircraft engine parts have helped to more than quadruple the manufacturing payroll over the past 20 years. Benton County, Oregon, has doubled its factory payroll in the same period by making an increasingly common product—Hewlett-Packard printer cartridges. In Iowa, Marion County has built a diversified economy on the strength of Pella Windows, 3M, and Vermeer Manufacturing, a builder of landscaping and tree removal equipment. Pontopoc County in northeastern Mississippi has capitalized on its proximity to hardwood forests to specialize in the manufacture of wood flooring and furniture.

Minnesota's McLeod County is a special place. Bill Asp and Dan Mraz might not be fodder for a profile in *Wired* magazine, but they and others like them make things work there. Asp passed up a four-year degree for a tech school diploma, started his own machine shop, grossed $150,000 in his second year of business, and managed to teach a full load of tool-and-die courses at Ridgewater College. Then he chucked his 100-hour work weeks and sold his business to concentrate on teaching. The new owner is Sam Marz, another alum from Ridgewater, a two-year community college in Hutchinson, Minnesota, the seat of McLeod County.

McLeod County is 60 miles west of the state's principal metropolitan area, the Twin Cities. Yet, the county stands on its own, because its growth has been built on the achievements of its two largest industrial employers, 3M and Hutchinson Technology. Both companies and many small job shops in the region have benefited from the worker flow and customized training programs run by Ridgewater College. In 1996, *Money* magazine named Hutchinson, the county seat, one of America's "50 Hottest Little Boom Towns."

Scores of Ridgewater graduates have flocked to the payrolls of 3M and Hutchinson Technology. The school has also forged customized training partnerships with both companies and with manufacturers across the country. Its instructors travel to Seattle to teach courses in the science of measurement to Boeing employees. Ridgewater's "Nondestructive Testing" program, which turns out technicians able to detect tiny cracks in airplane wings or structural flaws in oil pipelines, is regarded as one of the best for that discipline in the world.

Hinterland Highspots are not very complicated places. People work hard, get along, and have specialties. Companies and governments cooperate within a spirit of community well-being.

FREEWAY FLYERS

Interstate highways slice through the non-metropolitan counties we call Freeway Flyers. Quick access and speedy transport have attracted many manufacturers. Interstates pass through 716 nonmetropolitan counties, yet only 20 did well enough to make this category. Often, these counties flourish courtesy of a single manufacturer or industry. Overall, manufacturing employment in Freeway Flyer counties has grown 80 percent since the early 1980s while payroll has tripled. (See Figure 5.2.)

FIGURE 5.2   Freeway Flyers

COUNTY	METRO AREA	MFG. EMPLOYMENT 1977	MFG. EMPLOYMENT 1999	% MFG. EMPLOYMENT CHANGE 1977–1999	% MFG. PAYROLL CHANGE 1979–1999
Steuben, IN	None	2,100	7,890	275.7%	592.8%
Monroe, TN	None	2,300	5,530	140.4	752.7
Granville, NC	None	3,200	6,525	103.9	344.0
Pontotoc, MS	None	3,200	6,455	101.7	420.0
Dubois, IN	None	7,400	14,715	98.9	314.7
Hardin, KY	None	3,700	7,231	95.4	408.3
Rockingham, VA	None	5,200	9,927	90.9	373.7
Steele, MN	None	4,500	8,309	84.6	317.4
Maury, TN	None	6,200	11,355	83.1	650.8
Hall, GA	None	10,000	18,294	82.9	338.5
Walworth, WI	None	6,300	10,970	74.1	272.1
Logan, OH	None	3,800	6,575	73.0	439.5
Saline, KS	None	4,000	6,921	73.0	236.6
Henderson, NC	None	4,800	8,000	66.7	306.9
Jackson, IN	None	4,100	6,375	55.5	312.6
Dodge, WI	None	8,700	13,432	54.4	220.1
Portage, WI	None	3,500	5,313	51.8	222.6
Pope, AR	None	3,300	4,642	40.7	172.6
Coffee, TN	None	4,500	5,682	26.3	288.7
Mississippi, AR	None	6,400	7,115	11.2	218.7

Mississippi County, in the northeast corner of Arkansas about 70 miles north of Memphis, is a Freeway Flyer. It was once almost totally dependent on farming and jobs generated by Eaker Air Force Base. In 1992, the base closed, but by then Big Steel had arrived. Nucor, attracted by easy access and a good workforce, built two huge minimills at Blytheville and Hickman in the 1980s. Scrap steel moves down the Mississippi River to the mills, which transform it into rolled steel that is then loaded onto trucks heading to Interstate 55 and on to industrial customers. Today, 2,500 employees work at the two mills and for recently arrived related industries in Mississippi County. Cecil Holifield, president of the Blytheville-Gosnell Chamber of Commerce, says the new industry has turned an economically impoverished county into a growth area. "This used to be total farmland," he says. "Now, it's all heavy industry."

Wood means good in Dubois County, nestled deep in the hills of southern Indiana. Manufacturing jobs in the county rose 30 percent from 1988 to 1995. Workers stream into the county from towns an hour or more away to jobs at woodworking plants in or near Jasper and Huntingburg. As a result, Jasper's daytime population of more than 30,000 is roughly three times its count at night. Kimball International, the one-time piano-maker based in Chicago, moved its headquarters to Jasper years ago and evolved into a major producer of office furniture. Kimball has 11 plants in the county. Huntingburg-based Styline Industries, which also makes office furniture, has another 9 there. Woodworking has been the county's mainstay industry for decades, a role that intensified with the opening of Interstate 64 along the county's southern border. "I-64 really opened up southern Indiana," says Styline Chairman Robert Menke Sr.

Maury County, Tennessee, is home base to Saturn Corp.—the start-with-a-clean-sheet-of-paper car division of General Motors that opened in the 1980s. It has the distinction of having the highest average manufacturing pay of any Freeway Flyer in 1999—$57,400 per employee per year, or 6.5 times what it was in 1977. Granville County, in North Carolina, supplements its regional capability in the textile industry by employing nearly 2,000 workers to make cosmetics and toiletries for Revlon. Rockingham County in the Shenandoah Valley of Virginia processes poultry and prepares pharmaceuticals for Merck.

The Freeway Flyer counties, like the Hinterland Highspots, have gained economically by carefully and consistently cultivating specialized manufacturing capabilities that have become distinctive on a national scale. They tend to be manufacturing intensive with manufacturing averaging nearly 38 percent of all county jobs and 48 percent of total county payroll. Manufacturing employment in the Freeway Flyer counties increased 76 percent from 1977 to 1997 during a time when the nation as a whole lost 2 million manufacturing jobs.

> *Manufacturing employment in the Freeway Flyer counties increased 76 percent from 1977 to 1997 during a time when the nation as a whole lost 2 million manufacturing jobs.*

METRO MOVERS

Metro Movers are high-industrial-growth communities within metropolitan areas. Overall, metropolitan counties lost more than 1.3 million industrial jobs between 1977 and 1997, while the Metro Mover counties added 460,000 jobs—doubling their manufacturing employment. Only 5 percent of the nation's metropolitan counties made the Metro Movers list. (See Figure 5.3.)

FIGURE 5.3   Metro Movers

COUNTY	METRO AREA	MFG. EMPLOYMENT 1977	MFG. EMPLOYMENT 1999	% MFG. EMPLOYMENT CHANGE 1977–1999	% MFG. PAYROLL CHANGE 1979–1999
Collin, TX	Dallas-Fort Worth, TX	4,700	24,208	415.1%	1828.9%
Williamson, TX	Austin-San Marcos, TX	2,000	9,685	384.3	1136.3
Carver, MN	Minneapolis-Saint Paul, MN-WI	2,100	9,309	343.3	787.8
Scott, KY	Lexington, KY	2,600	10,318	296.8	1524.1
Montgomery, TX	Houston-Galveston-Brazoria, TX	2,100	7,280	246.7	616.5
Warren, OH	Cincinnati	3,800	13,018	242.6	723.3
Clark, NV	Las Vegas, NV-AZ	5,400	18,430	241.3	499.6
Placer, CA	Sacramento-Yolo, CA	2,400	8,131	238.8	834.4
Gwinnett, GA	Atlanta, GA	8,300	27,468	230.9	534.1
Travis, TX	Austin-San Marcos, TX	17,800	53,728	201.8	826.7

FIGURE 5.3   Metro Movers, *continued*

COUNTY	METRO AREA	MFG. EMPLOYMENT 1977	MFG. EMPLOYMENT 1999	% MFG. EMPLOYMENT CHANGE 1977–1999	% MFG. PAYROLL CHANGE 1979–1999
Snohomish, WA	Seattle-Tacoma-Bremerton, WA	21,400	62,102	190.2	377.6
St. Charles, MO	Saint Louis, MO-IL	5,000	14,387	187.7	458.6
St. Croix, WI	Minneapolis-Saint Paul, MN-WI	2,100	5,965	184.0	460.1
Ada, ID	Boise City, ID	6,800	19,169	181.9	456.3
Marion, FL	Ocala, FL	3,400	9,420	177.1	390.0
De Kalb, IN	Fort Wayne, IN	5,100	13,706	168.7	464.1
Manatee, FL	Sarasota-Bradenton, FL	4,100	10,995	168.2	468.8
Davis, UT	Salt Lake City-Ogden, UT	3,200	8,144	154.5	386.1
Livingston, MI	Detroit-Ann Arbor-Flint, MI	4,100	10,047	145.0	494.9
Sonoma, CA	San Francisco-Oakland-San Jose, CA	11,000	26,391	139.9	470.4
Denton, TX	Dallas-Fort Worth, TX	5,700	13,277	132.9	452.8
Lapeer, MI	Detroit-Ann Arbor-Flint, MI	2,900	6,420	121.4	442.4
Riverside, CA	Los Angeles-Riverside-Orange Co., CA	23,400	49,509	111.6	307.7
Boone, KY	Cincinnati	4,600	9,387	104.1	286.8
Kenton, KY	Cincinnati	4,000	7,777	94.4	460.3
Durham, NC	Raleigh-Durham-Chapel Hill, NC	16,000	30,780	92.4	284.8
Washington, AR	Fayetteville-Springfield-Rogers, AR	7,900	15,014	90.1	399.9
Sacramento, CA	Sacramento-Yolo, CA	17,700	31,865	80.0	232.6
Cass, ND	Fargo-Moorhead, ND-MN	3,800	6,745	77.5	282.5
Johnson, IN	Indianapolis, IN	3,700	6,551	77.1	260.9
Madison, KY	Lexington, KY	3,600	6,331	75.9	298.0
Johnson, TX	Dallas-Fort Worth, TX	3,700	6,437	74.0	345.1
Fairfax, VA	Washington-Baltimore	7,600	13,050	71.7	284.1
Fort Bend, TX	Houston-Galveston-Brazoria, TX	6,600	11,091	68.0	159.8
Minnehaha, SD	Sioux Falls, SD	7,600	12,725	67.4	172.1
Canyon, ID	Boise City, ID	6,500	10,790	66.0	319.8
Hamilton, IN	Indianapolis, IN	4,100	6,604	61.1	210.5
Washington, OR	Portland-Salem, OR-WA	23,100	37,147	60.8	258.8
Chesterfield, VA	Richmond-Petersburg, VA	7,400	10,357	40.0	239.7
Larimer, CO	Fort Collins-Loveland, CO	9,800	12,718	29.8	303.5

Metro Mover counties added 460,000 jobs—doubling their manufacturing employment. Only 5 percent of the nation's metropolitan counties made the Metro Movers list.

These counties are often characterized by industrial diversity, with their manufacturing employment spread across many companies and industries. They are not as manufacturing-intense as the Hinterland Highspots or the Freeway Flyers, but some specialization is evident. Sometimes industrial swarming—a heavy concentration of companies in a particular industry—occurs in these counties on a broader scale than in the Hinterland Highspots or the Freeway Flyers. Oregon's Washington County, near Portland, is noted for employers of distinction in the electronics industry. Intel employs 17,000 workers there, and Epson, NEC, and Tektronics are also large employers. Snohomish County, north of Seattle, has Boeing's largest plant.

Some of these counties are woven into the fabric of large metropolitan areas. Examples are Riverside east of Los Angeles, Gwinnett near Atlanta, Livingston near Detroit, Carver in the Minneapolis-St. Paul area, St. Charles near St. Louis, three Kentucky counties near Cincinnati, and Collin and Denton north of Dallas. The industrial areas north of Dallas count among their industrial employers Raytheon Systems, Boeing, the main plant for Peterbilt's highly successful heavy-duty truck, and a raft of emerging telecommunications equipment makers.

North Carolina's Durham County is the home of the Research Triangle Park, which is packed with manufacturers' research and development arms. Many of the employers in the park—Cisco Systems, Nortel, JDS Uniphase, and more—are seen mostly as information technology companies. Others—GlaxoSmithKline, Covance Biotechnology Services, Biogen, and others—tend to be viewed as pharmaceutical or medical research firms. All share a common goal: to make and then to sell tangible products.

Other Metro Movers, like Durham, are core counties for smaller and often-vibrant metro areas. Among them: Travis County in Texas (Austin), Larimer in Colorado (Fort Collins), Ada in Idaho (Boise), and Cass in North Dakota (Fargo). The Austin area, in particular, claims a long list of electronics industry leaders including IBM, Dell Computer, Motorola, Advanced Micro Devices, and Applied Materials.

Manatee County, on Florida's Gulf Coast south of Tampa Bay, is home to another household word: Tropicana, which employs 3,200 at an orange juice plant there. Many of the most highly regarded companies in these counties grew and prospered with their communities, after being founded or started up as relatively small satellite plants. Nearly two-thirds of the Metro Mover counties are in states with counties losing momentum. Thus, it seems unlikely that state policies played a major role in attracting them. Instead, as with so many companies in other counties gaining momentum, one of the principal forces driving their success may well be the quality of the company itself.

GRADUAL GROWERS

Gradual Grower counties exhibit less dramatic but still steady growth in manufacturing. They can be urban, suburban, or rural. Many are in stable and sometimes rapidly growing metro areas. Most, but not all, are on interstates. Taken together, the Gradual Growers accounted for more than 650,000 manufacturing jobs in 1997. (See Figure 5.4.)

FIGURE 5.4   Gradual Growers

COUNTY	METRO AREA	MFG. EMPLOYMENT 1977	MFG. EMPLOYMENT 1999	% MFG. EMPLOYMENT CHANGE 1977–1999	% MFG. PAYROLL CHANGE 1979–1999
San Luis Obispo, CA	San Luis Obispo, CA	2,400	6,894	187.3%	447.9%
Pima, AZ	Tucson, AZ	11,100	29,214	163.2	375.1
Rockdale, GA	Atlanta, GA	3,100	6,912	123.0	368.9
Hidalgo, TX	McAllen-Edinburg-Mission, TX	5,500	11,865	115.7	265.3
Sumner, TN	Nashville, TN	5,000	10,447	108.9	368.6
Ottawa, MI	Grand Rapids-Muskegon-Holland, MI	20,100	41,072	104.3	354.7
Allegan, MI	Grand Rapids-Muskegon-Holland, MI	9,100	17,959	97.4	374.5
San Bernardino, CA	Los Angeles-Riverside-Orange County	36,200	68,909	90.4	211.7
DeSoto, MS	Memphis, TN-AR-MS	3,400	6,385	87.8	249.4

(Continued)

FIGURE 5.4   Gradual Growers, *continued*

COUNTY	METRO AREA	MFG. EMPLOYMENT 1977	MFG. EMPLOYMENT 1999	% MFG. EMPLOYMENT CHANGE 1977–1999	% MFG. PAYROLL CHANGE 1979–1999
Guadalupe, TX	San Antonio, TX	3,100	5,787	86.7	426.0
Boone, MO	Columbia, MO	3,100	5,757	85.7	239.5
Merced, CA	Merced, CA	4,500	8,322	84.9	290.2
Stearns, MN	Saint Cloud, MN	7,200	13,170	82.9	281.6
Washington, MN	Minneapolis-Saint Paul, MN-WI	6,200	11,034	78.0	331.6
Lee, FL	Fort Myers-Cape Coral, FL	3,000	5,293	76.4	266.2
Shelby, IN	Indianapolis, IN	4,200	7,349	75.0	328.1
Washoe, NV	Reno, NV	6,800	11,773	73.1	221.8
Ellis, TX	Dallas-Fort Worth, TX	5,700	9,854	72.9	268.2
Portage, OH	Cleveland-Akron, OH	8,000	13,775	72.2	256.0
Franklin, MO	Saint Louis, MO-IL	6,400	10,857	69.6	267.9
Geauga, OH	Cleveland-Akron, OH	6,500	11,018	69.5	337.3
Henderson, KY	Evansville-Henderson, IN-KY	4,300	7,237	68.3	240.6
Lauderdale, AL	Florence, AL	4,200	7,037	67.5	313.9
Rockingham, NH	Boston	10,700	17,033	59.2	231.2
Tippecanoe, IN	Lafayette, IN	10,900	17,213	57.9	235.5
Harford, MD	Washington-Baltimore	4,200	6,484	54.4	376.9
Madison, TN	Jackson, TN	8,300	12,734	53.4	259.4
Union, NC	Charlotte, NC	8,800	13,239	50.4	284.8
Whatcom, WA	Bellingham, WA	6,400	9,495	48.4	175.2
Dane, WI	Madison, WI	18,200	26,681	46.6	217.2
Medina, OH	Cleveland-Akron, OH	7,800	11,317	45.1	257.0
Washington, WI	Milwaukee-Racine, WI	10,900	15,333	40.7	227.1
Dyer, TN	None	4,600	6,473	40.7	225.5
Marathon, WI	Wausau, WI	13,200	18,368	39.2	184.4
Montgomery, TN	Clarksville-Hopkinsville, TN-KY	5,600	7,401	32.2	272.8
Outagamie, WI	Appleton-Oshkosh-Neenah, WI	16,700	21,422	28.3	184.6
Tuscaloosa, AL	Tuscaloosa, AL	10,100	12,460	23.4	318.2
Shelby, AL	Birmingham, AL	5,000	6,021	20.4	214.6
Lake, IL	Chicago-Gary-Kenosha	50,400	59,746	18.5	206.4
Henrico, VA	Richmond-Petersburg, VA	9,200	10,768	17.0	144.3
Dakota, MN	Minneapolis-Saint Paul, MN-WI	15,100	17,319	14.7	149.0

While metropolitan counties in general lost more than 1.3 million manufacturing jobs between 1977 and 1997, the Gradual Growers added nearly 360,000—a 60 percent gain. These counties have nurtured a broad spectrum of basic industries. They are more diverse than either the Hinterland Highspot or Freeway Flyer counties, though manufacturing still accounts for a larger share of total employment than the nation as a whole (25% versus 18% in 1995).

While metropolitan counties in general lost more than 1.3 million manufacturing jobs between 1977 and 1997, the Gradual Growers added nearly 360,000.

Alabama's Tuscaloosa County produces tires, motor vehicles, fabricated wire, pipes and fittings, petroleum products, and heating equipment. Benton County, in Arkansas, makes bread, bags, machine tools, plastic hose, and motors. Minnesota's Washington County turns out Andersen Windows, plastic products, printing machinery, and 3M abrasives. Madison County, in Tennessee, makes potato chips, power-driven hand tools, lawn equipment, hardwood flooring, air compressors, and household appliances. These examples suggest that successful manufacturing does not have to be exotic. The operating paradigm is the efficient production of high-quality products continuously sold for common use.

When manufacturing momentum begins, it can build quickly if the companies come to view their community as a good place to do business. The Jackson, Tennessee, area in Madison County offers a wonderful example. Maytag first came in 1990, then followed with expansions in six of the next nine years. Owens Corning Fiberglass arrived in 1993 with a $40 million shingles plant; two years later, it tacked on a $48 million addition. Pentair Corp., parent of Porter Cable, Delta, and Devilbiss, recently decided to concentrate those operations there.

Marathon County in Wisconsin tells a similar story. This county and its major city of Wausau, 70 miles west of Green Bay, are home to two major millwork companies—SNE and Kolbe & Kolbe—with a combined employment of more than 3,000. The county also has three paper mills, a Marathon Cheese plant, a Fiskars scissors plant, an electric motor plant, and the Greenback Fan Corp., which employs 1,200 workers.

South of Green Bay, Outagamie County and its principal city of Appleton have benefited from the wealth spawned by industry in the Fox River Valley. Paper mills are at the heart of the valley's prosperity, but workers there make a wide variety of other products—fire trucks, sausage, frozen pizza, refined petroleum, and plastics.

Core counties in the Gradual Growers group in the South and Southwest include Pima (Tuscon) in Arizona, Washoe (Reno) in Nevada, Lee (Fort Myers) in Florida, and Hidalgo (McAllen) in Texas. Others, in the Midwest, are home to university towns: Stearns (St. Cloud) in Minnesota; and Dane (Madison) in Wisconsin.

SPECIAL CASES

Counties in all of the seven categories, and others outside of our sample, turned out to be special cases worthy of more attention. The more familiar we become with their characteristics and trends, the better we can understand the manufacturing sector.

Cluster Counties

Clusters—also known as industrial swarming—are concentrations of similar businesses that seek to perpetuate themselves by developing a strong network of support services. The term is currently in fashion in academic and economic development circles, but the concept has been around for centuries. In medieval times, merchants and tradesmen formed guilds to provide mutual aid systems and maintain standards for their specialized activities. Today, an example of a strong cluster would be a growing medical device industry in a particular region. The industry would be built on one or more strong manufacturers. They would be supported by job shops supplying them with parts, specialized university courses and training programs in medical technology, skilled employees, trade groups that tend to the concerns of the industry, patent lawyers, specialized investment bankers, securities analysts, and business-friendly governments. Often, a single company— for example, Hewlett-Packard in Silicon Valley, Medtronic in the Twin Cities, Digital Equipment in the Boston area—has acted as a flywheel, spinning off startups in related fields as talented employees get the itch to leave and strike out on their own.

We found such a cluster thriving in Indiana's prosperous Elkhart County. Fifty-three percent of the county's workers hold manufacturing jobs, four times the national average. They have made the county one of the wealthiest in the state. Manufacturers there make everything from pharmaceuticals to band instruments, but at the center of it all is the county's motor home and recreational vehicle (RV) industry. In 1998, *Time* magazine named Elkhart one of the nation's seven "secret capitals" for producing a specific product—RVs. Elkhart manufacturers are a major power in the state's trade associations for RVs and motor homes. In Elkhart's entrepreneurial climate, heavy-handed regulation is not welcome. Dennis Harney, former planning director for both the city and the county of Elkhart, says citizens would get on his back when he worked with small businesses on zoning regulations. "They'd say, 'Why are you messing with that guy? He's just trying to make a living.'"

Dalton, 90 miles northwest of Atlanta on Interstate 75 in Whitfield County, touts itself as "the Carpet Capital of the World." The forerunner to I-75 through the county, US 41, once carried the nickname "Bedspread Alley"; salesmen and Florida-bound tourists would see the colorful cotton bedspreads hung out to dry on clotheslines, then stop to buy them off the lines. Later, the industry, aided by cheap power, became more sophisticated as textile experts introduced new machinery and manmade fibers—polyester, nylon, acrylics, and tufted yarn products—to turn out durable carpets. Today, the Dalton area claims more than 80 percent of U.S. tufted carpet production. The industry employs more than 20,000 workers in the county. Thousands more work for catalog publishers, chemical and plastics firms, and other businesses that support the carpet industry. In 1998, blessed by the wealth generated by the carpet industry, Dalton State College became a four-year school. "It's been the backbone of what we do," George Woodward, vice president of business services for the Dalton-Whitfield Chamber of Commerce, says of the industry.

The woodworking factories of Dubois County, Indiana, provide another example of a successful cluster. Manufacturing clusters also prosper in Sonoma and Napa County, centers of California's wine country. In Minnesota, Medtronic's successes have given rise to a medical device cluster in the Twin Cities area, and a concentration of composite materials producers have given Winona County a cluster in that industry.

Unfortunately, for certain communities, clusters don't always grow. Sometimes they shrink. Stark evidence of that condition comes from the steel industry. Support networks strengthened steel clusters in Pittsburgh, Gary, Youngstown, and Birmingham, but such backing was not enough to protect the industry from serious decline in those cities. Ultimately, the source of the problem was the industry itself, which failed to invest in the new equipment and technology it needed to prosper and grow.

Globalizers

Globalizer counties are places that have attracted substantial foreign investment in manufacturing. This has been particularly so in the auto industry. Producers from abroad have built factories in the United States, dubbed transplants, in order to get closer to the lucrative American market. Ten counties—Union, Logan, and Shelby Counties in Ohio; Tippecanoe and Gibson in Indiana; McLean in Illinois; Scott in Kentucky; Rutherford in Tennessee; Tuscaloosa in Alabama; and Spartanburg in South Carolina—have captured billions of dollars in transplant investments from Japanese and German automakers. Investors from abroad have also sunk their capital into other U.S. industries by buying factories outright or through joint ventures. In many cases, these outlays have led to the creation of support businesses in and beyond the manufacturing sector.

In 1982, Honda became the first Japanese company to build a U.S. auto plant. The factory rose in Marysville, Ohio, about 30 miles northwest of Columbus. Logan County, one of the counties in what has come to be known as the "Honda Corridor," surfaced as a Freeway Flyer on the strength of Honda's growth. Manufacturing payrolls there rose 440 percent from 1979 to 1999.

Innovators

Innovators are counties whose manufacturers have made sizable research commitments. Typically, this has occurred at research parks, the granddaddy of which is Research Triangle Park in North Carolina. The second largest of these developments is Cummins Research Park, in Madison County, Alabama (Huntsville), with more than 20,000 jobs. Many other smaller parks, usually affiliated with universities, are growing rapidly. The jobs in these centers are good jobs—well-paid, high-tech workers in the Triangle Park pull up Durham County's average annual pay for manufacturing to $44,500, significantly above the averages for each of the four geographical categories of well-performing counties. Mostly, the research park jobs are at manufacturers, because this part of the economy dominates the nation's private sector research and development effort.

Near Misses

Some counties just missed the list of counties gaining momentum, but still exhibited favorable characteristics. One of them is Marshall County, Indiana. Leaders in Marshall County wanted to avoid dependence on a single company. They had learned their lesson from nearby South Bend, where long-dominant Studebaker finally closed it doors in 1964 after years of production inefficiencies, troubled labor relations, and internal bickering that compounded quality problems. County leaders sought diversification by developing a large industrial park that catered to many small to midsized manufacturers, instead of courting a single large employer. The strategy worked. From 1989 to 1994, Marshall County ranked ninth among Indiana's 92 counties in the pace of job growth. Manufacturing earnings, a relatively small part of the county's economy in the 1950s, grew to account for nearly half of the county's wages by 1994.

One of the physically largest U.S. counties is Arizona's Maricopa County, which sprawls across an area twice the size of Connecticut. This rapidly expanding county very nearly made the Gradual Growers list with more manufacturing jobs than in each of 18 states.

MANUFACTURING IN SEARCH OF GOOD PLACES

Other counties benefited from decentralization policies pioneered by 3M, Deere, IBM, and other large corporations, mostly after World

War II but some of them much earlier. Frank Berdan, manufacturing strategy manager for 3M, traces this policy to the company's move to Cumberland, Wisconsin, in 1948. The company couldn't find enough workers near St. Paul, then its main production site. Thus, it turned to Cumberland, a town with a population of just 2,000 about 50 miles northeast of the Twin Cities. Good experiences there encouraged the company to adopt a strategy of building or acquiring plants in small towns, sometimes distant from larger cities. Among them: Nevada, Missouri, 80 miles south of Kansas City; Guin, Alabama, 70 miles northwest of Birmingham; Brownwood, Texas, 135 miles southwest of Dallas; and Hutchinson, Minnesota—now a Hinterland Highspot county.

"What we found was there were a number of people in more rural areas who had innovative skill sets," says Berdan. "There were a lot of people looking for work as agriculture consolidated." They had tinkered in the barns, operated mechanical equipment, and made their own payrolls.

After the early 1970s, 3M's location strategy changed. The company built fewer new factories in the United States, because it was growing more rapidly overseas and more slowly overall. Managers preferred larger areas, because cultural and educational attractions seemed better there and opportunities for job-seeking spouses were greater. Midsized areas such as Austin, Texas or smaller university towns like Columbia, Missouri, became more popular. But, says Berdan, the company remains quite satisfied today with its many plants in small towns.

In the serious pursuit of lower cost and higher quality, manufacturers are forced to assess all of their operating characteristics, including geographic location. These competitive pressures are resulting in great changes. The nation's most successful steel company has plants in several predominantly rural states, but none in Pittsburgh. The latest and most modernized auto plants are no longer restricted to Detroit, but are in places like Georgetown, Kentucky, and Smyrna, Tennessee. Computer manufacturing, once concentrated in a few urban centers, has now spread out to some of the most rural sections of the United States and to many locations overseas. In general, these changes are gradual, but for some communities, they are precipitous.

Prosperity, however welcomed, is not guaranteed to any county. Benton County, Oregon, for instance, has a huge Hewlett-Packard plant that helped the community to prosper for many years. Manufacturing employment doubled there in 20 years and manufacturing payroll increased almost by a factor of five. Now that industry is less robust and future growth is not assured.

> *Prosperity, however welcomed, is not guaranteed to any county.*

Minnesota's McLeod County has benefited greatly from the highly specialized expertise of Hutchinson Technology—the manufacturing of suspension assembly arms for disk drives. Nobody in the world does it better, but with the increasing capacities of computer disk drives, not quite as many suspension assemblies are needed per gigabyte. The company, hurt by flagging demand for its products, turned to mass layoffs in 2001. By September of that year, the layoffs had become a major cause of a 7 percent decline from a year earlier in the county's employment.

Manufacturers will continue to search for good places—places that will allow them to compete effectively providing quality products at reasonable costs. The counties described above have had a pretty good ride the past 20 years and their successes are encouraging. However, success is neither ensured nor universal. In the next chapter, we will discuss the counties losing momentum.

CHAPTER 6

Counties Losing Momentum

When a storm heads for your town, it can be hard to get out of the way. That is pretty much how things have gone in many of the slider counties—those where manufacturing sectors have clearly slipped in recent years. The forces that led to these slippages were often beyond the full control of the communities, though repelling forces were often present. Still, city councils and public-minded citizens were not equipped to do much about downturns in particular industries, intensified overseas competition, and shifting markets. These were among the forces that adversely affected production in these communities.

The counties losing momentum were divided into three groups based on their manufacturing employment in 1995. Smaller Sliders had from 4,800 to 9,999 manufacturing employees, Midrange Sliders from 10,000 to 34,999, and Sliding Goliaths 35,000 or more. In general, the manufacturing losses in these counties were substantial. During the 20 years from 1977 to 1997, the counties losing momentum lost an average of 40 percent of their manufacturing employment. Manufacturing payroll from 1979 to 1997, not adjusted for inflation, increased 41 percent in these counties, while payrolls roughly doubled in the United States overall and grew by 335 percent in the counties gaining momentum. As described in Chapter 4, the counties losing momentum constituted roughly the bottom sixth of the 704 large employment sample counties in terms of manufacturing payroll and employment changes during the 1977 to 1997 sample period.

During the 20 years from 1977 to 1997, the counties losing momentum lost an average of 40 percent of their manufacturing employment.

Many of the counties identified here as losing momentum made profound contributions to U.S. manufacturing in earlier times. Some of these early manufacturers remain prominent today, a few of them in their third century of industrial accomplishment. Among these 116 counties are those in the anthracite coal regions of eastern Pennsylvania that were so integral to the launching of U.S. manufacturing in the early 19th Century. The beginnings of the textile industry in colonial times can be traced to Samuel Slater's mill in Pawtucket, Rhode Island, now part of a Sliding Goliath county. Shipbuilding, photocopying and photography, wagon production, machine tools, agricultural equipment, and a variety of other crucially important U.S. industries took shape in the counties we now identify as losing momentum. Many of the country's high-technology defense systems were developed in the sliding counties of Connecticut, Massachusetts, and Pennsylvania. It is not an exaggeration to suggest that America would not be much of an industrial power without the inventiveness and resourcefulness of the people who created industries that sometimes still function, though less vigorously, in these communities.

It is not an exaggeration to suggest that America would not be much of an industrial power without the inventiveness and resourcefulness of the people who created industries that sometimes still function, though less vigorously, in these communities.

It would be wrong to say that leaders in the Slider counties have written off manufacturing. In many cases, they have kept and attracted manufacturing jobs by assembling and setting aside land, innovative pollution cleanups, one-stop permit shopping, and various other programs. Creative officials in Buffalo resolved a transportation problem, which arose from the proposed renovation of an older plant, by turning an older section of Conrail tracks into the Northeast Buffalo Highway. St. Paul's Port Authority has developed financing tools and partnerships that have helped to retain and attract more than 50,000 jobs since 1962, mostly in manufacturing, at 15 industrial parks. Many cities are working hard at the complex, lengthy, and often-unheralded task of reclaiming polluted land to make it suitable for small and midsized manufacturers. Many have taken the advice of the Northeast-

FIGURE 6.1   Average Year Established of Manufacturing Employers with 500 or More Employees in 1999

CATEGORY	NUMBER OF EMPLOYEES	AVERAGE YEAR ESTABLISHED
Hinterland Highspots	62,122	1954
Metro Movers	276,030	1960
Freeway Flyers	38,485	1964
Gradual Growers	348,759	1947
Smaller Sliders	80,457	1942
Midrange Sliders	309,476	1935
Sliding Goliaths	759,123	1927
Total Sample	1,874,452	1941

SOURCE: Manufacturing News Database, 1999, and University of St. Thomas

Midwest Institute, to empower "a strong local governmental entity" to restore older cities to economic health.

Industry counts for a lot even today in the Slider counties, where manufacturing still employs 3.2 million people representing 3 percent of all U.S. jobs and 4.1 percent of the country's total payroll. However, major employers in the counties losing momentum are significantly older than those in the counties doing better than average. Figure 6.1 shows the differences. Age alone does not determine a company's ability to compete. John Deere started in 1837, Levi Strauss in 1850, Armstrong in 1860, DuPont in 1802. According to the Manufacturing News Database of 1999, 1 of every 12 U.S. manufacturing employees works at a company more than 100 years old. Yet, because of their age, these companies often have operated older plants in core cities. Frequently, they elect to shut down or cut back their older plants when decision day arrives for where to put new investments, leaving the cities as losers unless they can attract new companies and new technologies.

One of every 12 U.S. manufacturing employees works for a company more than 100 years old.

SLIDING GOLIATHS

Easily the most recognizable of any of the seven groups is the Sliding Goliaths category—major urban counties adversely affected by industrial decline. Sliding Goliaths had 35,000 or more manufacturing employees in 1995. Three key points to note about these counties are the degree to which the declines have hurt their economies, how the declines have torn at the social fabrics of their core cities, and how much manufacturing investment and employment remains.

A quick tour of these counties is almost like looking at the cities that made up Major League Baseball before the 1950s. Then, there were just 16 big league teams, all in the country's northeastern quadrant near the rail lines that served this section of the country. Now, the core counties representing 15 of those 16 teams—in New York City, Philadelphia, Boston, Cleveland, Chicago, Detroit, St. Louis, Pittsburgh, and Cincinnati—are Sliding Goliaths. Four of these cities lost major league

---

FIGURE 6.2   Sliding Goliaths

COUNTY	METRO AREA	MFG. 1977	MFG. 1999	% MFG. EMPLOYMENT CHANGE 1977–1999	% MFG. PAYROLL CHANGE 1979–1999
Onondaga, NY	Syracuse, NY	47,800	33,015	−30.9%	45.3%
Dade, FL	Miami-Fort Lauderdale, FL	85,100	58,699	−31.0	41.0
Forsyth, NC	Greensboro–Winston-Salem, NC	41,700	26,819	−35.7	23.1
Middlesex, NJ	New York–Northern New Jersey	80,500	50,359	−37.4	42.5
Norfolk, MA	Boston, MA	54,900	33,781	−38.5	81.1
Hartford, CT	Hartford, CT	116,700	70,243	−39.8	43.3
Monroe, NY	Rochester, NY	126,200	72,961	−42.2	22.0
Erie, NY	Buffalo-Niagara Falls, NY	108,800	62,301	−42.7	26.7
Hampden, MA	Springfield, MA	55,700	31,710	−43.1	45.2
Jackson, MO	Kansas City, MO-KS	64,600	36,320	−43.8	6.8
Summit, OH	Cleveland-Akron, OH	75,600	41,784	−44.7	15.3
Providence, RI	Providence-Warwick-Pawtucket, RI	91,100	48,213	−47.1	33.3
Lucas, OH	Toledo, OH	59,900	30,757	−48.7	23.7
Hamilton, OH	Cincinnati, OH	139,600	71,679	−48.7	15.9

(Continued)

FIGURE 6.2   Sliding Goliaths, *continued*

COUNTY	METRO AREA	MFG. 1977	MFG. 1999	% MFG. EMPLOYMENT CHANGE 1977–1999	% MFG. PAYROLL CHANGE 1979–1999
Cuyahoga, OH	Cleveland-Akron, OH	226,100	114,898	−49.2	8.6
Queens, NY	New York-Northern New Jersey	94,100	47,671	−49.3	15.7
San Francisco, CA	San Francisco-Oakland-San Jose, CA	42,900	21,725	−49.4	−33.3
Bergen, NJ	New York-Northern New Jersey	109,100	55,157	−49.4	23.1
Baltimore, MD	Washington-Baltimore, DC-MD	57,900	29,243	−49.5	2.3
Cook, IL	Chicago-Gary-Kenosha, IL-IN-WI	687,500	345,873	−49.7	12.8
Passaic, NJ	New York-Northern New Jersey	65,300	31,029	−52.5	15.3
New Castle, DE	Philadelphia, PA	50,700	24,058	−52.5	3.3
Fairfield, CT	New Haven-Bridgeport-Stamford, CT	117,300	51,975	−55.7	8.6
Lake, IN	Chicago-Gary-Kenosha, IL-IN-WI	85,600	35,019	−59.1	−15.7
Union, NJ	New York-Northern New Jersey	92,600	37,648	−59.3	3.6
Nassau, NY	New York-Northern New Jersey	92,100	36,787	−60.1	1.2
Essex, NJ	New York-Northern New Jersey	86,100	34,015	−60.5	−6.4
Wayne, MI	Detroit-Ann Arbor-Flint, MI	334,500	128,741	−61.5	−11.6
Kings, NY	New York-Northern New Jersey	118,400	44,679	−62.3	−15.3
Allegheny, PA	Pittsburgh, PA	150,300	55,384	−63.2	−20.7
Baltimore city, MD	Washington-Baltimore, DC-MD	72,900	25,803	−64.6	−16.4
Suffolk, MA	Boston, MA	54,700	19,108	−65.1	−5.5
St. Louis City, MO	Saint Louis, MO-IL	92,600	30,792	−66.7	−28.5
Westchester, NY	New York-Northern New Jersey	62,200	18,355	−70.5	−48.3
Philadelphia, PA	Philadelphia, PA	157,500	44,023	−72.0	−33.3
New York, NY	New York-Northern New Jersey	359,400	70,559	−80.4	−57.0

teams as rising cities in the south and west won teams. Similarly, they lost much of their manufacturing bases as industry moved south and west. Today, just 12 of the 30 teams call the northeast quadrant home.

Some of their steepest slides came in the 1980s. Over that decade, manufacturing employment plunged at rates ranging from 22 percent to 43 percent in Brooklyn, Queens, Manhattan, Philadelphia, Cook County (Chicago), Wayne County (Detroit), Allegheny County (Pittsburgh), Baltimore, St. Louis, Erie County (Buffalo), Cuyahoga County (Cleveland), and Essex, Hudson, and Union Counties in New Jersey.

Generally, the slides have continued since 1990, although some Sliding Goliaths have fallen at a slower pace in more recent years. Manufacturers still have huge stakes in these counties despite the job losses. For example, manufacturing jobs in Cook County fell from 688,000 in 1977 to 346,000 (372,000 including publishing) in 1999, but nearly half of the decline came in the first 5 years of that 20-year period.

Cuts in defense spending have smacked a number of Sliding Goliaths. In New York's Nassau County on Long Island, Grumman Corp. employed 25,000 workers at its massive aerospace complex in 1986; by 1996, Northrup and Grumman had merged and only 3,800 jobs remained on Long Island. In Connecticut's Fairfield County, the largest employer in 1999 was Sikorsky Aircraft, whose workforce had fallen to 5,700 from nearly three times that total in the mid-1980s. Much defense employment remained, though. Boeing's McDonnell Douglas Division still remains a large manufacturing employer in the city of St. Louis.

The fall-offs in employment in the Sliding Goliaths are not limited to a few basic industries. Cook County, Westchester (New York), Passaic and Essex (New Jersey), Philadelphia, and Providence suffered manufacturing declines totally or nearly across-the-board, in all of the major manufacturing categories.

Often, the jobs lost have been good ones—high-paying jobs in promising industries. From 1988 to 1997, Cook County lost roughly half a billion dollars in annual payroll in each of three industries: instruments, electronics, and industrial machinery, and even more in printing and publishing. Over this same period, Manhattan lost more than 27,000 jobs averaging nearly $60,000 per year in printing and publishing.

Despite all of these declines, manufacturers retain huge investments in many of the Sliding Goliath counties. That's why their continuing struggles in these counties merit sympathy and concern.

MIDRANGE SLIDERS

Midrange sliders are counties with declining manufacturing employment, and between 10,000 and 34,999 jobs in this sector in 1995 (Figure 6.3). Almost all of them suffered significant industrial job losses from 1988 to 1997, but their showing was not as weak as that of the

FIGURE 6.3   Midrange Sliders

COUNTY	METRO AREA	MFG. 1977	MFG. 1999	% MFG. EMPLOYMENT CHANGE 1977–1999	% MFG. PAYROLL CHANGE 1979–1999
De Kalb, GA	Atlanta, GA	25,600	23,495	−8.2%	88.2%
Smith, TX	Tyler, TX	12,100	9,908	−18.1	88.3
Nash, NC	Rocky Mount, NC	12,400	9,899	−20.2	130.3
Rockingham, NC	None	16,700	13,164	−21.2	63.4
Racine, WI	Milwaukee-Racine, WI	27,200	20,032	−26.4	33.7
Clarke, GA	Athens, GA	10,200	7,464	−26.8	70.1
Knox, TN	Knoxville, TN	25,400	17,654	−30.5	70.5
Contra Costa, CA	San Francisco-Oakland-San Jose, CA	27,300	18,890	−30.8	63.1
Sullivan, TN	Johnson City-Kingsport-Bristol, TN-VA	25,500	17,568	−31.1	81.3
Kalamazoo, MI	Kalamazoo-Battle Creek, MI	30,000	20,619	−31.3	34.5
Etowah, AL	Gadsden, AL	11,800	8,066	−31.6	9.0
Delaware, IN	Muncie, IN	14,200	9,391	−33.9	34.7
Lorain, OH	Cleveland-Akron, OH	39,800	26,239	−34.1	33.9
Rockland, NY	New York-Northern New Jersey	14,800	9,731	−34.3	52.5
East Baton Rouge, LA	Baton Rouge, LA	17,800	11,574	−35.0	44.5
Lynchburg, VA	Lynchburg, VA	19,900	12,634	−36.5	92.7
Hinds, MS	Jackson, MS	14,200	8,991	−36.7	44.3
Penobscot, ME	Bangor, ME	14,300	8,931	−37.5	47.1
Pickens, SC	Greenville-Spartanburg-Anderson, SC	17,500	10,909	−37.7	66.7
Orange, NY	New York-Northern New Jersey	15,200	9,373	−38.3	64.0
Allen, OH	Lima, OH	16,800	10,330	−38.5	48.1
Lackawanna, PA	Scranton–Wilkes-Barre–Hazleton, PA	26,100	15,753	−39.6	55.8

FIGURE 6.3   Midrange Sliders, *continued*

COUNTY	METRO AREA	MFG. 1977	MFG. 1999	% MFG. EMPLOYMENT CHANGE 1977–1999	% MFG. PAYROLL CHANGE 1979–1999
Broome, NY	Binghamton, NY	30,700	18,378	–40.1	30.8
Richmond, VA	Richmond-Petersburg, VA	34,800	20,727	–40.4	44.9
La Porte, IN	None	16,800	9,973	–40.6	39.1
Madison, IL	Saint Louis, MO-IL	29,300	17,379	–40.7	24.9
Denver, CO	Denver-Boulder-Greeley, CO	42,400	24,640	–41.9	9.2
Caddo, LA	Shreveport-Bossier City, LA	22,200	12,647	–43.0	44.3
Jackson, MS	Biloxi-Gulfport-Pascagoula, MS	30,100	16,660	–44.7	57.0
Luzerne, PA	Scranton–Wilkes-Barre–Hazleton, PA	40,500	22,159	–45.3	52.0
Steuben, NY	None	14,200	7,467	–47.4	13.8
Jefferson, TX	Beaumont-Port Arthur, TX	28,400	14,540	–48.8	18.5
Dutchess, NY	New York-Northern New Jersey	27,400	13,491	–50.8	1.4
New London, CT	New London-Norwich, CT	39,200	18,805	–52.0	95.3
Lehigh, PA	Allentown-Bethlehem-Easton, PA	47,800	22,722	–52.5	14.6
Berkshire, MA	Pittsfield, MA	18,800	8,447	–55.1	–2.2
Delaware, PA	Philadelphia, PA	44,800	19,613	–56.2	11.1
Orleans, LA	New Orleans, LA	21,400	9,366	–56.2	–1.8
Northampton, PA	Allentown-Bethlehem-Easton, PA	39,300	16,996	–56.8	–10.4
Monmouth, NJ	New York-Northern New Jersey	26,600	11,280	–57.6	–4.0
Peoria, IL	Peoria-Pekin, IL	32,900	13,519	–58.9	–17.2
Madison, IN	Indianapolis, IN	25,600	10,279	–59.8	–2.2
Rock Island, IL	Davenport-Moline-Rock Island, IA-IL	26,700	9,676	–63.8	–32.6
Bronx, NY	New York-Northern New Jersey	33,100	11,675	–64.7	–18.6
Hudson, NJ	New York-Northern New Jersey	72,200	20,840	–71.1	–25.8
Mercer, NJ	New York-Northern New Jersey	35,900	9,805	–72.7	–32.8

Sliding Goliaths. Sometimes these counties experienced declines in the basic industries of steel, paper, and chemicals, but typically the declines are more general. Often, Midrange Slider manufacturers are satellite facilities—operating arms of larger corporations. These counties, typically lacking major corporate headquarters and buffeted by strategic shifts put into place by geographically distant CEOs, often fall prey to restructurings. In some cases, such moves could be expected, because so many plants are old and have outdated equipment. Other times, plants have suffered through years of neglect by detached managers in faraway cities who seldom invest in and rarely visit the plants.

Upstate New York's Broome County, on the Pennsylvania border about 170 miles northwest of New York City, has an illustrious manufacturing history. Situated at the junction of the Susquehanna and Chenango Rivers on the former Erie Railroad mainline, the county's "Triple Cities" of Binghamton, Johnson City, and Endicott have been major industrial centers since the early 19th Century. Endicott-Johnson, once one of the nation's leading shoe manufacturers, gave the region its largest employer and a Fortune 500 headquarters for many years. The defense-aerospace industry flourished during the Cold War at General Electric, a Link training simulator plant, and at an IBM plant in adjoining Tioga County, but the region was best known as the birthplace of IBM, in Endicott. Broome County manufacturing employment fell from a peak of 33,000 in 1982 to 21,000 in 1997. At IBM, the decline in the two counties was more pronounced with jobs falling to just 5,000 from 15,000 in the early 1970s. Eventually, GE and Link sold their plants. Endicott-Johnson is long gone. The situation illustrates a common dilemma for Midrange Sliders: They are rarely masters of their own destiny.

Dutchess County, New York, is another Midrange Slider. There, the impact of shrinkage at IBM has been even greater than in Broome County. The company's extensive operations turned Poughkeepsie into a company town during IBM's glory years of the 1960s and 1970s. Its employment in the region peaked at 31,300 in 1984, but by 1993 the head count was down to 10,000, and the unemployment rate up to 11 percent. Leaders rallied, touting the space and skilled workers left behind by IBM. They stressed the region's location, just a two-hour drive from New York City, and pushed economic incentives in three state-backed economic zones. They offered customized training at a new technical institute. By 1995, the jobless rate was back down to where it had been in 1990—3 percent. However, while the development corporation's efforts helped to halt the manufacturing job decline in Dutchess County, they failed to significantly reverse it. Manufacturers employed 17,500 workers in the county in 2000, just 600 more than the low in 1993 and far below levels that prevailed before IBM so greatly reduced its employment in the region.

SMALLER SLIDERS

Smaller Sliders are counties with 1995 manufacturing employment ranging from 4,800 to 9,999 that have experienced substantial declines in such jobs over the past two decades (Figure 6.4). As with the other classes of momentum-losing counties, these counties have often been whipsawed by the constant restructuring that has been occurring at major corporations. In many cases, the Smaller Sliders suffered declines because their manufacturers failed to come up with products of distinction at reasonable cost. Extended mediocrity ultimately led to either radical downsizing or complete meltdowns of key industries.

About 15 percent of the job losses in the Smaller Sliders over the decade ended in 1997 came in the apparel and textile industries, as they lost business to overseas producers. Four counties in Pennsylvania lost 12,000 such jobs. Hudson County in New Jersey lost 7,000 and Bronx County in New York City lost 2,000. Pickens County in

---

FIGURE 6.4   Smaller Sliders

COUNTY	METRO AREA	MFG. 1977	MFG. 1999	% MFG. EMPLOYMENT CHANGE 1977–1999	% MFG. PAYROLL CHANGE 1979–1999
Harrison, MS	Biloxi-Gulfport-Pascagoula, MS	4,900	4,435	−9.5%	116.9%
Columbus, NC	None	5,200	4,269	−17.9	69.8
Ulster, NY	None	7,900	6,414	−18.8	−20.7
Wabash, IN	None	6,600	5,322	−19.4	89.2

(Continued)

FIGURE 6.4   Smaller Sliders, *continued*

COUNTY	METRO AREA	MFG. 1977	MFG. 1999	% MFG. EMPLOYMENT CHANGE 1977–1999	% MFG. PAYROLL CHANGE 1979–1999
Richmond, NC	None	6,300	4,800	−23.8	80.3
Alcorn, MS	None	6,200	4,647	−25.0	86.1
Talladega, AL	None	9,400	7,017	−25.4	63.4
Adams, IL	None	8,500	6,224	−26.8	25.5
Rensselaer, NY	Albany-Schenectady-Troy, NY	7,100	4,872	−31.4	81.9
Henry, VA	None	11,200	7,614	−32.0	102.6
Washington, RI	Providence, RI	10,100	6,804	−32.6	93.8
Androscoggin, ME	Lewiston-Auburn, ME	12,900	8,387	−35.0	91.3
Vance, NC	None	6,800	4,411	−35.1	65.2
Oswego, NY	Syracuse, NY	8,400	5,279	−37.2	23.9
Montgomery, NY	Albany-Schenectady-Troy, NY	7,700	4,775	−38.0	53.1
Humboldt, CA	None	8,800	5,262	−40.2	27.8
Lawrence, PA	None	9,700	5,778	−40.4	5.1
Kershaw, SC	None	7,900	4,699	−40.5	41.4
Northumberland, PA	None	13,200	7,652	−42.0	47.8
Warren, NJ	New York-Northern New Jersey	12,600	7,076	−43.8	52.1
Cattaraugus, NY	None	9,100	5,094	−44.0	18.0
Atlantic, NJ	Philadelphia	8,700	4,656	−46.5	19.7
Vermilion, IL	None	14,100	6,980	−50.5	−1.0
Halifax, NC	None	5,900	2,912	−50.6	45.2
Colbert, AL	Florence, AL	9,800	4,832	−50.7	−15.5
Lancaster, SC	None	9,800	4,756	−51.5	29.0
Cambria, PA	Johnstown, PA	16,600	7,937	−52.2	−24.1
Kennebec, ME	None	9,900	4,491	−54.6	4.1
Union, SC	None	7,500	3,393	−54.8	7.7
Kanawha, WV	Charleston, WV	14,300	6,447	−54.9	2.7
Cabell, WV	Huntington-Ashland, WV-KY-OH	13,100	5,871	−55.2	−11.9
La Salle, IL	None	14,300	6,215	−56.5	2.3
Tazewell, IL	Peoria-Pekin, IL	18,100	6,944	−61.6	−11.0
Schenectady, NY	Albany-Schenectady-Troy, NY	24,400	5,209	−78.7	−48.9

South Carolina lost 2,500 jobs. In North Carolina, Richmond and Vance Counties lost 2,800 jobs. In Mississippi, Monroe, Harrison, and Alcorn Counties lost 2,600 such jobs; in Alabama, Talladega County lost 1,100. In Pennsylvania, Northumberland County lost 930.

Sometimes, the presence of one or two companies hit by foreign competition dragged these counties down. Transportation equipment jobs fell in St. Joseph County, Indiana, and in several counties near New York and Philadelphia. More often, though, the declines have come across the board, rather than in single industries where the case could be made that the United States has a comparative disadvantage.

Schenectady County in New York was hurt by General Electric's downsizing, while Newport County in Rhode Island suffered losses in shipbuilding. Glass container manufacturing in La Salle County, Illinois, was hurt by stepped-up competition, including new challenges from substitute products. In Virginia, Henry County suffered when competitive pressures hit its furniture industry.

Tazewell County in Illinois got caught up in the consolidations and labor difficulties at Caterpillar. The county lost 62 percent of its manufacturing employment from 1977 to 1997, as Caterpillar adjusted to volatile markets and intense pressure from Komatsu and others abroad. Foreign producers of shoes and textiles put stress on manufacturers in Maine's Androscoggin County.

Elsewhere, declines occurred in higher-tech industries. Kanawha County (Charleston) in West Virginia is a base for chemical producers DuPont, Rhone-Poulenc, and Union Carbide. The county lost 765 jobs in that industry.

In spite of widespread cutbacks, most Smaller Sliders remain manufacturing-intense counties. Nearly 30 percent of their workers are in the industrial sector, accounting for 39 percent of payrolls. Textile mills and apparel companies are still active in Union County, South Carolina. Inco continues to refine nickel in Cabell County, West Virginia. Caterpillar workers in Tazewell County still make construction equipment.

The issue with the counties losing momentum is whether new companies and new technologies are being attracted to the same communities. Some of these areas are being reclaimed, often with expensive and highly subsidized redevelopments filled with big-box discounters, clinics, and other service businesses. Thus, the job decay so visible today may be a temporary condition, but the jobs offered by these new enterprises often fail to provide the pay and benefit levels of the industrial work that disappeared. Can these counties attract activity more valued than the manufacturing that they lost? Often, the answer is no.

We now move in for a closer look at the causes and consequences of industrial declines in some of the nation's largest cities.

CHAPTER 7

Big-City Blues—
Philadelphia and Beyond

 The industrial ruins of Philadelphia bear a striking similarity to the decay that has replaced the busy factories of New York City, Chicago, Detroit, and many other urban cradles of American manufacturing. Once-bustling plants sit abandoned with their windows cracked, their facing crumbled, and their signs faded. Frequently, entire plants have been demolished, only to be replaced by open fields crawling with weeds, littered with waste, and blotched by pollution. Nearby, proud working-class neighborhoods have fallen into disarray. Longtime residents who kept up their properties have scattered, perhaps for better opportunities, perhaps not. Those who remain find themselves battling for survival amid poverty and crime.

The big cities of the Northeast and Midwest have become signatures for the losses that occur when industry goes away. They are the cores of the Sliding Goliaths—the counties where manufacturing declines have been deepest relative to national averages. They are the places where the forces repelling manufacturing, as noted in Chapter 4, have come together to overwhelm the attracting forces. These are also the locales that provide the most visible signs of manufacturing change, for better or for worse, in any of our seven classes of counties. Tour almost any of these cities, and you can't miss the deterioration. In Philadelphia, the descent has been particularly painful, because of the city's storied history as a maker of almost everything. For decades, Philadelphia's manufacturing strength led the city to proudly carry the moniker, "Workshop of the World." Then the workshops faded. Manufacturers of all kinds left town. Manufacturing jobs plunged to 44,000 from 400,000. The resulting losses of wealth and income became a principal cause of steep declines in the city's school system and in various city services.

A CITY'S GLORIOUS HISTORY

In manufacturing's heyday, Philadelphia was a model of new-world entrepreneurial spirit.

If there had been lists of America's greatest places to work a century ago, the Henry Disston Saw Works in northeast Philadelphia surely would have ranked high. Employees walked to work from their homes, which the company built. They prospered from a superior employee benefit package. The company supported local businesses, a community park, a music hall and library, churches, and a clinic. In 1879, President Rutherford B. Hayes toured the Disston factory. As the president arrived, company officials showed him a flat piece of steel. Two hours later, as the president was leaving, they handed him a saw made from that same piece of steel. Pennsylvania's secretary of the interior hailed the neighborhood as the ideal industrial setting, a place that flourished because of a near-perfect relationship between the factory's owners, its workers, and its community.

By 1915, the company claimed the largest saw works in the world, with 3,600 workers in 58 buildings. Today, only a trace of the Disston Saw Works remains. Philadelphia's reputation as a world-class manufacturing center has been shattered by massive hemorrhaging of its industrial base. The City of Philadelphia and Philadelphia County, one of our Sliding Goliath counties, are contiguous. Manufacturing jobs there fell 61.4 percent over the 20 years ended in 1997, to just 60,835 from 157,500. Today, one of every four jobs in the city is a government job.

The City of Brotherly Love has survived, but not without considerable strain. After flirting with bankruptcy in the early 1990s, Philadelphia made a comeback as the national economy rebounded. In its midyear economic report for 2001, the city controller's office noted that fiscal restraint and other factors had produced record budget surpluses. Gentrification fueled a rebound in the center city and a few adjoining neighborhoods. The city's high concentration of "meds and eds"—medical schools and institutions of higher education—remain as a strength.

Nonetheless, warnings about the state of the city punctuate the controller's report. The report notes that Philadelphia's bond ratings recovered by 2001 from below investment grade (bonds judged strong enough that banks are allowed to invest in them) during 1990–1995, but only to levels slightly above that status. Philadelphia didn't see annual employment growth after the 1990–1991 recession until 1998, six years after the nation and five years after the region. The city's population, 1.52 million in 2000, was down 26 percent from its peak of 2.07 million in 1950. Relief greeted this latest census figure, because city officials had been expecting a notably greater decline than census-takers found. Still, the overall population decrease in the last half of the 20th Century was one of the steepest recorded by any American city, and the decline is not expected to stop anytime soon. Says the report: "Looking ahead, it is likely that future Philadelphia will be populated by fewer residents and that those residents will be older and poorer." The controller calls abandoned property a serious problem, noting that more than one-fifth of the 25,000 vacant buildings in the city have been designated as dangerous. The city spent more than $100 million over the previous five years to demolish 13,000 structures. Even so, it has been unable to significantly reduce its inventory of such buildings. The report says this problem is likely to grow in the years ahead despite increased funding. Most worrisome of all, the controller's office warns that Philadelphia's growing municipal debt burden could soon force the city to slash services or boost taxes. Already, says the report, the city takes too much from its businesses and residents, sometimes taxing them "right out of existence."

In his 1997 book about Philadelphia, *A Prayer for the City*, Buzz Bissinger counts the casualties. By 1990, 60 percent of the city's children had been born to single mothers, 40 percent of those enrolled had dropped out of high school, and 20 percent of the city's households were operating at poverty levels. By 2001, the city's school district was projecting a $1.5 billion deficit over the next five years. More than half of the system's students were scoring near the bottom on statewide reading and math tests. School buildings were decaying. The city's faltering school system was on the brink of becoming the largest in the country ever to be run by its state government, according to Todd Ziebarth, a policy analyst for the Education Commission of the States. Noting the school crisis, state legislator Mario Civera warned: "You cannot let Philadelphia fall into the Delaware River."

Similar troubles have plagued other great American cities. What caused the problems? Almost everyone who has studied the question agrees that one of the principal causes is the erosion of manufacturing. William Julius Wilson, an eminent sociologist, has done extensive studies of the ghettos of Chicago's South Side. He attributes many of the economic woes of the urban poor to the loss of manufacturing jobs for unskilled workers in the core cities. In Detroit, author Thomas Sugrue tied that city's extended decline firmly to a traumatic, long-running process of deindustrialization. In his 1996 book, *Origins of the Urban Crisis*, Sugrue traced Detroit's decline to auto industry cutbacks that intensified in the 1950s. He recounted the congressional testimony of workers who lost their jobs in Packard's 1956 shutdown of a plant in Detroit. "I felt someone had hit me with a sledgehammer," said one worker. "It was such a shock. . . . They just threw us out on the street," another declared. "It hit and hit hard, hit the man who was the common assembler the hardest," said a worker with 30 years of seniority. Sugrue went on to describe how similar cutbacks kept hitting the city, year after year, right up to the end of the century.

> *What caused the problems that led to declines in Philadelphia and other great Americans cities? Almost everyone who has studied the question agrees that one of the principal causes is the decline of manufacturing.*

Philadelphia's manufacturing history is legendary. In March of 2001, WHYY, the region's main public television station, aired a 70-minute documentary on the topic, entitled "Workshop of the World," as part of its pledge week fundraising campaign. The show stirred nostalgia and civic pride. Calls for tapes of the program, offered in return for $60 pledges, inundated the station.

Manufacturers established themselves in Philadelphia late in the 18th Century. Entrepreneurs and craftsmen took advantage of the city's location on the Delaware River. The city became a center for furniture producers, shipbuilders, and assorted crafts, and grew as a portal to the developing Northwest Territory. In 1797, workers at a private ship-yard in Philadelphia launched the first ship built for the U.S. Navy. Four years later, the Navy chose the city as the site for its first ship-yard. The completion of the Erie Canal in 1825 blunted Philadelphia's status as the gateway to the West, but the rise of the Pennsylvania Railroad and of a wide band of industries helped to rebuild that role.

By 1880, the city's leading industry was clothing and textiles, yet a re-markably diverse range of industries—machine tools and hardware, shoes and boots, paper and printing, iron and steel, lumber and wood, glass—had come to differentiate Philadelphia from other manufactur-ing centers. Buzz Bissinger noted that the Englishman Arthur Shadell studied manufacturing in England, Germany, and the United States, then concluded that Philadelphia was "the greatest manufacturing city in the world." Unlike Detroit, no single product or entrepreneur stood out. Nondurable industries, specialized manufacturing, family-run businesses, and partnerships, rather than large industrial corpora-tions, prevailed. Decade after decade, persistence and stability marked the city's industrial base.

In a lengthy 1936 profile of Philadelphia, *Fortune* magazine mar-veled at the city's industrial clout. Philadelphia, *Fortune* estimated, pumped out nearly 5 percent of U.S. production. "Probably nowhere else in the United States, with the possible exception of the New York area, have so many industries reached first or second rank," the mag-azine declared. First in knitwear, petroleum refining, sugar refining, paper products, cigars, carpets and rugs, radios, Bibles, false teeth, plumbers' supplies, and clay products; second in men's and boys' clothing, leathers, druggists' preparations, ice cream, and ships.

Manufacturing peaked in Philadelphia during World War II. The city had been one of the principal suppliers in the nation's military effort, with the focus of its activity at the bustling Naval Shipyard. Workers at the yard assembled 53 ships, including the largest ever built for the U.S. Navy, the battleship *New Jersey*. Monstrous rush-hour traffic snarled the streets leading to the yard. The federal government rushed construction of housing developments throughout the city and beyond. The civilian workforce at the shipyard reached a high of 58,434 in 1943; by the end of 1946, it was down to 7,500. The following year, manufacturing still accounted for 47 percent of the city's work-force, almost five percentage points above manufacturing's share of the U.S. workforce. But in the 1950s, an unrelenting storm of manu-facturing job losses began buffeting Philadelphia and other big cities. "In the 1960s alone, the number of blue-collar jobs lost in the country's four largest cities—New York, Chicago, Detroit, and Philadelphia—had been more than one million," Bissinger wrote. By 1992, it was appar-ent that the decline would continue in Philadelphia. "The Workshop of the World," he wrote, "had become the Manufacturing Mausoleum of the World." As the 1990s ended, only about 10 percent of the city's workers were in manufacturing, roughly four percentage points below the U.S. average.

Among those convinced that the unusually steep manufacturing decline seriously damaged the city were members of a team, mostly at Temple University, that scrutinized Philadelphia's problems in the 1991 book, *Philadelphia: Neighborhoods, Division and Conflict in a Postindustrial City*. To those urbanologists, the word "postindustrial"—often used approvingly to describe an economy that no longer has to deal with messy, outdated factories—was not a term of endearment.

"Philadelphia's shift to postindustrialism has increased the divisions among classes, races, and neighborhoods in both the city and suburbs," the team concluded. "The preindustrial and industrial economies operated as the glue that held the region together. The vast web of economic interconnections between firms and sections of the city helped to establish social and political cohesion in a diverse citizenry."

> *Philadelphia's shift to postindustrialism has increased the divisions among classes, races, and neighborhoods in both city and suburbs. The preindustrial and industrial economies operated as the glue that held the region together.*

Few can speak to that point with more authority than Frank Maguire, a social worker for the Veterans Administration in Philadelphia. For 28 years, Maguire worked for Kelsey-Hayes, an auto and aircraft parts supplier that once flourished in the city. He grew up in Kensington, a blue-collar Philadelphia neighborhood then laced with busy factories. After high school and a stint with the U.S. Army, he joined the company. He worked as a laborer, rigger, machine operator, and tryout machinist. Then he moved into a full-time position as the leader of the company's United Auto Workers local. When a wave of factory shutdowns swept across the city in the 1970s, Maguire and other labor leaders campaigned successfully for legislation requiring advance notice of the closings.

He fought to retain worker benefits after the plant struggled through ownership changes, bankruptcy, and, finally in 1994, a shutdown. Then, he embarked on a second career, earning undergraduate and graduate degrees in social work from Temple University. At Temple, he interviewed scores of former manufacturing workers for a research project on what it's like to lose a job. Now, he spends much of his time helping the downtrodden in the city's soup kitchens and homeless shelters.

Maguire drove one of the authors through the city's crumbling manufacturing neighborhoods. It was almost like listening to a tour guide describe a European city struggling to dig out from under the rubble of World War II. Along the way, he alluded frequently to the decline and fall of Kelsey-Hayes:

Philadelphia is in real trouble. Just look. Suppose you lose a plant with 1,000 people. What's the ripple effect? Years ago, Tioga Street was packed. Now it's all dead. This is not only in North Philadelphia. It's in West Philadelphia. It's in Kensington. Now we're on 11th Street. You're probably in the poorest of the poor. See that building over there? That used to be a manufacturing site. It's falling apart, but the city can't afford to take it down. It'd cost them too much money. It'd be interesting to see what they are paying a year for fires in these buildings. You used to find everything here. You'd find Kelsey-Hayes. You'd find Budd, Yale and Towne, Cross Brothers. You'd find SKF, which made ball bearings. You'd find ITE, which made electrical circuits, and Philco Ford. Fleer's Chewing Gum was another. The list was endless. Suppose you had a plant with a thousand people. Who supplied them? The trucking outfits? The steel mills? On any given Monday or Tuesday, we would have 30 to 35 trucks of steel waiting outside of Kelsey-Hayes. We reached our peak here, with about 1,100 workers, in the late 1970s. Then the company diversified and put a wheel plant in Sedalia, Missouri. They had a one-million-square-foot plant here, but the machines became antiquated. Fruehauf owned the company, piled up a lot of debt, didn't reinvest.

Maguire's descriptions of the past owners of Kelsey-Hayes were not pretty:

Fruehauf sold it to William Stoecker. *60 Minutes* did an investigative report on him a few years ago. Check it out. The management decided to keep one product line here, aerospace. Bottom line: We gave the company back $1.25 an hour in wages in the late 1980s. That saved 500 jobs. Now it's 1990. Along comes Ralph David Ketchum. He buys it from the banks. In 1994, the plant closed. We went bankrupt. He walked away. People lost everything. It's so demoralizing to see everyone but the workers getting paid. It's a shame.

We're on Erie Avenue. You used to go from factory to factory here. There's where Frankford Unity was, the city's largest supplier to ma and pa shops. They went out of business. Look at this—the amount of vacant property in the city—it's unbelievable. People living here left the city if they could afford to. We'll be going into Feltonville. I'm going to show you blocks and blocks of houses that were taken out. The Center City is coming back, but who's moving there? A one-bedroom condo will cost you $170,000. Who can afford that? It's like every other center city in the United States—we improve the central location but what do we do to improve the rest of the city? We're getting two new stadiums. They'll create mainly temporary jobs for construction workers, who mostly don't live in Philadelphia.

What could have been done? I don't know if Philadelphia could have competed. Suppose you were running a plant. The southern states got the plants. The plants didn't pay real estate taxes, or for the water or the roads. This was state versus state. They put up your plant. What would you have done? There were too many factors in the equation. There wasn't enough foresight in this in the beginning.

Still more deterioration came into view as we swung west onto Wyoming Avenue . . .

It just goes on and on like this. It's not only in North Philadelphia. It's in Kensington. It's in West Philadelphia. Kensington was textiles, rugs, plants after plants after plants. When you were a kid, if you didn't work down the street, you went up the street. There's where Mrs. Smith's Pies was. Now it's gone. Out of business. The Fairless Steel plant was outside of Philadelphia, but the cutbacks there had to affect suppliers in the city.

You know what bothers me? We don't care. We don't think we need manufacturing. There's a pool hall, a nightclub, a hospital building. Once, this was all Kelsey-Hayes. There were five different buildings—auto, aircraft, a wheel shop, R&D. Now just one is still standing, offices. They couldn't tear it down. The real culprit here is Kelsey-Hayes. The problem was that we were old and we were not reinvesting. If you're taking money out, you've got to put it in.

That yellow building over there was Exide Batteries. Now it's Dollarland. Now we're back in North Philadelphia. That sign says "William Penn—sheet metal products—$1-square-foot rent immediate possession." But it's shut down. This was all industry, as far as you can see. Over there was Stetson Hat, Stetson Hospital, Stetson this, Stetson that. Stetson owned this neighborhood. Look what it did. That used to be the John Hofbrau Restaurant, one of the biggest restaurants around. Now it's an abandoned building and this is one of the poorest neighborhoods around. This is an empowerment zone, but do you see much empowerment here?

Kensington Avenue used to be a corridor. It used to be retail, and the retail was fed by the manufacturing. The people around the corridor all worked in little ma and pa industries. Now they're all closed. Probably the biggest industries along Kensington Avenue now are prostitution and drugs. There was the Packard plant; it's an apartment building. There was the Ford plant, at Broad and Lehigh. Now, that's a burnt-out area. Temple is a major employer. The University of Pennsylvania is a major employer. We're lucky to have them.

This used to be Columbia Avenue. Now it's called Cecil B. Moore Avenue. He was a famous civil rights leader in the city. This is another soon-to-be-rebuilt district. It's where the riots were in Philadelphia. I hope they make it.

Maguire began talking about lessons learned . . .

We have to own up to some of our own mistakes. Looking back, what would I do over? I would have researched the two buyers for Kelsey-Hayes to death, to find out if they were for real. We bent over backward for those two deals.

Here's Red Lion Road and the old Budd plant site. They made railroad cars here. Now a German company owns Budd. They made this over into a golf course. That's the only thing they could do because of environmental problems. This was probably one of the most expensive pieces of property in Philadelphia, and they couldn't sell it.

Companies will say the unions drove them out. They'll say taxes did. It wasn't either, but there were problems. The cost of workers compensation was a disgrace. You can't just fix the hubcaps and say you don't want to change to another job. You couldn't have six guys changing a hose. All that had to be changed at the end. Companies needed flexibility. The labor movement is rough. You can't always be telling the worker he or she is right. You do what you can.

The stock market went crazy. American banks let people buy plants when they really didn't have any money.

I like what I'm doing now. I get a $250-a-month pension, for twenty-eight-and-a-half years of work. I'll have to work 'til I drop. This is just a second career, that's all. I did a paper on what it feels like to lose a job. I did a lot of interviews. Workers no longer have the loyalty they once did. I think American workers always took a lot on the chin. How do you take 28 years and just throw it out of your life—all the people you met? You spent more time there than you actually spent with your family. There were up to 400 workers at Kelsey-Hayes when it closed. Their average age was early fifties. On average, they took about a 30 percent pay cut. A few went back into manufacturing and others took different jobs altogether. You know what astonished me the most? The so-called braintrust children that the company had in management. They didn't go back into manufacturing. They opened their own businesses or went to Home Depot—service jobs. Not many of them retired. They couldn't get enough of a pension. Only those who were at the company before it was sold got benefits. I went into research to see if it's the same all over. I knew people who didn't get jobs, families that broke up. I knew people who committed suicide.

URBAN INDUSTRIAL DECLINE—A MULTITUDE OF WHYS

Why has manufacturing fallen so steeply in so many big cities? Some, like Maguire, place much of the blame on industry itself and on Wall Street. In Philadelphia, Baldwin Locomotive, once one of the world's most vaunted manufacturers, failed to renew itself through investment and innovation. When the steam engine died, so did the company. Later, some of the city's manufacturers fell victim to financial and legal manipulation, as exemplified by the Kelsey-Hayes saga. In 1997, Chicago businessman William Stoecker was convicted of bilking 25 banks out of more than $150 million in a case described by federal prosecutors as the largest such fraud ever in Illinois. Stoecker acquired Kelsey-Hayes and Fruehauf in 1988. Then, by age 31, he had built up his industrial conglomerate, Grabill Corp., into a $750 million empire of more than 30 companies. By 1990, though, Grabill had collapsed. The *Chicago Tribune* reported that Stoecker had defaulted on $65 million of bank loans in 1986—fully two years before he acquired Fruehauf. At Stoecker's sentencing, assistant U.S. attorney Gillum Ferguson called him a "bad man" who displayed "an entire lack of scruples." The Kelsey-Hayes story sounded one of many sour notes for Philadelphia in the 1980s, when the city limped through a wrenching deindustrialization.

The team of urbanologists that studied Philadelphia's problems stressed technological improvements that enabled manufacturers to boost production with fewer workers; producers who cut costs either by contracting business to suppliers beyond the city or by moving to lower-cost regions of the country; and tougher competition from abroad. The team found that 79 percent of the city's factory job losses from 1947 to 1986 came in the textile and apparel industries. The city's textile industry actually began its skid in the 1920s, when lower wages, subsidies, tax breaks, and cheaper utilities attracted manufacturers to southern and western states.

Ted Crone, an economist at the Federal Reserve Bank of Philadelphia, cited shifting markets and high costs of doing business. Relatively slow population growth in the Northeast led manufacturers to go where the growth was faster, in order to get closer to more customers. Crone also noted that the move of goods from rail to truck dealt a particular blow to Philadelphia's manufacturers, because the city's streets are so narrow. Philadelphia's wage tax, which provides the city with more than half of its revenues, is often mentioned as a significant disincentive. The tax, on wages earned in the city, is nearly 5 percent on residents and about 4 percent on nonresidents. A 1999 review of the wage tax by the Pennsylvania Economy League called it a factor in the manufacturing exodus. The league cited a 1992 analysis done for the Philadelphia Fed by Professor Robert Inman of the Wharton School. Inman estimated that the wage tax had cost the city 100,000 jobs since 1966.

TROUBLES IN OTHER CORE CITIES

Philadelphia is not alone. Many large and midsized cities in several parts of the country have experienced sharp declines in manufacturing—declines approximately as sharp as those seen in Philadelphia. Over the years, critics have suggested that misguided municipal leadership intensified these declines, but each city has its own story. Chicago's downtown and many of its neighborhoods have shown considerable vigor in recent years. Still, a close look at the vast stretches of decay beyond Chicago's glittering lakefront shows how seriously the city has been hurt by plant shutdowns. Similarly, new projects and neighborhood rebounds have helped New York City. Yet, manufacturing employment in the nation's largest city plunged from 1.1 million jobs in 1951 to 757,000 in 1972 and just 227,400 in 2001. There, city policies have drawn harsh criticism from Jason Epstein, a longtime publishing industry leader who cofounded the *New York Review of Books*.

In a 1992 article for the *Review,* Epstein charged that for decades, city officials embraced policies that discouraged manufacturing. "New York's manufacturing economy for years served a double purpose," Epstein wrote. "It turned immigrants into workers and workers into a bourgeoisie, and it provided abundant public and private wealth." In the 1960s and 1970s, he argued, the city still had the greatest concentration of factory jobs the world had ever known. In Brooklyn, manufacturers made everything from Brillo soap pads, Kirkman's laundry soap, and Eberhard-Faber pencils to Topps chewing gum and Rockwell's candy bars. Thanks to the jobs at these companies, the city was able to assimilate its newcomers. Its industries financed its schools and hospitals, its public university, a generous welfare system, a spectacular cultural life—things that only the richest city on earth could afford. Then, Epstein argues, New York City's manufacturing sector moved into a steep decline, turning black and Hispanic immigrants into the first major groups of newcomers in the city's history to face a shrinking industrial base.

Epstein concedes that city leaders had no control over changing technology. They couldn't simply order the companies making pencils and chewing gum to switch into production of semiconductors and microwave ovens. Yet, had city officials recognized the significance of such changes, he contends, they could have done more to attract newer industries and remain more competitive. Instead, the city bulldozed industrial districts to make way for subsidized office towers, glitzy development projects, and highways.

Epstein traces these policies back to the 1920s, when planners elevated their distaste for manufacturing to an ideological principle. The planners, "disturbed by the apparent mess of New York's pulsating industrial economy and immigrants whom it employed . . . were determined to replace both the workers and their factories with something more orderly, less congested, and cleaner." Their "Regional Plan for New York and Its Environs" anticipated the city's transformation "from a polymorphous manufacturing center to a highly specialized and fragile world financial headquarters manned by people who soon learned to speak, dress, and otherwise behave like the regional planners themselves." One of the planners complained that "a stone's throw from the stock exchange, the air is filled with the aroma of roasting coffee." Another planner, upset by the very presence of 420,000 factory employees working south of 59th Street, many of them near the upscale stores along Fifth and Madison Avenues, groused that "such a situation outrages one's sense of order. Everything seems misplaced. One yearns to rearrange the hodgepodge and put things where they belong." Epstein notes that one critic of the regional plan, Robert Fitch, went so far as to liken it to Stalin's Five-Year Plans.

Others agree with elements of Epstein's critique. In his 1985 book, *The Rise and Fall of New York City*, former city housing commissioner Roger Starr charged that residents constantly used city rules and regulations to stop manufacturers' projects. In a chapter titled "The Unmaking of Manufacturing," Starr argued that the controversies created such uncertainty that they either killed off the factory or left company officials so angry that they simply packed up and left town.

New York City's Taub Urban Research Center concluded in a 1996 study that the same pressures leading to industrial declines in the cities—technological change, foreign competition, aging and inefficient plants, lack of space, high land costs, and congestion—also battered New York City's manufacturers. The Taub Center's study added that many of the difficulties were of the city's own making. The study cited high taxes and fees; bureaucratic hassles with city agencies; prohibitively expensive environmental regulations; long delays in selling city-owned property to space-squeezed small businesses; zoning laws that favor large real estate developers over light industry; and weak ties between public schools and manufacturers.

Manufacturing's big-city blues in the Empire State reach well beyond New York City. Three of the state's eight Sliding Goliath counties are boroughs of the city, but two more (Westchester and Nassau) are in the suburbs and the rest (Erie, Monroe, and Onondaga) include the three largest cities in upstate New York (Buffalo, Rochester, and Syracuse). Moody's Investors Service says New York's sagging industrial sector is one of the reasons why the state shares with Louisiana the dubious distinction of having the worst state bond rating in the country. State officials, finally acknowledging in the mid-1990s that high taxes and burdensome regulations were pushing manufacturers out of New York, began cutting taxes and regulations. By then, though, they were paying a heavy price to lure industry back. In 1997, Mayor Rudolph Giuliani hailed the arrival of the city's first significant new manufacturer in 50 years, a $150 million paper recycling factory on Staten Island. Luring the project to the city, however, required an enormous package of incentives: $240 million in bond financing, 20 years of property tax abatements, sales and use tax exemptions, $1.4 million in grants and loans, and $1.4 million for barges.

COULD INDUSTRY COME BACK?

Despite steep declines in their industrial bases, the large cities of the Northeast and Midwest retain a significant industrial activity. This is apparent at small specialty manufacturers, where dramas of tough times, resilience, and success have been quietly unfolding for years. Messinger Bearings Corp., which employs 32 workers at a nondescript plant in North Philadelphia, has lived on the edge time and again. The company began doing business in 1912 as a blacksmith shop. Its payroll peaked at 160 workers during World War II, when it made bearings for gun mounts on aircraft carriers and battleships. Messinger struggled in the 1970s, eventually falling into receivership, but it survived and has endured under new ownership. Today, the company successfully works a niche market: custom-made bearings for special uses. Messinger's president, Robert Mathews, says leaving the city wouldn't make economic sense because of the company's investment there. In 1998, NASA asked the company to make a bearing nearly 16 feet in diameter for a flight simulator. Messinger responded, turning out what Mathews describes as the largest bearing ever built in the United States, in just five months. Philadelphia Mayor Ed Rendell came to the factory to celebrate the occasion. Ed Hook, a machine operator who has been with the company since 1965, won't forget that day. Hook joined Messinger after working as a short-order cook. "I felt there was something better out there," he says. Today, he makes $40,000 a year plus good benefits—enough, it's turned out, to raise five children. "We never get laid off," says Hook. "Just hearing that bearing was headed for NASA and to help the country—that was one of my greatest moments."

Joe Houldin heads the Delaware Valley Industrial Resource Center, a partnership that helps the region's manufacturers to become more competitive. Once a marketing executive for the city's industrial development agency, he retains his commitment to Philadelphia by keeping the center's offices just inside the city. Houldin clings to a fascinating vision for Philadelphia. He thinks the city could reinvent itself as a center for small, growing specialty manufacturers—much like it was in the early days of the industrial revolution. Eventually, he believes, new technologies will enable some of these producers to grow up as high-volume specialty manufacturers.

Houldin's vision is still pretty much of a dream. The city needs more educated workers. It must find the resources to clean up polluted sites and then to assemble sites large enough to draw new factories. Many manufacturers continue to prefer lower-cost, outlying sites.

Yet, many Philadelphians undoubtedly would like to see Houldin's dream come true. They worry, like urban residents in other big cities, that the postindustrial society is not dealing their city a good hand.

Or, as the public television station put it in its "Workshop of the World" program, "Today, the city that used to be an industrial giant takes a look around and wonders what happened."

CHAPTER 8

Manufacturing and Community Prosperity

 There are two overriding reasons why manufacturing jobs are important: they pay well and they generate growth in other sectors. When manufacturing thrives, so does the rest of the economy. When it declines, the balance of the economy weakens. Mining, agriculture, and a few other industries also transfer prosperity to other sectors, but manufacturing—with 23 percent of the nation's payroll—is the most significant multiplier of jobs.

JOBS VERSUS POVERTY

We tested this hypothesis for the 232 manufacturing counties in our sample. Figure 8.1 shows the results. Overall, employment grew in all seven categories of counties, but rose far more rapidly in the four groups gaining momentum in manufacturing than in the three groups doing less well in this sector. In the categories where manufacturing was gathering strength, every major employment sector grew substantially. Total employment increased from 37 to 63 percent. The increases were less than 10 percent in the groups where manufacturing was declining.

In the Slider county groups, construction, wholesale trade, and F.I.R.E. (finance, insurance, and real estate) all either lost jobs or showed minimal job growth. Services was the only sector to show sizable gains, but there is more to that story. Health care accounted for virtually all of the service category job gains in the Slider counties. These increases came as an aging population sought more medical services.

FIGURE 8.1   Percent Employment Changes by Major Sector,* 1988 to 1997

CATEGORY	MFG.	CONST.	TRANSPOR-TATION & UTILITIES	WHOLE-SALE	RETAIL	F.I.R.E.	SERVICES	TOTAL
Hinterland Highspots	33.3%	59.4%	24.1%	14.6%	32.2%	19.5%	70.8%	36.7%
Metro Movers	53.8	54.6	50.9	63.5	46.8	43.4	92.2	62.8
Freeway Flyers	40.8	37.1	33.2	21.9	29.3	13.8	77.4	43.0
Gradual Growers	33.0	22.1	47.8	46.8	32.4	34.0	69.1	42.7
Smaller Sliders	−20.2	8.6	6.9	3.5	10.9	0.4	40.8	9.2
Midrange Sliders	−20.3	−3.3	2.2	−0.1	6.7	9.5	42.8	9.8
Sliding Goliaths	−25.1	−15.6	5.8	−3.8	−0.1	1.9	25.0	2.4
Total United States	−3.3	11.6	18.5	13.9	17.0	10.6	48.7	12.7

SOURCE: University of St. Thomas and U.S. Census Bureau, County Business Patterns, 1988 and 1997
* Standard Industrial Classification (SIC)

In the categories where manufacturing was gathering strength, every major employment sector grew substantially. Total employment increased from 37 to 63 percent. The increases were less than 10 percent in the groups where manufacturing was declining.

Nationally, nearly a fourth of the 18.8 million jobs the United States added from 1988 to 1997 were in health care. Manufacturers and other private sector companies have provided much of the tax money that supports the new health care jobs—but that can only continue with the underpinning of healthy industry. Bill Maxwell, executive vice president of the Fairview Hospital chain in Minnesota, puts it quite bluntly: "Government underfunds its portion of medical expense and then relies on private industry to make up the difference. We couldn't make it with an erosion of industry."

Government underfunds its portion of medical expense and then relies on private industry to make up the difference. We couldn't make it with an erosion of industry.

The stronger manufacturing counties had lower unemployment rates. The four momentum-gaining groups had jobless rates from .7 to

1.7 percentage points below the U.S. rate. The three losing groups had rates from .3 to 1.6 percentage points higher.

Poverty rates also reflect striking differences between the momentum-gaining counties and those that are losing steam (Figure 8.2). Counties gaining momentum in manufacturing are reducing poverty, while those weakening in manufacturing are seeing their poverty stabilize at higher levels or else worsen. This is most evident in the Hinterland Highspot counties, where the poverty rate fell 14.9 percent from 1989 to 1997. Meanwhile, the poverty rate in the Sliding Goliaths rose 9.8 percent. Generally, this pattern worsens in the core cities. In New York's Kings County—the Borough of Brooklyn, where manufacturing has been in a long, steep decline—the poverty rate rose nearly 17 percent over this period.

Counties gaining momentum in manufacturing are reducing poverty, while those weakening in manufacturing are seeing their poverty stabilize at higher levels or else worsen.

Household income, a figure not adjusted for inflation, also grew about 60 percent faster than the nation as a whole in the momentum-gathering counties (Figure 8.2). Household income in the Sliding Goliath counties grew more slowly than in the nation.

FIGURE 8.2   Poverty Rate and Household Income Changes 1989 to 1997

CATEGORY	POVERTY RATE 1989	POVERTY RATE 1997	CHANGE 1989 TO 1997	HOUSEHOLD INCOME 1989	HOUSEHOLD INCOME 1997	% CHANGE 1989 TO 1997
Hinterland Highspots	13.4%	11.4%	Down 14.9%	$24,424	$35,225	44.2%
Metro Movers	9.1	8.8	Down 3.3	34,331	46,737	36.1
Freeway Flyers	12.0	11.1	Down 7.5	26,345	36,452	38.4
Gradual Growers	11.6	10.7	Down 7.8	31,277	41,851	33.8
Smaller Sliders	13.9	13.7	Down 1.4	25,685	33,398	30.0
Midrange Sliders	13.7	13.6	Down .7	29,485	37,613	27.6
Sliding Goliaths	12.3	13.5	Up 9.8	34,211	41,151	20.3
Kings County, NY	22.7	26.5	Up 16.7	25,684	26,108	1.7
Total United States	13.1	13.3	Up 1.5	30,056	37,005	23.1

SOURCE: University of St. Thomas and U.S. Census Bureau, 1989 and 1997

The impact of rising poverty rates and less robust income growth is visible in the expenditures of local governments, according to the Census Bureau. County and local government expenditures per capita in 1992 averaged $1,871 in the Hinterland Highspot counties, $1,892 in the Metro Mover counties, $1,702 in the Freeway Flyer counties, and $2,449 in the Sliding Goliath counties.

MANUFACTURING AND TAXES

Not surprisingly, local taxes follow suit. First, we looked at city taxes when industry declines, using 1997 data from the U.S. Bureau of the Census. Those cities with more people employed in manufacturing have distinctly lower per-capita city taxes, as illustrated in Figure 8.3.

We also tested the relationship between the percentage of employment in manufacturing and taxes at the county level, which includes local taxes. County and local taxes were 4.5 percent of income for the total United States in 1992 but, as with the cities, taxes go up as manufacturing declines (Figure 8.4). Among the 690 counties we exam-

---

FIGURE 8.3   Manufacturing Intensity and City Taxes

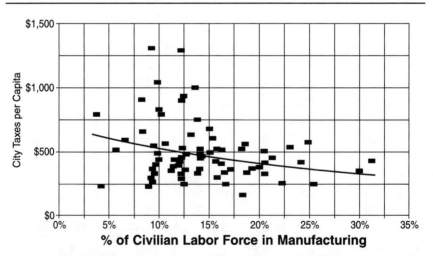

SOURCE: U.S. Bureau of Census, 1997
Each dot represents one U.S. city

FIGURE 8.4   Manufacturing Intensity and Per-Capita Taxes

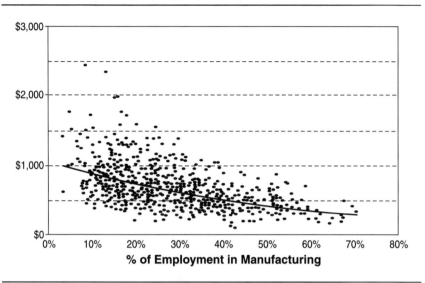

SOURCE: Counties USA 2000 and University of St. Thomas

ined, those with 10 percent of civilian employment in manufacturing averaged about $1,000 in county and local taxes per person in 1992 while the counties with 30 percent averaged $650 and those with 40 percent averaged $562.

> *Among the 690 counties we examined, those with 10 per-cent of civilian employment in manufacturing averaged about $1,000 in county and local taxes per person in 1992 while the counties with 30 percent averaged $650 and those with 40 percent averaged $562.*

MANUFACTURING AND INCOME DISPARITY

We pointed out in Chapter 2 that fringe benefits and wages vary greatly from one industry to another—within manufacturing. The differences across the broad spectrum of all industries within the U.S. economy are greater still. Although the United States is a wealthy country, legions of social scientists and professionals have found rising disparities in both wealth and income. Jared Bernstein, Lawrence Mishel, and John Schmitt of the Economic Policy Institute described growing disparities in their book, *The State of Working America 2000–2001.*

Not surprisingly, some people lay the problem of income disparity at the door of our political systems. From one perspective, taxes on the wealthy are too low, executives are overpaid, and wages should be increased. From another, taxes should fall to promote entrepreneurship and greater opportunity, and the government should be shrunk to keep from gumming up the free enterprise system. However, both viewpoints beg the question of whether the social problems can be solved solely through redistribution—one way or the other. As the late economist Franz Mueller wryly observed, "It is hard to redistribute something that hasn't been produced in the first place."

The relationship between manufacturing prominence and income equality should be studied further. In a study entitled "The Loss of Manufacturing in America," manufacturing manager Paul T. Carson observed that U.S. income equality increased in the late 1940s through the late 1960s, when U.S. manufacturing was quite strong. When the United States began to lose its manufacturing edge after the 1973 oil embargo, income gradually became more unequal.

Carson's analysis makes intuitive sense. In places where well-paid jobs historically provided by manufacturing are decreasing, it may be no coincidence that disparities are rising.

In summary, poverty rates are worsening, unemployment rates are climbing, populations are aging, nonmanufacturing jobs are growing more slowly, and taxes are climbing higher in areas of our sample where manufacturing is in relative decline. The reverse is occurring in counties where manufacturing is gaining strength. Manufacturing job losses can also lead to rising disparities of income and wealth. For both social progress and fiscal solvency, healthy industry is still the critical variable. The future prosperity of many regions and the quality of life experienced by citizens is likely to depend on the expansion or contraction of local industry.

PART THREE

Coping in a World Economy

The rapid emergence of an economy with increasingly global dimensions brings not only opportunities but additional stresses capable of affecting U.S. prosperity and leadership position. Not all of these forces are negative, but coping in a world economy does provide challenges. The prosperity of the United States and its status as the world's largest open market has attracted the attention of aspiring producers in many countries. As these aspiring producers become more active in certain markets, they gain skills that are often useful in other markets. Industrial capabilities that helped make the United States a fortress of democracy in past wars are now shared with other counties. And, other countries are finding it appealing to invest in the United States in ways that are helping both the U.S. economy and the fortunes of individual communities.

Part Three of this book deals with the dynamics of coping in a world economy and how U.S. industry has been faring in this changing environment:

Chapter 9 breaks down the U.S. trade deficit by industry and by country, explains how the strong dollar has worked to increase the size of the deficit, and looks at how specific companies have been dealing with competition from abroad.

Chapter 10 considers the thickening of supplier and skills networks in other lands, explains why it's important to retain suppliers, shows how changing economics and technology give foreign rivals more flexibility, and cautions against the current fashion of farming work out to contractors.

Chapter 11 shows how the nation's changing defense industrial base has affected U.S. manufacturing.

Chapter 12 explains how investment by foreign competitors, most notably in the auto industry, has helped to reinvigorate certain regions of the country.

CHAPTER 9

A Deeper Look at the Trade Deficit

 Outside, politicians, union members, and just plain folks on Minnesota's Iron Range gathered, on the steps of Virginia High School, to belt out "Solidarity Forever." Inside, in the school's Goodman Auditorium, labor leaders, mayors, congressmen, small business owners, corporate executives, state bureaucrats, and even a Catholic bishop gave testimony to the need to stop the flood of steel from China, Russia, Brazil, and other faraway lands. The U.S. Commerce Department had called a hearing to help determine whether the imports threaten national security. If so, quotas would be imposed on steel imports. Some 900 people had asked to testify. Time allowed for 34, in an impassioned proceeding that stretched on for seven hours.

Among them was 18-year-old Samantha Grippe, a member of the Class of 2001 at Mesabi East High School. Both of her parents had just lost their jobs in the shutdown of LTV Steel's taconite mine in nearby Hoyt Lakes, situated on top of Minnesota's vast deposit of iron ore known as the Iron Range. "The stubbornness and persistence in our ancestors' European blood that built these towns from the ground up is still running through the veins of the Iron Range," Grippe told the crowd. "Our towns are built up around these mines and I believe that if our mines fall, so will the towns. I worry not only for the future of the Iron Range, but also for the future of our nation."

Similar protests have erupted from a host of steel towns from Gary to Youngstown, and from other locales where companies have lost business to rivals from abroad. Just as on Minnesota's Iron Range, workers elsewhere often see themselves as victims of unfair trade practices. In such cases, the trade deficit takes on a personal dimension. It has come to symbolize their fears, even though job declines at many of these companies are often due to circumstances other than imports. Frequently,

119

poorly run companies, hostile communities, intransigent labor groups, or any of a host of other factors pave the way for plant shutdowns or cutbacks. Yet, when foreign competition is part of this mix, the number of jobs affected sometimes can be large and the outcries loud.

Competing in world markets is a family affair. Everyone's productivity counts, because the costs for all of us ultimately must be absorbed by a nation facing more international competition. The industrial economy is closely tied to the rest of the economy. Industries provide a robust market for the service businesses. That sector and others transfer many costs—taxes, mandates, legal fees, assessments, health insurance—onto industries. Sometimes, the collective burden of these costs weighs more heavily on U.S. manufacturers than on their foreign rivals.

A nation's balance of trade is a principal index of how well it competes internationally. Explored in depth, trade figures lead to questions about how industrial infrastructures—suppliers, schools, and other support systems—reflect on a nation's competitiveness. The United States has a large trade deficit, one that has been reaching record highs by various measures in recent years. Any nation will always buy more than it sells in some goods and services, but consistently huge overall trade deficits for long periods portend trouble. In such circumstances, a nation can find both its wealth and industrial expertise draining away. Mysterious to some and boring to others, the U.S. trade balance—the difference between exports and imports—ran close to even in the postwar years until the mid-1970s when oil imports began to mount. Since the mid-1990s, the trade balance has turned to a consistent and accelerating deficit as the nation's consumers gobbled up lower-priced imports, markets for exports to lands abroad lagged, and the strong dollar put American exporters at an increasing disadvantage.

BALANCE SLIPPING IN KEY INDUSTRIES

U.S. exports have been increasing but, in recent years, at a pace far behind imports. With the exception of one year, 1972, the country maintained a positive balance of trade on non-oil goods and commodities for roughly 90 years until 1983. Then imports of automobiles and other goods began to accelerate. By 1987, the non-oil trade deficit had reached

$116.7 billion. But American manufacturers, motivated by the need to survive, invested heavily, trained workers, and adopted new methods. Their new ways of doing things had blossomed earlier, as an outgrowth of the 1980–1982 recession, but it took a few years for everything to work as intended. By the late 1980s, U.S. products were again winning respect. Caterpillar and Deere were providing exemplary heavy equipment. Ford's Taurus had become North America's best-selling car. From 1987 through 1991, the non-oil trade deficit declined by 81 percent, from $116.7 billion to $22.4 billion.

Then the slide began. From 1991 to 2000, the country's non-oil merchandise trade deficit shot up sixteen-fold to $360 billion. With petroleum imports included, the total trade deficit in goods reached $450 billion by 2000—worsening by $100 billion in 1999 and that much again in 2000 (Figure 9.1). U.S. exports were increasing, but at a pace far behind imports. American citizens entered the 21st Century importing $1.2 trillion worth of merchandise—an average of $4,350 per man, woman, and child in the country—about one-seventh of our gross domestic product. We were exporting, too, of course, $773 billion, or $2,750 per person.

FIGURE 9.1   U.S. Trade Balance with and without Oil ($ Billions)

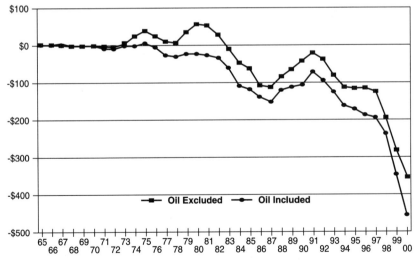

SOURCE: Economic Report of the President, 2001

Many observers, often people with vested interests, offer reasons why the U.S. trade deficit is worsening so badly. Foreign producers hire cheap labor and do not consider the environment. Foreign currencies are kept artificially low versus the dollar in order to make goods produced abroad more attractive to buyers. U.S. trade negotiators have not effectively represented U.S. interests. Financially driven corporate America doesn't care about keeping industry at home.

Not to worry, say the free trade advocates. Comparative advantage should rule and, ultimately, the world will be better off if we all trade freely.

Though there is certainly some truth to these claims, more light and less heat should be applied to the trade discussion. There are three fundamental questions to consider:

1. Are the industries being affected important to the country?
2. Is the deficit broadly based geographically or specific to a few countries?
3. Which companies are able to operate successfully within the current system?

LARGER DEFICITS IN KEY INDUSTRIES

Many of the larger deficits are in key industries. In primary metals, the United States has a $19 billion annual deficit. This industry has world-class competitors in Alcoa and Nucor. Still, its $42 billion of primary metals imports is more than seven times the annual sales of U.S. Steel, the largest home-based steel producer.

In the vital area of computers and office equipment, the United States was the unchallenged pacesetter for decades, led by companies such as IBM, Control Data, Univac, and Digital Equipment. In 2000, however, the trade deficit in computers was $46 billion—the value of imports was twice that of exports. That same year, the United States had a $13 billion deficit in machinery, also a strength 20 years ago when companies such as Cincinnati Milicron, Westinghouse, and Bausch & Lomb were in their prime. Within the machinery category, the United States ran trade deficits in electrical machinery in 2000, general industrial machinery, metalworking machinery, optical goods, power generating equipment, time pieces, and photographic equipment. Surpluses remain in scientific instruments and specialized industrial machinery.

The $75 billion deficit in clothing, shoes, and textiles, and the $14 billion in furniture and bedding, while not insignificant, are in labor-intensive industries. Yet, trade balances are also worsening in technically important industries: $105 billion in vehicles (from Toyota, Daimler-Benz, Volkswagen, Nissan); $59 billion in consumer appliances (Sony, Samsung, Matsushita Electric); and $3 billion in rubber and plastic products. Even in paper, where the United States has a strong concentration of technologically advanced companies, the deficit is now $3 billion. The aircraft industry's traditional surpluses continue, but fell to $22 billion in 2000 from $33 billion in 1999 reflecting the growing strength of the European consortium Airbus Industries. Figure 9.2 shows U.S. imports and exports by industry, and imports' share of total trade, for 2000.

Some of the deficits are occurring in goods where the country's needs are greatest. At a time when the United States faces acute shortages in electrical distribution and generation, two of its largest long-time producers of this equipment no longer have a presence in the market. Allis-Chalmers went bankrupt and Westinghouse withdrew. General Electric has focused on other endeavors at the same time that Europe's Siemens and ABB have stepped up their activity. In 2000, the U.S. trade deficit on power generation machinery was $1.3 billion—more than twice its size the year before. In electrical machinery, the deficit rose 42 percent to $19.1 billion. Where strong companies exist, in medical devices and scientific instruments, chemicals, and specialized industrial machinery, trade balances are positive. For these industries, the U.S. trade surplus was $23.3 billion.

The authors respect the many first-rate economists, industrialists, and labor leaders who have been grappling with trade issues and do not wish to enter the heated debates on U.S. trade policies. We do argue that the trade balance is an important indicator of future U.S. industrial strength. Given the wages paid to the employees of some of the industries being affected, the trade balance may also be a long-term leading indicator of U.S. prosperity.

FIGURE 9.2   U.S. Exports, Imports, and Trade Balance in Goods for 2000 ($ Millions)

ITEM	2000 EXPORTS	2000 IMPORTS	2000 TRADE BALANCE	IMPORTS AS A % OF TRADE
Total Balance of Payments Basis	$1,222,772	$ 773,304	$(449,468)	1.58%
Net Adjustments	6,029	(9,125)	(15,154)	–0.66
Total Census Basis	1,216,743	782,429	(434,314)	1.56
Manufactured goods	623,986	1,013,480	(389,494)	61.9
Agricultural commodities	50,387	37,755	12,632	42.8
Mineral fuels	13,134	133,590	(120,456)	91.1
Selected Commodities				
ADP Equipment; Office Machines	$46,661	$92,165	$(45,504)	66.4%
Airplanes & Parts	39,760	17,943	21,817	31.1
Alcohol & Tobacco	4,957	3,772	1,185	43.2
Metals	22,573	41,532	(18,959)	64.8
Chemicals	79,918	73,633	6,285	48.0
Clothing, Shoes & Textiles	19,377	94,325	(74,948)	83.0
Crops	25,724	15,667	10,057	37.9
Cork, Wood, Lumber	4,321	8,235	(3,914)	65.6
Machinery	230,950	244,236	(13,286)	51.4
Animal Products	12,457	15,784	(3,327)	55.9
Furniture and Bedding	4,744	18,927	(14,183)	80.0
Gems, Diamonds	1,289	12,060	(10,771)	90.3
Jewelry	1,565	6,459	(4,894)	80.5
Glass	2,486	2,250	236	47.5
Glassware	865	1,920	(1,055)	68.9
Lighting, Plumbing	1,392	5,106	(3,714)	78.6
Metal Manufacturers	13,272	16,228	(2,956)	55.0
Fossil Fuels	12,737	130,879	(118,142)	91.1
Paper and Pulp	15,373	18,565	(3,192)	54.7
Pottery	115	1,806	(1,691)	94.0
Printed Materials	4,778	3,698	1,080	43.6
Rubber & Plastic Products	11,667	14,779	(3,112)	55.9
Ships, Boats	1,044	1,178	(134)	53.0
TV, VCR, Media, Games	36,930	95,670	(58,740)	72.2
Travel Goods	351	4,432	(4,081)	92.7
Vehicles	56,873	161,682	(104,809)	74.0
Wood Manufacturers	1,856	7,222	(5,366)	79.6

SOURCE: Report FT900 (CB-01-31), Bureau of the Census, Foreign Trade Division, December 2000. Detailed data are presented on a Census basis.

The U.S. trade balance is an important indicator of future U.S. industrial strength. Given the wages paid to the employees of some of the industries being affected, the trade balance may also be a long-term leading indicator of U.S. prosperity.

DEFICITS WITH WHOM?

From a geographic perspective, the U.S. trade deficit is concentrated with a few trading partners. Figure 9.3 shows imports and exports, net trade balance, and the ratio of imports to exports for each country. Of the 33 trading partners for which the Census Bureau routinely publishes data, the United States has a favorable or roughly equal trade balance with 10: Belgium, Netherlands, Spain, United Kingdom, Switzerland, Australia, Hong Kong, Argentina, Brazil, and Egypt. Another 8 countries, including prominent Asian producers such as Singapore and Korea, sell from $1.08 to $1.47 to the United States for every dollar purchased from the United States. U.S. trade is seriously out of balance with only a few countries: oil producers Indonesia, Nigeria, Saudi Arabia, and Venezuela; Germany and Italy in Europe; China and Japan. The latter two lands account for more than $80 billion each. The U.S. trade deficit with China, $83.8 billion in 2000, was the largest for any single country. In 1999 and 2000, more

FIGURE 9.3 U.S. Imports and Exports by Country in 2000

REGION AND COUNTRY	IMPORTS ($ MILLIONS)	EXPORTS ($ MILLIONS)	TRADE BALANCE ($ MILLIONS)	RATIO IMPORTS TO EXPORTS
North America	$365,120	$290,507	$(74,613)	1.26
Canada	229,209	178,786	(50,423)	1.28
Mexico	135,911	111,721	(24,190)	1.22
Western Europe	241,031	181,270	(59,761)	1.33
Austria	3,233	2,554	(679)	1.27
Belgium	9,931	13,960	4,029	0.71
Finland	3,250	1,571	(1,679)	2.07
France	29,782	20,253	(9,529)	1.47
Germany	58,737	29,244	(29,493)	2.01

(Continued)

FIGURE 9.3   U.S. Imports and Exports by Country in 2000, *continued*

REGION AND COUNTRY	IMPORTS ($ MILLIONS)	EXPORTS ($ MILLIONS)	TRADE BALANCE ($ MILLIONS)	RATIO IMPORTS TO EXPORTS
Italy	25,050	11,000	(14,050)	2.28
Netherlands	9,704	21,974	12,270	0.44
Spain	5,731	6,323	592	0.91
Sweden	9,603	4,557	(5,046)	2.11
United Kingdom	43,459	41,579	(1,880)	1.05
Other EU	21,888	11,811	(10,077)	1.85
Norway	5,710	1,544	(4,166)	3.70
Switzerland	10,174	9,942	(232)	1.02
Eastern Europe	16,227	6,144	(10,083)	2.64
Hungary	2,716	569	(2,147)	4.77
Poland	1,040	757	(283)	1.37
Russia	7,796	2,318	(5,478)	3.36
Pacific Rim Countries	418,187	203,245	(214,942)	2.06
Australia	6,439	12,460	6,021	0.52
China	100,063	16,253	(83,810)	6.16
Japan	146,577	65,254	(81,323)	2.25
Hong Kong	11,452	14,625	3,173	0.78
Korea	40,300	27,902	(12,398)	1.44
Singapore	19,186	17,816	(1,370)	1.08
Taiwan	40,514	24,380	(16,134)	1.66
Other Pacific Rim (3)	53,655	24,554	(29,101)	2.19
South America & Central America	73,301	59,257	(14,044)	1.24
Argentina	3,102	4,700	1,598	0.66
Brazil	13,855	15,360	1,505	0.90
Colombia	6,969	3,689	(3,280)	1.89
Other S/C A (3)	49,375	35,509	(13,866)	1.39
OPEC	67,028	19,235	(47,793)	3.48
Indonesia (3)	10,385	2,547	(7,838)	4.08
Nigeria	10,549	718	(9,831)	14.69
Saudi Arabia	14,219	6,230	(7,989)	2.28
Venezuela (3)	18,648	5,552	(13,096)	3.36
Other OPEC	13,226	4,187	(9,039)	3.16
Other Countries	65,028	30,909	(34,119)	2.10

SOURCE: U.S. Trade Balance on Goods, U.S. Bureau of Census, 2001 Detailed data are presented on a Census basis.

than $6 in imports from China flowed into the United States for every dollar of exports sent there.

> *In 1999 and 2000, more than $6 in imports from China flowed into the United States for every dollar of exports sent there.*

CHINA AND THE PACIFIC RIM

The vast potential of trade with China and other Pacific Rim countries is well acknowledged by both companies eager to sell there and by economists who recognize the intrinsic value of free trade. Some disconcerting questions are surfacing in other circles. Is China employing an explicit strategy to pile up and sustain huge trade surpluses in order to build up its manufacturing base? Federal Reserve Research Officer James Orr, writing in the Federal Reserve Bank of New York's *Quarterly Review,* perceives deliberate efforts to hold down the value of the yuan, China's currency, relative to the dollar. Many China watchers feel these and other policies are making Chinese manufacturing somewhat artificially more competitive because of the undervaluing of the Chinese currency. Bob Goldfarb, president of the widely respected Sequoia Fund, told the mutual fund's 2001 annual meeting that "an area of risk to American manufacturing companies that I do not believe has received appropriate recognition is the continuing evolution of Chinese manufacturing." Goldfarb said numerous manufacturers have told Sequoia executives that Chinese products could soon fare better against U.S.-made products, "even high-value-added products." Chinese manufacturers "may pose an increasingly large risk to the sustainable competitive advantage of many outstanding manufacturers," he concluded.

Will entry into the World Trade Organization (WTO) provide the basis for more mutually beneficial trade with China? Opinions are divided. Writing in *Asian Survey,* Professor Richard Holton and Research Scholar Xia Yuan Lin, of the University of California at Berkeley, provide five reasons why China is unlikely to adjust its behavior as readily as the agreement requires:

1. The lack of an established legal bedrock in China
2. Widespread general ambiguity in the interpretation of laws
3. A paucity of people trained in either international law or contracts
4. The existence of corruption that thwarts enforcement efforts
5. Court systems that are not independent of local party politics

Assistant Secretary of Commerce for Market Access and Compliance William H. Lash is less concerned. "One thing is certain regarding China's compliance with WTO rules. We will have plenty of help watching them," Lash noted in a question and answer period after a 2001 speech in Minneapolis. "The entire world will be looking at China to see if they do comply."

CONTRASTING EXPERIENCES

In spite of vagaries and inconsistencies in the operating conventions surrounding world trade, it is clear that individual U.S. companies have responded differently.

At the hearing on Minnesota's Iron Range, no one objected to shoring up the troubled steel industry through quotas or other protectionist measures. Indeed, to the workers there whose jobs have been lost or threatened, the trade deficit is part of a witch's brew of forces that have devastated a treasured way of life. While new jobs are being created in other industries and other locales, the workers on the Iron Range can't easily find jobs that match the wages and benefits that the mining companies paid. There's no question that worldwide overcapacity in the steel industry has intensified their problems by forcing down prices.

Yet, a closer look at the domestic industry suggests that quotas alone won't eliminate the pain. Eighteen U.S.-based steel manufacturers declared bankruptcy from the fall of 1999 through the spring of 2001, and employment in the primary metals industries declined by 85,000 in three years. Critics argue that in many instances, stockholders and managers did these companies in by failing to invest and innovate. Steel imports have increased their share of the domestic market by only about seven percentage points in the past 30 years. The big integrated producers—US Steel, LTV, Bethlehem, and others—lost four times that share of the market. Much of their loss in market position was to the better-managed and better-equipped U.S.-based minimills.

LTV was a poorly run company for most of the past 20 years, and in January of 2001, it initiated its second bankruptcy proceeding in 15 years. The first one lasted for 7 years, from 1986 to 1993. The company's stock hit $16 per share in 1994, but by 2000 it was worth just 38 cents. The American steel industry's problems are complicated; steel workers are hard workers, doing tough jobs, and they deserve sympathy. Yet, Alan McCoy, vice president of public affairs at A.K. Steel, was not alone when he told *Industry Week* that weaker companies unable to survive on their business plans and outdated production facilities ought to go under. "We don't think the government and taxpayers should be the bank of last resort for failed steel companies with a flawed business plan," McCoy said.

Eighteen U.S.-based steel manufacturers declared bankruptcy from the fall of 1999 through the spring of 2001.

Long-time metallurgist Robert Nichols, now retired in Oregon, is not surprised at the fate of some of the large steel companies. "Each of the companies had some good people but quite a few of the vice presidents didn't know anything," Nichols remarked. "I bet one of the Bethlehem vice presidents a dollar that the company would have to make free machining steel in response to market conditions. He said it wasn't necessary. They finally did have to make it and I won the bet, but I never got my dollar."

Other U.S. manufacturers have proven to be strong, resilient global competitors. Consider Deere & Co., which has worked its way through severe adversities to become a solid exporter. The company's stock fell from $690 to $4 during the 1930s, but Deere survived by coming up with better products, improving its efficiency, and keeping its best employees on the payroll. In the 1980s, farm income plummeted and interest rates soared, hurting sales. Even now, Deere's annual revenue has been hovering around $12 billion for five years, yet the company manages to annually export about $2 billion in high-quality farm and construction equipment.

A TALE OF TWO NEIGHBORS

The experiences of two Minnesota manufacturers, both with operations along the Mississippi River, illustrate how differently companies respond to world markets. Red Wing Shoe, a domestic producer in Red Wing, has flourished in the shadow of a near-complete takeover of shoe manufacturing by foreign companies.

In fact, imports have captured more than 90 percent of the U.S. shoe market. Hundreds of domestic producers have closed their doors, driving employment down to a fifth of what it was in the 1960s. Yet, Red Wing's consolidated volume of $374 million in 2000, most of it from sales of the shoes it makes, has tripled since 1985. About 15 percent of total sales come from abroad. Red Wing sells to customers in more than 100 countries on all seven continents. How has the company accomplished this feat? CEO Bill Sweazy says the employees mastered a niche: work boots and shoes, purchased mostly for comfort, range of sizes, and safety rather than price.

Typically, prices for its shoes range from $90 to $250. "From AA to EEEE: Fitting feet around the world," boasts a slogan at the company museum in downtown Red Wing. "Where you find tough work environments—from oil fields and opal mines to hospitals and factories—you find our hard-working shoes." Some have soles that guard against electrical hazards; others have metal plates to protect firefighters from nails on the floors of burning buildings. Chances are good that if you see a construction worker perched on an eight-inch-wide girder of a high-rise, he'll be wearing Red Wing shoes. "He's not going to go to Kmart to find out which pair of shoes is the cheapest today," Sweazy says. Importers can't match the diversity of sizes and styles that the company offers, thereby leaving much of the huge domestic market for work shoes to Red Wing.

Self-sufficiency has been another key factor. In 1987, as more domestic tanneries shut down, Red Wing Shoe purchased the S.B. Foot Tannery in Red Wing. In 1998, the sudden closing of the Pfister & Vogel tannery in Milwaukee, a key supplier to Red Wing, underscored the value of the decision to buy the Foot operation. The company stepped up production at its Foot tannery, which maintained the flow of leather into its plants. Today, S.B. Foot is one of a handful of remaining domestic tanneries supplying leather to shoe manufacturers.

Loyal, productive employees, working in a stable, union-management environment, have also been part of the recipe at Red Wing. The company employs about 2,500 workers mostly at four shoe plants, including two in Red Wing. The workers produce by hand 90 percent of the shoes they make, in at least 150 distinct operations. Jim Nash, who retired in 2001, started at the company after graduating from high school in 1955. Six of his ten brothers and sisters have worked there and, he adds, "at least four nieces and nephews." By retirement, Nash was making $16.25 an hour plus good medical and dental coverage. Over the years, he did well enough to see his two sons through to college degrees. His pension will come to nearly $2,000 a month. Nash's experience goes against the grain of careers more common among today's younger workers, who often switch jobs time and again. Amazingly enough, Nash has been a cutter, stamping out pieces of leather by hand—a process that hasn't changed since 1955—ever since he walked in the door. And he's worked the same day shift since he started out. "I still enjoy coming to work," says Nash.

Red Wing Shoe has been privately owned by the Sweazy family for most of the years since it was founded in 1905. Bill Sweazy, representing the third generation of the family to run the company, intends to keep it that way. "We enjoy being private," he says. "I think it allows a longer-term perspective on a lot of things because you aren't trying to please analysts." The company keeps its overhead low by locating its stores almost entirely in low-rent strip malls. Its customers want only Red Wing shoes, and will go wherever they are sold to buy them.

Red Wing Shoe has accepted and dealt with the complexities of playing in an international economy. In 1998, it established its WORX line of industrial-strength shoes. While U.S. workers still produce the overwhelming majority of the company's shoes, contractors in China make the WORX shoes and then export them to the United States and other countries. In 2000, Red Wing Shoe established an international code of conduct, which provides for human rights audits of its contractors overseas. Years ago, sudden crises that slashed Red Wing's exports to Libya and Iran helped the company learn to live with the volatile swings that can jolt sales abroad. Most domestic shoe producers gave up years ago, Sweazy says. "They quit the battle about imports, because they lost." Does this suggest that Red Wing Shoe, the rare exception, will still be around 20 years hence? Sweazy won't give odds, either way.

Sixty miles southeast in Winona, Winona Knitting Mills shut down in 2000—a melancholy windup to 57 years of producing cardigan and crew-neck sweaters for people the world over. Winona Knitting Mills had good workers, too, and its sweaters were known far and wide. Mister Rogers wore them regularly on his popular *Mister Rogers' Neighborhood* public television show. In 1983, the company ranked 375th among *Inc.* magazine's 500 fastest-growing small businesses. By 1995, it employed 850 workers. When the shutdown was announced, the count was down to 230. Over the years, they had made 66 million high-grade sweaters for prestigious brands.

The company's cavernous plant is empty now, a monument to an era when the country's domestic producers made the apparel needed by its citizens. Winona Knitting once ranked among the 25 largest U.S. apparel manufacturers, but the strains mounted as foreign rivals gained the upper hand with lower-priced sweaters. In 1960, notes owner Pete Woodward, imports accounted for about 20 percent of the U.S. market; by 2000, their share was above 80 percent. When the plant closed, 18 semi-loads of equipment were shipped to factories in Puerto Rico and the Dominican Republic. Everett Mueller, a 43-year employee who was vice president of manufacturing, stayed on to button things up. "We thought it might happen some day, but most people did not expect any shutdown for at least 10 or 15 more years," Mueller says. Adds Woodward, "The invasion was relentless. It just kept coming."

Woodward says sharply reduced trade curbs, the high dollar, and cutthroat price competition heavily favored low-wage importers in the late-1990s. These factors zapped his incentive to produce in the United States. In 1995, when Winona Knitting and another firm merged, the combined operation had 2,800 U.S. workers in ten apparel plants. It had sales of $100 million and was selling sweaters to retailers for an average price of $21. By 2001, the combined firm had no plants and just 280 workers, was importing all of its sweaters, and was selling them for only $13.75. Yet sales were $280 million, and the company was much more profitable than in 1995. As American consumers opted for lower-priced imports, Winona Knitting was unable to carve out a niche for its American-made sweaters like Red Wing did for its domestically produced work shoes.

HOW THE DOLLAR COUNTS

The value of the dollar influences the nation's trade balance, and the performance of manufacturing in general. When the dollar is strong, U.S. exporters face price pressure and the loss of sales to foreign producers. When it's weak, U.S. manufacturers are more likely to sell abroad. For companies abroad, the reverse is true in that a strong dollar means they can more easily compete against U.S. producers. Figure 9.4 shows the relationship of national currency values to U.S. imports as a percentage of exports. There appears to be about a two-year lag but when the dollar strengthens, imports gain ground on exports a short time later. When the dollar weakens, exports' share of U.S. international trade increases.

American manufacturers are acutely aware of these patterns. In 1994, General Electric CEO Jack Welch took note of a flurry of articles hailing manufacturers for their rebound from the bad old years of the 1980s. "The American manufacturing sector has been getting some

FIGURE 9.4   U.S. Imports and Currency Values

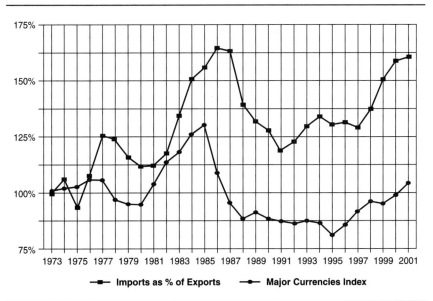

— ■ — Imports as % of Exports   — ● — Major Currencies Index

SOURCE: Economic Report of the President, 2001

pretty good press lately, even from those busy writing its obituary just a few years ago," Welch wrote in the *Wall Street Journal.* "We've been described as 'back with a vengeance,' 'tough, farsighted, clever,' even 'the envy of the industrialized world.'" Welch went on to note that exports as a share of gross domestic product were up more than 50 percent from a decade earlier. Then he argued that the declining value of the dollar was a major reason for the rebound. But, by July of 2001, with the dollar approaching its 1985 highs, both Jerry Jasinowski, president of the National Association of Manufacturers, and John Sweeney, president of the AFL-CIO, wrote President Bush expressing their concerns about the impact of the high dollar on U.S. manufacturing.

Just what moves the dollar can be a mystery. Generally, though, much of the strength it gathered since 1995 was due to the perception of the United States as a "safe harbor" that offers foreigners a huge, prosperous market for investment and goods. Money from abroad helped to finance the U.S. trade deficit at a time when Americans were saving very little. The Asian financial crisis influenced dramatic exchange rate changes from 1995 to 1998, as shown in Figure 9.5. The dollar gained strength against both Asian and European currencies. This left U.S. manufacturers with a dramatically less competitive cost structure versus their rivals in Asia and Europe. The labor that cost $22 an hour in Germany became valued at $17.16, about the same as

FIGURE 9.5   Currency Changes from 1995 to 1998

COUNTRY & CURRENCY	1995 UNITS PER U.S. DOLLAR	MARCH 1998 UNITS PER U.S. DOLLAR	PERCENT CHANGE IN VALUE
Malaysian Ringgit	2.5	3.6	−31%
Taiwan Dollars	26	33	−22
Indonesian Rupiah	2,000	8,300	−76
Singapore Dollars	1.4	1.6	−12
Thai Baht	25	38	−34
Indian Rupees	32	39	−18
Japanese Yen	90	130	−31
Swiss Franc	1.15	1.5	−24
French Franc	5	6.1	−19
German Mark	1.45	1.85	−22
Mexican Peso	6.2	8.5	−29

in the United States. Labor costs of $17 an hour in Japan fell to $11.84. The labor that was $4 per hour in Indonesia plummeted to $1.

After other major currencies weakened with the Asian financial crisis of 1997, the U.S. trade deficit on goods fell off a cliff from a record level of a $196 billion deficit on goods in 1997 to $345 billion in 1999 and $450 billion in 2000.

So far, the strong U.S. dollar has been a two-edged sword. It allows American consumers to buy things cheaply and to travel abroad inexpensively, but it hurts U.S. manufacturers and their communities. One widespread concern about the high trade deficit is that it makes the dollar more vulnerable to large, sudden devaluations if foreign investors become pessimistic about the U.S. economy or the associated investment opportunities. In such a circumstance, these investors might withdraw their resources from the country. That, in turn, could lead to higher prices for imports, more inflation, higher interest rates, and less economic growth—in short, an upheaval that would not be good for the U.S. economy.

As we shall see in the next chapter, the critical issue in trade events is not the money, though the financial impact of ongoing trade deficits is likely to be felt over time. The critical issue is the subtle transfer of wealth-producing skills from countries that have them to those who are working hard to achieve them.

CHAPTER 10

Globalization and the Transfer of Skills

 In 1974 at Control Data, 22 vice presidents, a general manager, and a reliability engineer turned controller met to review an order for one of the company's huge supercomputer systems. The order was a large one, an $11 million system for processing oil exploration data in the Soviet Union. It was a highly profitable order, with all of the cash up front. The terms required the company to build a data tape controller capable of reading Russian seismic magnetic tapes. Building the tape controller was not particularly difficult, but the engineering department wanted extra money because the documentation was in Cyrillic. There were other aspects of the order that needed attention. Finally, the controller said, "Why don't we turn the order down? They have no place else to get this system. We can go back and negotiate a little better deal." After a long silence, the general manager asked a question. "Are you sure we have the authority to turn the order down?"

His question turned out to be a precursor of the bureaucracy that eventually did so much to bring down Control Data. And not just Control Data, but much of the U.S. computer industry as well. As the technology changed and many of the industry's critical suppliers moved overseas, more and more of the industry's expertise also drifted abroad. A closer look at Control Data and its industry is instructive. Back in the 1960s and 1970s, there was no question about the company's technical expertise. It was the unabashed leader in making the world's fastest and most powerful computers. With nearly 60,000 employees worldwide, and operations in many countries, CDC was a major technical force in aerospace, weather forecasting, oil exploration, and scientific computations of all sorts. The company's computers were installed in virtually every national laboratory.

The expertise of Control Data started in St. Paul shortly after World War II at a company called Engineering Research Associates, which later became Univac. The early computers were named after engineering projects, such as Univac 1 or Univac 2. When the number got up to 13, the engineers thought it would be unlucky so they put the number in binary arithmetic and the new computer became the 1101. Then they built the 1102 and the 1103, which sold quite well. But Remington Rand swooped in to acquire Univac and some of the people left to form a new company called Control Data Corporation (CDC), which opened its doors at 501 Park Avenue in Minneapolis. Not knowing what to call their new computer, the pragmatic Midwestern engineers added 501 (their address) to 1103 (their last computer) and the new computer became the 1604. The CDC 1604 computer sold very well and launched the company. The 3000 series followed, then the ultra-fast, liquid-cooled 6000 series, which later became known as the Cyber family.

The technical expertise of Control Data soon spawned other companies in the upper Midwest. Cray Research was launched by Seymour Cray, CDC's chief computer architect, while Network Systems was formed by his associate, Jim Thornton. Data 100, Lee Data, National Computer Systems, and many other companies also had Control Data roots. Univac remained and became Unisys. Fellow Minnesota company Honeywell had acquired the GE and RCA computer operations to also become prominent in the industry. Medical device manufacturers such as Medtronic and Guidant also benefited from CDC's cultivation of electronic expertise. St. Paul–based 3M supplied magnetic tape and data storage expertise. Among the largest employers in Minnesota in the mid-1970s were Control Data, Honeywell, Univac, and the IBM plant in Rochester, Minnesota.

The general vigor of Minnesota's computer-based economy spilled over to other sectors. Computer executives, salespeople, and technical personnel flew to distant locations on one of two major airlines home based at the Minneapolis/St. Paul International Airport. Lawyers, accountants, consultants, and a variety of other service professionals flew with them and contracted much work locally. Component suppliers like Fabtech, Basic Industries, Advanced Circuits, American Machine, Gage Tool, and Bermo benefited as well. In August of 1973, then Minnesota Governor Wendell Anderson was featured on the cover of *Time* magazine with the title, "Minnesota, the State that Works" as if the governor did it.

Along the way, however, Control Data and several other major computer manufacturers became high-cost and inefficient. The rapid advance of technology, which these companies helped to lead, drove down prices and imposed a subtle profit squeeze that would ultimately curtail the affluence brought on by technology. Unfortunately, the emergence of this squeeze escaped the attention of both company and public officials. Soon, the companies were forced to reduce costs. They began depending more on foreign suppliers for parts. Core memories were the first to go, because they were labor intensive. Electrical components and other parts soon followed. Prices dropped further. Layoffs spread through the industry. Control Data suffered huge losses.

There is no Control Data anymore. Pieces of the company, which once employed 60,000 workers, have been parceled out, dismembered, or shut down. Remnants exist here and there, with the principal survivor being Seagate's disk drive operations.

Control Data was particularly important because of its vast size and extensive technical expertise. The company, which failed to keep pace with changes in its major markets, did not have to die. Control Data lost ground because of ill-advised diversification, failure to strengthen its technical lead, increasingly out-of-touch management, and lavish spending on activities unrelated to what customers were buying.

Honeywell has left the business. Univac, Cray Research, Network Systems, and IBM's Rochester plant were either acquired or downsized. Many suppliers went out of business. The computer industry in Minnesota, and in other parts of the country as well, was once highly acclaimed for its large scientific computers and its expertise in networking, multitasking, storage devices, and peripheral equipment. Today, many computers carry American names, but the vast share of critical computer components—memories, motherboards, disk drives, monitors, and peripherals—are made beyond our borders.

THE BIG PROBLEM WITH THE TRADE DEFICIT

The big problem with the trade deficit is the transfer of expertise—in the computer industry and others—to emerging lands beyond the

United States. The rise of overseas networks that support these skills is helping these nations to become more competitive in manufacturing. Steadily, these networks—engineering schools, suppliers, and other elements of emerging infrastructures—are becoming more numerous and more capable.

Productivity consultant James Harbour described this development in his 1998 Harbour Report. Workers in Mexico's auto factories have honed the skills they need to make effective use of available technologies. At GM's plant in Silao, they make Suburbans, Tahoes, and Yukons—the company's largest sports vehicles—and ship most of them to the United States. The Silao factory has just 6 percent of the automation that its sister plants claim and labor costs of only $2.50 an hour, yet the plant's records for quality, safety, productivity, absenteeism, and employee turnover are among the best to be found anywhere in GM. Elsewhere in Mexico, Chrysler's Lago Alberto plant boosted its productivity 25 percent between 1994 and 1998, while Ford's Cuautitlan truck plant and GM's Ramos Arizpe plants showed 13 percent gains. Chrysler's Saltillo plant saw a 10 percent improvement in 1997, and is now 14 percent more productive than its sister plant in St. Louis.

Once, partly because of the prominence of U.S. industry and its support for strong postgraduate programs in engineering, the United States was the epicenter of manufacturing technology. Companies like Timken prospered in part because nobody knew how to make tapered roller bearings with the expertise and quality of those the workers made at Timken's Canton, Ohio, plant. Timken is still an excellent company, but now production expertise is very widespread. Important metallurgical, manufacturing, and engineering principles are taught many places—often to students more aggressive in their pursuit of knowledge than their American counterparts. Universities like Nonyang in Singapore or the Czech Technical University in Prague have won international recognition for both their research and the quality of their programs.

In much of Europe and most of Asia, engineering is the predominant degree. It accounts for 5.3 percent of all bachelor's degrees awarded in the United States but 19.4 percent in Japan. The differences are even more striking at the master's degree level. Engineering accounts for 6.8 percent of master's degrees in the United States but 47.4 percent in Japan. Each year, Japan graduates about 50 percent more engineers than does the United States, to support an economy half the size. More than 60 percent of students in Russia and Brazil earn their first university degrees in engineering and science fields. The comparable number in China is 72 percent.

For the past 50 years, the United States has been home to some of the world's finest technical universities. Gradually, that superiority is being challenged. The country's share of refereed articles in major scientific and technical journals fell from 37 percent in 1990 to 33 percent in 1997. Engineering showed a particular decline, with the U.S. share dropping from 38 percent to 29 percent. In mathematics, it fell from 41 percent to 32 percent, in physics from 28 percent to 22 percent. With world-renowned universities like M.I.T., Stanford, and Purdue, the United States will maintain considerable technical prowess for some time to come. Yet, technological expertise is rapidly proliferating. Universities in Brazil, China, India, Mexico, Singapore, and many other countries have already joined or will soon be joining the ranks of highly respected technical institutions.

In China, manufacturers have also been cultivating their expertise at making high-quality aircraft components. In his book, *Boeing: The First Century*, retired Boeing executive Eugene Bauer described the operations of a Chinese subcontractor for Boeing in Xian as a model of efficiency. In one contract, the Chinese firm shipped 1,680 forward-access doors with no defects, Bauer noted. He also quoted Larry Dickenson, a senior vice president at Boeing, as saying: "The quality of parts coming out of China is better than that coming out of our Wichita plant."

SUPPLIERS ARE KEY BUILDING BLOCKS

The development of sophisticated suppliers in emerging industrial countries is strengthening manufacturers there. In some instances, countries abroad are building up their supplier bases through "offload," or "offtake," agreements. In these deals, U.S. multinationals win major contracts in countries abroad only if they guarantee that much of the work will be *offloaded* to subcontractors in those countries. In today's highly competitive global economy, companies and their governments abroad expect to get something back for awarding multi-million-dollar contracts to American firms. For example, Asia has been a strong market for Boeing, so Boeing has reciprocated by awarding substantial subcontracts to Asian manufacturers. Boeing's unions protested. Offload is a revered or hated word, depending on whether you are in aircraft sales or in a union representing American workers.

As emerging manufacturing countries expand their exports, their supplier bases are gradually being strengthened. Reliable sources of pre-plated steel, for instance, are put in place so that cabinets can be made for computers that are being exported. Copper and bronze coil stock is made available to support the electronics industry. Steel suppliers and heat-treating and plating facilities are established to support die-making and specialty machining operations. Soon, a vast industrial network arises, not only to fulfill existing contracts but also to be available for the next new thing. Even the development of mundane consumer products leads to the establishment of formidable technical skills and investments, giving overseas exporters opportunities to exploit new markets.

Meanwhile, the same developments are often taking place in reverse in the developed countries. When manufacturers gradually move offshore, revenues of their domestic suppliers come under more pressures. This reduces the suppliers' ability to attract investment, particularly if the owners are nearing retirement with no enthusiastic successors in place. What incentive is there to make further investments if the business is not growing? Better-run companies in the 1990s were investing around $12,000 in capital expenditures per employee to keep their companies competitive. Using this figure as a threshold, a company with 300 workers might need to invest $3.6 million annually for new equipment, updated facilities, delivery vehicles, and other improvements. An owner faces this question: Should I keep the business competitive, or should I retire and enjoy life? Some make the investments, others don't.

Bill Kuban, owner of one of the country's largest job shops, Kurt Manufacturing in Minnesota, spent $4.5 million for one machine a few years ago. He remarked: "I thought long and hard about what kind of a cabin I could buy up North for four and a half million dollars." Kuban invested, but not everyone does.

This high rate of investment taking place in emerging countries coupled with modest investment in domestic manufacturing shows up in the U.S. trade balance on many keystone technical products, as discussed in Chapter 9. The U.S. trade deficit on rubber and plastic molds, a critical element in industrial production, now tops $1 billion. Deficits are also rising for solenoid valves, small electric motors, power supplies for computers and office machines, electric drills, motor-vehicle windshield wipers, resistance and arc welders, and cordless telephones.

Karl Hohlmaier, of Balfour Corp. in Massachusetts, was an early user of computer-aided engineering systems to make the tools and dies that are so important to the industrial value chain. Hohlmaier was renowned for his successes, which was surprising to some because of his unorthodox methods. Instead of recruiting degreed engineers to operate these highly sophisticated systems, he chose experienced machine operators from the shop floor. The results were phenomenal. This was what Hohlmaier expected because he knew the workers would learn what they needed to know to keep jobs much better than their previous jobs. These experienced machinists, with a profound understanding of how dies and molds were made, were able to use the new systems much more efficiently, and much faster, than people educated in engineering. It took the shop floor people surprisingly little time to understand the technology in depth. Hohlmaier summarized the situation simply: "People think this is all technology. It isn't all technology. It's maybe one-third technology and two-thirds skill."

In various ways, the issues raised by the trade deficit come as much to the transfer of expertise as to the transfer of wealth. More people abroad are learning the skills that only a few countries have dominated in the past. The discipline of making exportable products cultivates and refines new skills. As people in emerging lands build these skills, they apply them to make higher-valued products. The often-expressed viewpoint that the United States can sustain a prosperous economy through services or by conceptualizing high-value products while workers in other countries make them has yet to be tested over time. The workers most likely to come up with new or improved products next year may turn out to be those who gained experience making last year's version.

People think this is all technology. It isn't all technology. It's maybe one-third technology and two-thirds skill.

The rapid progression of late-arriving foreign competitors has not escaped the attention of U.S. manufacturers. "They, the foreign competitors, are going to get better at it. It is just a matter of being more involved," says Peter McGillivary, co-owner of a precision molding shop near Minneapolis. Just as practice prepares people for sporting events, it enables them to compete more effectively in world markets. Those who work harder at making things can end up making better things. The United States has much technology, but its colossal accomplishments have left many Americans with the sense that technology can do nearly everything by itself. It takes skill to use the technology, and skills are becoming more geographically dispersed.

SHRINKING AND SHIFTING ECONOMIES OF SCALE

The rapid accumulation of skill by developing economies is easier now because the rapid advancement in manufacturing technology makes it easier to achieve economies of scale. Economies of scale develop because manufacturers are able to amortize the cost of equipment, facilities, the time it takes to set up, and production over a sufficiently large number of units to produce at costs below the average for the industry. Company size is not a factor in economies of scale. It makes no sense to consider economies of scale on a firm-wide basis. Economies of scale are particular to individual production processes—not companies. Many large companies, though not all, have accomplished economies of scale because of good product design, appropriate manufacturing strategy, and competent implementation, but it doesn't happen just because revenue is high.

Today, many companies are under assault as new competitors, new methods, and new technologies continually challenge both cost and quality leaders. Modern methods reduce the time and cost it takes to set up production. In the 1970s, setting up for a major production job could consume hours or even days. Now, it often takes seconds. It is now technically practical to have very small economical lot sizes—sometimes lot sizes of one. The implications of this change are huge, because it works to the disadvantage of historically large producers. Modern technologies and shifting markets open the door for smaller, more nimble competitors. If setup costs are low, and economies of scale are rare or insignificant, manufacturing can be almost anyplace and established producers are far less insulated than they once were.

Take Bermo, for instance. As one of the larger producers of computer cabinets in the United States and one of the best equipped, Bermo has long been a supplier to premium brands within the computer industry. IBM, Hewlett-Packard, Compaq, Cisco, Sun Microsystems, Dell, and others have been customers for products shipped from Bermo's one-time network of six plants worldwide. But, assembly patterns on the part of Bermo's customers are greatly altering economies of scale and affecting the way the company does business. At this writing, there is a rapidly shrinking number of computer products assembled in the United States and Bermo's four domestic plants have been reduced to two. Computer cabinets and cases are precision products made to exacting specifications with extraordinary attention to aesthetics, but they sell for only about $40. When the assembly of the final product took place in Silicon Valley or St. Paul, Bermo could easily supply the customer from its California or Minnesota plants. When the final assembly takes place in Singapore, Malaysia, or China, the economies of scale are radically different. It is impractical to ship a $40 computer cabinet, with all the necessary protective packaging, from the United States to Southeast Asia for final assembly. Suddenly, the huge modern and well-equipped plants in Minnesota are a long way from potential customers in Asia.

The fact that it is now much easier for more and more new entrants to achieve low-cost economies of scale provides a siren's call to established companies wishing to lower their manufacturing cost by farming out production. Often, with far less trouble than would be incurred running a manufacturing plant, the end-product company can outsource both the production of its products and important design work. But, in doing so, these companies may compromise their future existence.

HAS OUTSOURCING GONE TOO FAR?

Stepped-up international competition has driven the rise of *outsourcing*, today's buzzword for farming out more and more work to suppliers. In 1986, *Business Week* voiced concern about this trend in a special report entitled "The Hollow Corporation," which argued that the United States had given birth to a new kind of company: manufacturers that do little manufacturing. "Instead," declared the big type on the publication's cover, "they import components or products from low-wage countries, slap their own names on them, and sell them in America." The magazine warned that this trend did not bode well for the country.

Such concerns soon faded. The idea of the hollow corporation won acceptance as a rational response to rising pressures from abroad. Another term, "supply chain management," came into vogue mostly to describe the practice of managing suppliers who make what manufacturers once made. These are hardly new concepts. Detroit's automakers, once highly integrated producers, now use suppliers for many components they once made on their own. In many cases, manufacturers do so to cut costs. Other times, producers have concluded that specialized suppliers can handle certain functions better. In the 1990s, however, outsourcing took on a life of its own as managers, consultants, business school professors, and authors hyped the concept. The *Outsourcing Journal*, the Outsourcing World Summit, the Outsourcing Research Council, the Outsourcing Institute, and even a 12-Step Outsourcing Guide were all created. Functions ranging from research and human resources departments to cafeteria jobs, security guard work, and public relations became targets for outsourcing. A new industry— fast-growing contract manufacturers such as Solectron, Flextronics, SCI Systems, and Celestica—grew by taking over production from large companies.

Lawrence T. Levine, a partner with the Fairfield, Connecticut, firm Creative Services, told the trade publication *Appliance* late in 2000 that globalization will force more outsourcing by exposing new technologies to the world faster and shortening the time companies have to exploit them effectively. "The global environment will also make it easier to effectively outsource by making more qualified suppliers available to address a company's needs," he said.

Some companies have quietly resisted this trend. One is S.C. Johnson, the privately held, Wisconsin-based consumer products giant. The *Johnson Journal*, an employee publication, put it this way in describing its supply chain practices: "While other consumer marketers see manufacturing as a cost center to be outsourced, we see our world-class product supply operation as an increasingly valuable competitive advantage." The article quoted Nico Meiland, the company's long-time director of global manufacturing, as saying, "We have absolutely no intention of outsourcing manufacturing."

Motorhome manufacturer Winnebago also regards its proprietary manufacturing as a key strength. The smooth flow of the industry's most modern plant has allowed Winnebago to rank high in quality, profit rates, and dealer satisfaction for several years. Elsewhere, the horror stories have mounted as manufacturers have found they must pay a price for outsourcing too much.

In the 1980s, IBM broke from its longtime practice of making its primary products in-house when it decided to outsource the principal components of its personal computer. As author Charles Fine tells it in his book, *Clockspeed*, that decision reshaped the emerging personal computer industry. Instead of becoming a vertically integrated industry, with each PC maker designing and controlling its proprietary technology, the industry assumed a horizontal structure. PC makers such as Compaq and Dell used industry-standard components—notably Microsoft's MS-DOS operating system and Intel's microprocessors—to build compatible systems. Eventually, they routed IBM.

Chicago's once-dominant Schwinn Bicycle Company virtually outsourced the entire company to Asian suppliers. In their book, *No Hands*, about the fall of Schwinn, authors Judith Crown and Glenn Coleman attribute much of the company's decline to botched relations with Taiwan's Giant Manufacturing and, on the Chinese mainland, China Bicycles Company. Schwinn mistakenly felt its brand name would offset the price advantages of bicycles made by lower-cost Asian competitors. In the early 1970s, Schwinn built ties with Giant by buying accessories and replacement parts from the firm. By 1980, Schwinn was importing one-fifth of its bicycles from Asia. Then, spurred by a four-month strike at its Chicago plant, Schwinn stepped up its imports from Giant, began sharing more of its know-how with the company, and built a plant in Mississippi to cut costs. The move to Mississippi backfired. The remote site boosted the cost of importing parts from abroad, didn't have the needed metal workers, and couldn't attract managers. It became cheaper to import entire bikes than to bring in the parts alone. By 1986, Giant was supplying more than 80 percent of Schwinn's bicycles. Then Schwinn forged similar ties with China Bicycles and closed both U.S. plants. The company came to depend almost entirely on the producers in Asia, where the parts were being made. Late in 1992, Schwinn filed for Chapter 11 bankruptcy protection.

In Silicon Valley, Cisco Systems became the model for high-tech "virtual manufacturing"—manufacturers that farm out most of what they sell. Yet, now, the tech stock crash has dimmed the glow that built up around outsourcing by showing that this strategy is not without problems. In the summer of 2001, consultants from the Booz Allen Hamilton firm suggested in an article, "Why Cisco Fell: Outsourcing and Its Perils," that much of the company's stunning $2.1 billion write-off of inventory was due to Cisco's sweeping embrace of outsourcing. Jeffrey Young, a journalist who has followed Valley companies for years, attributes some of Cisco's difficulties to its love affair with outsourcing. He notes that several upstart competitors have begun to take bites out of Cisco's business by stressing their research, engineering staffs, and manufacturing prowess as strengths Cisco lacks. In his early 2001 book, *Cisco Unauthorized*, Young describes the presentation of a "ponytailed forty-something" from Cisco at an Avis technology conference held in Spain in mid-2000:

"Outsource everything!" he declares as though he had just discovered the secret to the universe. "Get others to do it for you. You don't need a core of competency. You don't need people who understand the technology on which your company stands. That's Old World thinking. That's yesterday. Today, the hollow corporation reigns supreme."

The Avis crowd was not impressed. Young asks what a manufacturer is left with after it contracts out the crown jewels. "Outsourcing is one of those ideas that sounds good on paper around the conference table in the entrepreneuring fantasyland of Stanford's business school. But the real world is actually about selling something or delivering some tangible service to a customer and doing it better than anyone else can."

Outsourcing is often not pretty for domestic suppliers. Many smaller vendors are being squeezed as multinationals attempt to pass their competitive woes on down the supply chain. As president of the National Tooling and Machining Association, Matt Coffey listens to many tales of the pressures being imposed on these suppliers. On the one hand, he says, they are being pressed to guarantee price reductions on future work. On the other, they are being asked to provide givebacks and rebates for work they have already done. "The big companies are strapping a lot of vendors to the point that they do not want to run a company," says Coffey. He goes on to lament what he calls "the philosophy to squeeze suppliers until they fail" and then get new ones.

Today, with worldwide auctions on the Internet, it's not hard to get offshore companies to bid on work that loyal suppliers have done for years. "Internet auctioning now means that you are competing with everyone in the world," says Coffey. Suppliers complain privately that they are often asked to provide, as part of these bids, detailed information on methods and procedures that might be regarded as trade secrets. Some suppliers fear that their proprietary information will be distributed to others if they lose the contract.

"People would have to be crazy to go into this business today," remarks the owner of a nationally respected manufacturer of specialized components who wishes to remain anonymous. He provided us with a copy of a letter received from a major company demanding a 5 percent rebate on the prior year's purchases. "Please remit a check to my attention by November 15, 2000. If this amount is not received, we will subtract it from our payments to you," the letter said.

Outsourcing theories often neglect one of the most important determinants of how companies succeed: the accumulation of skills. When companies contract out, the contractors teach the workers. The workers then think up new ways to do things and, ultimately, become first-class competitors on a world scale. The assumption that America can maintain its prosperity by ceding its capacity to produce tangible products is a risky proposition.

In the course of creating this book, we received an e-mail from an interested manager at what was, at one time, one of America's most innovative and technically proficient companies. For practical reasons, the manager would like his quote to remain anonymous. Still, it is illustrative of the points we are making in this chapter:

Agilent Technologies was spun off from Hewlett-Packard (HP) and represents all the original HP test equipment businesses. At the time of the spin off, HP (printers, computing, software) had $40B in revenue and Agilent (test equipment and semiconductors) had $8B in sales. That was 1999. I work for Agilent. Last year we had revenue of $12B, mostly in semiconductor test equipment. Our revenues for 2001 will probably approach 50 percent reduction or close to $6B. This drastic reduction in revenues has forced Agilent to lay off 20 percent of its workforce. HP has announced similar layoffs, but at a smaller percentage. Both companies attempt to outsource as much production as possible, and where manufacturing is necessary it's generally done in Malaysia or Singapore, with new plants in China being considered. U.S.-based manufacturing has dwindled significantly to a few specialty shops like ours and another facility in Santa Rosa, California. We have some wafer fabs in California and Colorado as well, but all are in contraction right now.

Generally, the feeling from the "troops" is malaise, both from the corporate struggles, but probably more from the social issues we all face—the war on terrorism and displaced work in general.

CHAPTER 11

The Shifting Defense-Industrial Base

In the movie *Falling Down*, actor Michael Douglas plays a bitter defense worker gone berserk. He was once so proud of his career that he affixed a vanity license plate reading "D FENS" to his car. Then, as layoffs and plant closings swept through the industry, he was fired. The movie shows him running wild through the streets of Los Angeles. "I built missiles. I did everything they told me to," he declares. "But, now, I can't even support my own kid. I'm overeducated, underskilled, obsolete, not commercially viable."

That was in 1992. The Cold War had ended, and the United States was suddenly slashing defense spending. Now, little more than a decade after the Berlin Wall came down, another watershed event—the terrorist attacks on the World Trade Center and the Pentagon—is once again reshaping the U.S. commitment to its national security. Manufacturing was shaken by the first shift. From 1987 to 2000, the United States lost nearly 1.1 million defense manufacturing jobs—nearly 7 percent of manufacturing employment at the turn of the century (Figure 11.1). Almost 90 percent of these jobs paid high wages at companies producing durable goods.

Now, the sobering environment that has emerged in the wake of heightened concern about terrorism is leading to a new shift. It's still

FIGURE 11.1 Defense-Related Manufacturing Employment (Jobs in Thousands)

	1987	1996	1997	1998	1999	2000
Total Manufacturing Jobs	1838	902	819	758	753	740
Durable Manufacturing Jobs	1649	791	715	660	657	651

SOURCE: U.S. Bureau of Labor Statistics, 2001

too early to measure the shape and scope of the shift, but one thing is certain: Americans are more concerned about their security. Their sense of invulnerability was crushed after the attacks took more lives than were lost at Pearl Harbor. The country has decided that its "defense-industrial base" must change to strengthen its capacity to fight asymmetrical battles—unorthodox warfare waged by enemies who seek to circumvent the country's conventional military superiority.

Manufacturers have been at the heart of this base, often a critical part of the national economy, since the Revolutionary War. In a 1999 report, the National Research Council recounted their essential role in strengthening national security. The production of military goods has waxed and waned, but always maintained a presence. Powder and gun manufacturers supplied the colonial militia, and some of the original colonies established defense fleets. Before World War I, the United States generally avoided foreign wars, concentrating instead on guarding U.S. borders from direct attack. To that end, arsenals produced ground weapons and shipyards turned out vessels for the Navy to protect the coasts. When the war broke out in 1914, new inventions played an enormous role in the military effort. The radio enabled naval forces to communicate over long distances. Mass production techniques, perfected in new automotive plants, turned the country into a major supplier of arms, ammunition, and military vehicles.

During World War II, U.S. manufacturing created the vaunted "arsenal of democracy," so critical to the Allies' successes in winning the war. Scores of commercial factories were converted into defense plants. Ford built a plant at Willow Run, west of Detroit, to produce B-24 bombers. Kaiser Industries ramped up to the point where it was building one liberty ship a day at its shipyard in Richmond, California. As a group, factories across the country were turning out bombers at the rate of one every hour. When the war ended, the country demobilized, but in 1950 the Korean War broke out. Again, the country reversed gears, stepping up production at defense plants. In the 1950s, the first phase of the Cold War led manufacturers to provide long-range bombers, land-based missiles, and submarine missiles. The Soviet launch of Sputnik, the world's first artificial satellite, unleashed the space race. Eventually, that competition spawned a new industry, which enabled the country to land men on the moon. Next, the Vietnam War spurred production of more conventional equipment. Beginning in the 1970s, the demand shifted toward development of sophisticated high-tech weaponry.

A litany of innovations with broad commercial applications—radar, computers, global positioning systems, countless information technology advances—came out of the defense effort in World War II. After the war, the flow of this new technology into the marketplace continued. The National Research Council offers this list, far from complete, of postwar innovations:

- Development of the first numerically controlled machine tool
- Establishment of the basic building blocks of computer software
- Creation of manufacturing processes that have accelerated the growth of the microelectronics industry
- Development of isothermal forging for manufacture of titanium and superalloy parts
- Support for speeding up the development of computer-aided design, computer-aided manufacturing, and computer-integrated manufacturing
- Significant improvements in night vision systems

Then, of course, there's the Internet. In 1962, the Air Force asked the RAND Corp. to find a way the military could maintain command and control over its missiles and bombers after a nuclear attack. RAND came up with a proposal for a decentralized system that transmits information in packets which, if lost, could promptly be re-sent to other locations. The Defense Department's Advanced Research Projects Agency awarded a contract to a small firm, Bolt, Beranek and Newman (BBN), to develop a packet switching network. The company built a physical network linking four sites—the Universities of California at Santa Barbara and at Los Angeles, the Stanford Research Institute, and the University of Utah. Four years later, BBN developed the first e-mail program. In 1974, researchers Vinton Cerf and Bob Kahn named the system the Internet. All of this work, in turn, led to the creation of the World Wide Web. Finally, Netscape went public in 1995, unleashing a boom in the private sector.

Government-funded defense manufacturers have played a big role in regional economic development. It is often suggested that home-grown business entrepreneurs spawned many of the nation's most familiar clusters of high-tech businesses—Silicon Valley and Orange County in California, Seattle, the Route 128 beltway around Boston. For sure, the successes of these businesses count for plenty in these areas. Yet, economist Ann Markusen advances another view, that Pentagon defense dollars seeded much of this activity. Here's how she put it in her 1991 book, *The Rise of the Gunbelt*, in a comment she sticks with today: "This highly lauded 'post-industrial' organization of manufacturing in these regions, with its flexible specialization and small-batch, custom-made product, is erroneously ascribed to the commercial sector, when in fact these attributes originated in their defense-based industries."

Today, such seeding of economic growth by the Pentagon is less likely. That's because the pace of technology transfer from the defense industry to the commercial sector is not nearly as intense as it was in the 1950s and 1960s. "It's been falling since the 1970s," says Erik Pages, author of the 1996 book *Responding to Defense Dependence*. Pages cites an observation from Michael Sekora, former director of technology planning at the Pentagon. In 1991, Sekora noted that some composite materials used in weaponry are "not nearly as sophisticated as what you could buy in your local sporting goods store." In fact, many believe the Pentagon is likely to pick up innovations from the private sector more often than it creates and then transfers them to businesses. Defense wags have invented a term for this turnabout—"spin-on," as opposed to the spinoffs that use defense-funded R&D to build up companies. In his book, Pages points to Patriot missiles, which still use 1970s microprocessors that are several generations behind the commercial standards of the late 1980s.

> *This highly lauded "post-industrial" organization of manufacturing in these regions, with its flexible specialization and small-batch, custom-made product, is erroneously ascribed to the commercial sector, when in fact these attributes originated in their defense-based industries.*

Military spending hit a post–Vietnam War high in 1987. Driven by the Reagan era buildup, the nation's defense manufacturing payroll reached 1.84 million workers that year—twice its work force in the post-Vietnam low year of 1977. The largest concentration of these jobs was in the Los Angeles area. Thus, the flourishing defense industry of 1987, while providing a bonanza for the region, also set it up for a big fall. After the Cold War ended, defense industry cutbacks intensified.

Hollywood overstated the crisis in *Falling Down*, depicting Los Angeles as a Third World sinkhole almost as depressing as the city had been portrayed in *Blade Runner*. Yet, there's no denying that the defense cutbacks dealt a body blow to the region's economy. For decades, the Los Angeles area had served as the technological command post for the country's military effort to deter the Soviets. Southern California claimed the nation's largest concentration of military contractors and defense workers. In the early 1990s, steep declines in defense contracts sent the region into its deepest economic tailspin since the Great Depression.

In a 1996 report, a Rutgers University study team led by Markusen documented the extent of the decline in Los Angeles. From 1988 to 1994, durable goods employment in Los Angeles County plunged nearly 38 percent, to 355,400 jobs from 571,400. Almost half of the decline came in just two industries: aircraft and parts, and search and navigation equipment. The complex Cold War programs the region specialized in—the F117-A stealth fighter, the Peacekeeper and Trident missiles, the B-2 bomber—were terminated or trimmed considerably. The region, once the site of the headquarters or major divisions for 8 of the country's 25 largest Department of Defense contractors, lost sizable parts of all 8. Its largest defense contractors took huge hits: from 1992 to 1994, McDonnell Douglas cut 21,700 jobs; TRW, 16,835; and Northrup Grumman, 12,650. Membership in the United Auto Workers, the International Association of Machinists, and the International Brotherhood of Electrical Workers sank to 18,300 by the end of 1994 from 62,000 in the late 1980s. "It is no exaggeration to say that in 1990, the Los Angeles economy fell off a cliff," the Rutgers team concluded. "Employment in defense-related industries collapsed across the board. Hundreds of thousands of skilled, family-supporting jobs evaporated as the result of defense downsizing and corporate relocation."

The cutbacks reached far beyond California, battering the economies of St. Louis, Boston, Long Island, and other defense centers. Thousands of professionals in the industry's talented armada of engineers and scientists were not spared. McDonnell Douglas, the St. Louis region's largest employer, added nearly 13,000 jobs there during the decade ended in 1989. In the next four years, the company abruptly reversed gears, laying off 15,000 workers.

Today, the structure and size of the defense manufacturing industry looks very different from the late 1980s. Tighter defense budgets and government policies that encouraged consolidations helped to trigger 17 major mergers among defense industry contractors between 1990 and 1996. Over a longer stretch, from 1946 to 1994, the number of prime contractors fell from 26 to 7 for aircraft, 16 to 2 for tanks, and 22 to 9 for missiles. The rush of deals has continued since 1994, leaving a big three of survivors: Lockheed Martin ($18 billion in defense-related revenue), Boeing ($16 billion), and Raytheon ($14 billion). U.S. defense contractors have become more global. They are exporting greater portions of their production, forging strategic alliances and joint ventures, and in some cases merging with foreign defense contractors. Much as "global cars" evolved with parts made in many countries, final military products now contain parts from many countries. One of the principal examples is the F-16 fighter program. This plane is now built on three continents, with parts and expertise from the United States, Turkey, Greece, Israel, Denmark, South Korea, Belgium, the Netherlands, and Taiwan.

Concerns have been raised about the adverse effects of the consolidations. Michael Oden, a specialist in regional defense issues at the University of Texas in Austin, cites figures showing that while annual revenue of the 25 largest defense contractors fell 9 percent from 1989 to 1994, their employment dropped 25 percent. Oden says Wall Street pressures for short-term profits led to many "pure play" mergers—those that combine one defense contractor with another. He argues that this put a damper on diversification and technology transfer by large defense contractors into commercial markets, and by companies in commercial markets into defense work.

Over the years, many industries have attempted to win various forms of government support by defining themselves as part of the defense industrial base. Some have been more successful than others. Markusen notes that in 1989, aerospace, communications, and electronics firms won more than $23 billion in research and development funds from the federal government. That same year, the steel industry got only $21 million of such funding. Pages looked at efforts by four ailing industries—machine tools, semiconductors, ball bearings, and high-definition television—to land government backing during the 1980s. The semiconductor industry was the biggest winner, achieving trade protection and support for a manufacturing consortium. The tool-makers won voluntary restraint agreements limiting imports. Conversely, calls for direct support from the bearing and HDTV industries failed. More recently, the fledgling nanotechnology industry has gotten federal backing, but many other efforts struck out.

Yet, it is difficult to make the case that the decline of government subsidies is wholly responsible for shrinking capabilities of U.S. producers. Some company leaders have shown more of an interest in pleasing Wall Street than in making solid investments to expand the technical capabilities of their companies. Some unions have focused on the retention of perhaps unsustainable wage and benefit packages during an era when cost-containment became a national priority. And, over the past 20 years or so, foreign producers have greatly expanded their capabilities to deliver top-quality, defense-related goods at more reasonable costs. Subsidies might have helped some U.S. producers, but they may not have been sufficient without other changes in how the defense industry does business.

> *Yet, it is difficult to make the case that the decline of government subsidies is wholly responsible for shrinking capabilities of U.S. producers. Some company leaders have shown more of an interest in pleasing Wall Street than in making solid investments to expand the technical capabilities of their companies.*

Now, the terrorist attacks, which brought war-like devastation and great loss of life to American soil, are changing the very definition of the defense industrial base once again. Industries, ranging from steel to airlines, argue that they are essential to national security in efforts to win various forms of government support. A mighty national effort has arisen to make the country as safe as possible from terrorists. Homeland security, a term seldom heard before September 11, 2001, has suddenly become an important national priority. That means more public support for ships and planes that guard the country, and for security and surveillance devices of every kind. Efforts to defeat terrorism abroad will also heighten the need for a wide array of military and reconnaissance equipment.

In October of 2001, Lockheed Martin won what the *Wall Street Journal* called the "richest Pentagon competition in history"—the Joint Strike Fighter contract worth an estimated $200 billion in revenue. The award, which was a blow to competitor Boeing, raised new concerns about whether the nation has lost too much of its defense industrial capability. The world has changed and, to some as-yet-unknown extent, American manufacturing is adjusting to the new environment.

CHAPTER 12

Investment: Booster Shot from Abroad

In 1979, Japan's Honda Motor Co. ventured deep into the cornfields of Ohio to seed what would become one of the juggernauts of American manufacturing. The company put up its maiden U.S. plant, a motorcycle factory, about 30 miles northwest of Columbus. Then, in 1982, Honda built an auto plant there, the first of a parade of factories to be built by Japanese vehicle producers in the United States. Next came an engine plant, then a second auto plant. Currently, Honda employs 13,000 workers at the four sites plus ancillary operations sprinkled along a 40-mile "Honda corridor" from Marysville to Anna, in rural west central Ohio.

Today, these and other foreign-owned vehicle factories in the United States—dubbed "the transplants"—employ more than 50,000 workers at 18 plants in 9 states. When Honda first began making cars at Marysville, foreign producers made only 90,000 vehicles in the United States; they exported nearly 30 times that many to the states. Now, however, production at the transplants greatly exceeds the number of vehicles that overseas manufacturers export to the United States.

The foreign-owned vehicle industry is far from the only U.S. manufacturing sector to receive such investment. Two large diversified manufacturers, Germany's Robert Bosch and Denso of Japan, operate many American factories. Michelin, the French tire maker, has 8 plants. Other foreign companies own hundreds of plants in the United States. Some have had factories in the United States for generations. Indiana, which has worked hard to attract foreign investment, has 194 Japanese-owned facilities employing 38,000 workers.

Much of this investment has come since the 1970s. The transplants are probably the most visible instance, in a single industry, of where foreign investors have built factories in "greenfields"—virgin sites, often not in major metropolitan areas. Their performance is also easier to monitor than those of foreign-owned plants in other industries, because various consulting firms track the competitiveness of auto and truck plants closely.

They also reflect well the globalization of manufacturing—in this case, by direct foreign investment in construction of plants located in the United States. The government doesn't track the amount of foreign direct investment in new or expanded plants, so precise figures on this activity aren't available. In 2000, manufacturing accounted for 45 percent of the $321 billion in total foreign direct investment.

As a general rule, producers find it more practical to buy up existing production capabilities than to start fresh, from the ground up. In fact, mergers and acquisitions (M&A) account for most of the foreign investment. In 1999 and 2000, two years of frenzied M&A deals made up nearly 98 percent of $596 billion in such investment. Despite the dominance of M&A, though, the amount of foreign investment that has gone into the transplants since the early 1980s is considerable.

In an unintended way, some of the leading U.S. manufacturers provided useful models of how foreign producers could succeed in the

FIGURE 12.1   Foreign-Owned U.S. Vehicle Assembly Plants

MANUFACTURER	LOCATION	MODELS	CAPACITY	EMPLOYEES
Toyota	Georgetown, KY #1	Cars	236,504	2,536
Toyota	Georgetown, KY #2	Cars	236,504	2,536
Toyota	Princeton, IN	Trucks	150,000	2,400
Subaru/Isuzu	East Lafayette, IN	Cars/Trucks	248,160	3,000
Nissan	Smyrna, TN	Cars/Trucks	421,120	3,406
Nissan	Canton, MS	Trucks	250,000	4,000
Honda	East Liberty, OH	Cars	244,174	2,116
Honda	Marysville, OH	Cars	455,712	4,537
Honda	Lincoln, AL	Cars/Trucks	120,000	1,500
Nummi (Toyota/GM)	Fremont, CA	Cars/Trucks	355,696	3,663
Mitsubishi	Normal, IL	Cars	234,248	2,478
Auto Alliance	Flat Rock, MI	Cars	263,200	1,401
BMW	Spartanburg County, SC	Cars/Trucks	110,000	3,000
Mercedes	Tuscaloosa, AL	Cars/Trucks	100,000	1,900

SOURCE: The Harbour Report, Harbour and Associates, 2000 and other sources

United States. American multinationals built scores of plants around the world in the years after World War II. 3M sought out, trained, and developed country nationals in its overseas research laboratories, offices, and plants. GM, Coca-Cola, and IBM provided career paths abroad to the top levels of their empires. It wasn't surprising that foreign companies would do the same.

The first of the transplants, Volkswagen, was a failure. The German automaker came to western Pennsylvania in 1978, but closed after a few years. Employment reached only a fourth of its projected level—no doubt influenced by a weak product lineup presented to the U.S. market. Nissan arrived in 1983 with a pickup plant in Smyrna, Tennessee, seven months after Honda began production at Marysville. Toyota came the following year, partnering with General Motors in a joint venture at a plant near San Francisco.

Then came one plant after another, with Honda and Toyota leading the way. In 1998, the University of Michigan's Office for the Study of Automotive Transportation took a snapshot of the transplant industry for the Association of International Automobile Manufacturers. By then, BMW, Mercedes-Benz, and Subaru-Isuzu had joined the club. Moreover, the line of demarcation that separated the transplants from the U.S.-based producers had become fuzzier with two more joint ventures—Ford-Mazda and Chrysler-Mitsubishi—in production. All told, by 1996 the transplants were running ten assembly plants in the United States, either on their own or in joint ventures. By then, these factories had a total capacity of 2.72 million vehicles annually, employed nearly 38,000 workers, and represented an investment of $11.4 billion.

For the foreign car and truck makers, the U.S. market proved irresistible. It was by far the world's biggest market, in a country literally shaped by the automobile. Its workforce was productive and flexible. A richly experienced supplier base supported the industry. Foreign investment was generally welcomed, particularly as an alternative to imports. Because the plants created large, visible clusters of well-paying jobs, politicians backed them with hefty tax breaks. The plants rose mostly in rural areas or sites near smaller metro regions: Marysville; Georgetown, Kentucky; Tuscaloosa, Alabama; Lafayette and Princeton in Indiana. These locations offered ready access to major markets and suppliers via the interstates.

Local communities greeted the arrival of the transplants with gusto. When Toyota announced its $700 million truck plant in Princeton late in 1995, citizens flocked to the Princeton Community High School Auditorium for a celebration. Jerry Stillwell, the Princeton attorney who helped lead the long campaign to land Toyota, asked the audience: "Are we ready for 1,300 good-paying jobs in southwestern Indiana?" The crowd roared its approval. The high school pep band broke into a rousing rendition of the Princeton fight song. The red velvet curtain opened to reveal a stage occupied by dozens of local business and civic leaders. Indiana Governor Evan Bayh and Toyota President Hiroshi Okuda shook hands, standing in front of a T100 pickup and a gigantic map of North America. The *Princeton Daily Clarion* published a 50-page special edition with a gigantic headline saluting the company. "Toyota: We Love What You've Done for Us," the paper declared.

Honda came to Ohio in the depths of recession. In 1979, when its motorcycle plant opened, the unemployment rate in the Marysville area was about 9 percent. "It went to 15 or 16 percent in the early 1980s," Susan Insley, corporate planning vice president for Honda of America, recalled in an interview early in 1990. "Now, it's about 5 percent. We've rarely advertised for people. Right now, we have 32,000 qualified applications on file, and we'll hire about 1,000 people in 1990."

Honda's arrival and subsequent expansion spurred economic growth in a 14-county area of west central Ohio. Hundreds of homes went up. So did a new school building, a YMCA, and a library. The Benjamin Logan School District, once one of the poorest districts in the state, saw its annual budget rise nearly 50 percent thanks to the additional taxes generated by Honda's second plant.

Not everyone was happy. Residents had to learn to live with traffic jams. Smaller employers had to boost salaries to keep employees from going to better-paid jobs at Honda or its suppliers. In Lima, 25 miles north of the company's new engine plant, Mayor Gene Joseph charged that Japanese automakers were avoiding large cities with sizable black populations and strong union traditions. Honda denied the charge. Company officials said open land was the primary attraction. Honda was able to acquire much land from the state, including a transportation research center and a 6-mile auto test track.

In a 1999 interview, Nobuhiko Kawamoto, Honda's CEO and president from 1990 to 1998, was asked about the allegation that Honda deliberately avoided large cities when it opted for rural Ohio. He replied that the workers there were exceptionally qualified. An aide added that environmental restrictions in the big cities made finding good sites there a task that was next to impossible.

By many measures, Honda's performance at its Ohio plants is impressive. In 1998, an Economist Intelligence Unit study found that only 3 of the world's 20 most productive auto plants were in North America. Two of the 3 were the Honda plants in Ohio; the third was the General Motors-Toyota joint venture in California. Since it first came to Marysville, Honda has invested nearly $4 billion in its Ohio facilities. The company has gone on to open a power products plant in North Carolina, an all-terrain vehicle plant in South Carolina, and a third auto assembly plant in Lincoln, Alabama, 40 miles east of Birmingham. In some years, Honda has exported as much as one-sixth of its Ohio auto production. From 1992 to 1996, Honda exported nearly 400,000 autos from the United States versus 300,000 each for GM and Ford, 250,000 for Toyota, and 200,000 for Chrysler. In 2000, it shipped Ohio-made cars to 54 countries.

Despite such success, it would be wrong to conclude that foreign producers have achieved their inroads solely because of superior methods and more advanced technologies. There is something to that statement regarding Honda and Toyota, both of which are well-advanced technically and managerially. But several of the rest are only average companies, even though they have had money available for investment. Nissan has lost money for most of the past decade and is now managed by the French. Mitsubishi's productivity at the large plant in Normal, Illinois, was embarrassingly low for many years, resulting in several managerial and investment changes. Daimler's Teutonic management style has certainly not helped either Chrysler or DaimlerChrysler stock price, which declined from $110 to $40 from 1999 to 2001.

In 1999, profits per vehicle were higher at Ford's North American operations than at any company worldwide though tire problems and a slowing economy greatly reduced Ford profitability in subsequent years.

Productivity at the transplant factories has been good, but not always that much better than their American counterparts. According to the Harbour Report 2000, the most productive truck plant in the country was the Ford Ranger plant in St. Paul, Minnesota. Of the top ten North American truck plants, six were Ford plants, two were GM, one Nissan, and one Nummi (Toyota/GM). On the car side, Ford's Taurus plant in Atlanta led the list. Of the top ten car plants, four were Ford, two were GM, two Honda, one Toyota, and one Nissan.

But there was a difference that should be acknowledged. The transplants are newer. They have newer layouts, younger people, and often the very latest in equipment. The U.S. producers are not amateurs but they do have to deal with the practical aspects of taking what they have and making it work. They have been fairly successful.

The most productive truck plant in the United States in 1999, Ford's Twin Cities Assembly plant, reached the top of the list at age 74. DaimlerChrysler's Toledo Jeep plant has parts that are older yet and over its long history, it has been part of Willys-Overland, Kaiser Motors, American Motors, Chrysler Corporation, and DaimlerChrysler. Many General Motors plants date back to the 1930s, 1950s, and 1960s and, yet, it has been GM that registered the most impressive productivity improvement in the past decade.

The practical task of managing an older plant is quite different than managing a new one. Both workers and middle managers may be a little more set in their ways. Quite understandably, all equipment cannot be all new all of the time. Often, the plant manager struggles with equipment that might be a bit older and a bit slower than what is available at the new greenfield plant down the road.

From the standpoint of society, however, what are the options? Should companies abandon everything and just start over in new locations? Or, work cooperatively with those involved to make our existing factories more competitive? To their credit, both labor and management in the U.S. auto industry have tried to work well together. Not everything has been perfect, but much progress has been made. U.S. automakers, and their employees, have been able to effectively compete within an atmosphere of a very high dollar, more stringent environmental regulations than are present in many emerging industrial nations, and heavy investment by foreign companies seeking to purchase a foothold in the very large U.S. market. In general, U.S. auto manufacturers have been quite competitive.

The transplants' status as newly built plants gives them several advantages over the domestic producers. First, because they are so new, they have state-of-the-art equipment. Second, because their workforces are younger than those of the long-established U.S. producers, they face much less of a financial burden in paying pension and health care benefits to their workers. Third, many states competed for them, setting up bidding wars that sometimes led to hefty incentives for companies building these plants.

Labor-management systems vary also. Most foreign-owned U.S. manufacturing plants are not unionized and, in some cases, care seems to have been taken to locate in right-to-work states (states where employees are not required to join a union in a unionized facility) such as Alabama, Mississippi, and South Carolina. However, there are notable exceptions such as Honda's involvement in Ohio, Toyota in Indiana and Kentucky, Subaru-Isuzu in Indiana, Mazda in Michigan, Mitsubishi in Illinois, and Nummi in California. In 1999, less than 20 percent of transplant auto production took place in right-to-work states.

Local and state governments often tripped over one another trying to attract the next big transplant and associated suppliers. Toyota's Princeton plant received $73 million in tax training and infrastructure assistance. Mercedes-Benz's relatively small truck plant in Alabama won an initial subsidy of $253 million, plus another $120 million for expansion. Nissan received $295 million for its Mississippi plant. Honda's minivan plant in Alabama got $158 million.

It's true that some domestic auto manufacturers also got big packages. The state of Ohio and the city of Toledo assembled a $262 million package to keep DaimlerChrysler's Jeep plant from leaving the city. The transplants, though, have been more successful than the domestic producers at landing big subsidies, if only because they are the ones building plants these days.

The propensity of Japanese industry to invest outside of Japan has certainly attracted attention within that country. Complaints of Japan hollowing out have circulated in the Japanese media, and Japanese foreign direct investment placed outside of the country is currently running 12 times the foreign direct investment coming in. Japanese layoffs are beginning to mount as the world's proclivity to accept an ever-increasing volume of exports from Asia seems to be diminishing.

Many policy questions can be asked about the wisdom and efficiency of offering big incentives for the transplants. For sure, though, the economic impact of these plants in the United States—and of foreign direct investment in manufacturing in the United States—has been substantial for the U.S. economy. Big investments by foreign manufacturers certainly added to the vigor of the U.S. economy in the late 1990s.

During the past 20 years, when some U.S. companies were acquiring, divesting, merging, and laying people off, others were distinguishing their products, investing heavily, appreciating their employees, and gaining international prominence. In these pursuits, the better U.S. companies were joined by some respected foreign producers—companies that came to the United States because of its promise, and invested heavily. The investments have paid off. The 2001 Harbour Report suggests that 80 percent of Honda's operating profit came from North America, 10 percent from Japan.

Many policy questions can be asked about the wisdom and efficiency of offering big incentives for the transplants. For sure, though, the economic impact of these plants in the United States—and of foreign direct investment in manufacturing in the United States—has been substantial for the U.S. economy.

A Sector Still at Risk

The strength of U.S. manufacturing is sapped by strains within its own boundaries. Among the most prominent of these forces are the unappreciative attitudes of many Americans toward manufacturing, the frenzied urge to merge, and the need for better leadership.

Part Four describes these forces:

Chapter 13 considers the proposition that "factory" has become a dirty word in many circles of U.S. society. Too often, manufacturing has fallen out of fashion. On college campuses, science and engineering courses play second fiddle to MBAs and a host of other curriculums. "Not in my backyard," or NIMBY, groups often succeed in thumbing down proposals to build or expand needed power plants and factories.

Chapter 14 reports on the widespread criticism of mergers, then looks more closely at some that have not worked out well. This chapter also questions whether the rush to expand by acquisition will work out in troubled times.

Chapter 15 explains why good leadership is so important to success, and cites instances where illusory leadership has weakened manufacturers.

CHAPTER 13

Factories: An Unspoken Word

 Stephen Hardis frequently encounters disdain, even dismissal, of manufacturing at cocktail parties. "It's considered boring," says Hardis, the recently retired CEO at Eaton Corp. "The average American thinks of manufacturing companies as being dull, run by mediocre talent, very short-sighted. The bias is against joining industry. That would be dull."

Hardis believes this view is particularly prevalent on college campuses. In fact, he thinks students' images of manufacturing are so negative that they almost parallel students' adverse perceptions of ROTC during the anti–Vietnam War days of the 1960s.

To Hardis and others in many parts of U.S. manufacturing, Americans seem not to care. They have pushed the very word "factory" to the backs of their minds for years. Even manufacturers often shun the word. Instead, their publicists opt for "plant" or, in their least creative moments, "facility"—a beige-like word so neutral as to be virtually meaningless.

Manufacturing, as comedian Rodney Dangerfield might say, "don't get no respect." More than ever, people don't want to live near factories. Engineering and science education, so essential to industry, is not in vogue. Work experience on the factory floor doesn't count for as much as it once did. Thus, as more and more of the people who run factories approach retirement, some worry that fewer competent managers are moving up to replace them. This, despite the fact that today's American factories are, for the most part, far better places to work than the plants of yesteryear.

RUNAWAY NIMBYISM?

Consider the NIMBY, or "not in my backyard," phenomenon. Nobody knows the exact cost of NIMBY in blocking industrial expansion, but it is considerable.

We have no objection to orderly dissent if the arguments are well formulated and internally consistent. For instance, if someone wants to say, "I do not want air-conditioning and that's why I oppose the new power plant," that is a readily defensible position. Much less defensible are the views of power plant opponents using more and more energy, even as they oppose efforts to add generating capacity.

Early in 2001, days after California's first "rolling blackouts," industrial recruiters in Tennessee launched an unusual effort to lure prominent manufacturers from the Golden State. They sent them 1,000 battery-powered flashlights. It was a promotional gimmick, but one that made a telling point. Tennessee, they argued, offers reliable, lower-cost electricity that is no longer a sure thing in California. Why did the most populous state, with a giant economy, come to this? NIMBY is a reason.

The California Energy Commission did license nine large power plants, providing 6,278 megawatts, from 1994 until early 2001. By the latter date, six of the nine were still under construction. NIMBY has hardly been the only factor delaying approval. Competing utilities, unions concerned that construction crews won't be organized, and backers of alternative energy sources have more often been the primary opponents. The state also had an unusually long and potentially difficult approval process.

The NIMBY backers don't always win. In 2000, the San Jose City Council rejected a 600-megawatt, natural gas–fired power plant. Calpine Corp. had proposed to build the plant, designed to be environmentally friendly, near a site earmarked by Cisco Systems for a huge new corporate campus. Even the Sierra Club backed the plant, yet the mayor, city council, and Cisco—no small consumer of power—opposed it. In an editorial entitled "How Green Was Their Valley," the *Wall Street Journal* ripped Cisco for worrying more about the view from its new doorstep than about the companies that need more power to run Cisco's own routers and switches. In the *San Francisco*

Chronicle, writer Colin Jones called the opposition "runaway NIMBY-ism." Here's how Jones summed it up:

People want their SUVs but no roads, their cell phones but no towers, big shopping malls and office parks but no adjacent high-density housing, more flights but no added runways. And now, apparently, a huge industrial complex but no expanded power capabilities.

In the face of such criticism, the mayor and council reversed themselves and approved the project. At about the same time, though, voters in Southgate, near Los Angeles, thumbed down Sunlaw Energy Corp.'s proposal to build a 550-megawatt plant. The project featured a new technology that would have reduced emissions below those from diesel trucks entering and leaving a warehouse at the site. Air-quality regulators had approved the plant. In another victory for power plant opponents, developers backed away from a proposal for a smaller power plant in Baldwin Hills after running into a wall of opposition from Hollywood celebrities and neighborhood residents.

The NIMBY factor is not just a California problem. The New York Power Authority has the land and permits to build ten 40-megawatt plants in New York City, but, in 2001, a coalition of 11 neighborhood and environmental groups filed suit in the state's Supreme Court to halt construction of all of these plants. Nationally, the U.S. Department of Energy noted that from 1990 to 1999, peak demand rose 25 percent but capacity rose just 6 percent. The Northeast Power Coordinating Council has warned that operable capacity in New York and New England will not be sufficient to meet reserve criteria during some peak load hours.

"Nobody wants a power plant, and it's a hard reality," says Richard Kessel, chairman of the Long Island Power Authority. "But no matter how much we do with energy-efficiency programs, if we don't get several new power plants built in the next few years, the lights will go out." Although the demand for energy declined some with the recession of 2001, the electric infrastructure in some of the country's most populous regions is both old and fragile. Looking ahead, many of these regions will have to buy high-cost electricity from distant regions to satisfy future demand when the economy rebounds.

Yet, the nation's electricity transmission system is a frequent target of NIMBY critics. Tapani Seppa, a transmission consultant with the Valley Group in Ridgefield, Connecticut, is not optimistic. The electrical transmission system is in the same condition the highways were in before the 1950s, when President Eisenhower launched the nation's interstate highway system, he warns. "We are deregulating the market, but rearranging administrative boundaries will not remove transmission bottlenecks. We still have to deal with Ohm's Law." This famous law of physics, which measures the resistance that limits transmission of electricity, gives us something to worry about. We are attempting to send more electricity through aging generation and transmission systems that are nearing their theoretical load and temperature limits. Meanwhile, the political reality is that only power plants fired by natural gas can be built today. As demands for electricity rise, the nation's industries could be faced with both higher electrical costs and higher costs of natural gas now used as a generating fuel.

Oil refineries are another NIMBY problem. U.S. refinery capacity rose only 3.2 percent from 1988 to 1998. During the same period, refinery capacity rose 114 percent in China and 24 percent in Brazil. China now has about one-third as much capacity as the United States, while Asia's refining capacity now exceeds that of North America.

The last time a major refinery went up in the United States was in the early 1980s, when Valero Energy built a large complex in Corpus Christi, Texas. Refineries were critical to the nation during World War II. The country had 600 of them in 1945, but by 1981 the count had fallen to 324, and by 1993 to 187. At the end of 2000, there were only 155. Environmental regulations, low margins, and cheap foreign oil were major factors in the closings. Industry officials take it as a given, however, that any proposals to build a new refinery would automatically draw NIMBY-like opposition. Few people prefer to live near a refinery, but letting our refining capacity slip off to other lands can add to the costs hanging over U.S. manufacturers.

EVEN DESIRABLE GROWTH IS HARD TO SELL

Being a neighbor of window manufacturer Andersen Corp. might seem much less of a concern. Year after year, Andersen has won praise for providing one of the nation's best workplaces. Job applicants flock to Andersen's main plant in Bayport, Minnesota, drawn by the company's profit-sharing plan and its clean, orderly surroundings. Car dealers and stockbrokers queue up to solicit Andersen's workers when the company announces its annual profit-sharing bonuses, which can exceed $30,000 for an individual worker. Environmentally conscious Andersen is also a leader in recycling and the use of waste materials for clean fuel. Yet, none of these attributes counted for much when Andersen sought a permit to expand on land the company had developed with full cooperation of Minnesota's Department of Natural Resources. For reasons that were never obviously clear, local residents continued their opposition to the expansion. After strenuous effort for nearly a decade, Andersen finally dropped the proposal and expanded across the border, in Wisconsin.

In some instances, manufacturing has declined because communities don't want the growth that accompanies industrial expansion. We passed a large abandoned factory in Bennington, Vermont. Struck by its size, we inquired about it at the NAPA auto parts store across the street. "It was an old yarn and thread mill built in about the 1820s," the proprietor explained. "This whole area was filled with industry at one time." When asked about the status of industry in the year 2000, his answer was enlightening. "Well, you know, Vermont doesn't want much growth."

Unfortunately, NIMBY opposition is often more active in established older communities, where employment is most needed, than it is in the nation overall.

ENGINEERING—OUT OF FAVOR HERE, IN FAVOR OVERSEAS

As Hardis notes, manufacturing is not a poster child on our college campuses. Since the early 1980s, technology, engineering, and manufacturing have been losing ground to other fields as a percentage of total U.S. college degrees. From 1990 to 1996, bachelor's degrees rose by 6,012 in general studies; 6,241 in public affairs; 8,531 in natural resources; 9,364 in performing arts; 9,401 in recreation; 19,339 in psychology; 21,154 in health sciences; and 23,790 in biological sciences.

Computer science, engineering, and science were all down. The physical sciences now enroll fewer students than they did in the 1970s and 1980s. Out of the 2.3 million bachelor's degrees awarded in the United States in 1996, just 310,000, or 13 percent, were technology-related—a slightly smaller percentage than in 1980 (Figure 13.1). Technology growth has slowed at the graduate level, too. In 1996, U.S. schools granted 94,000 Masters in Business Administration degrees, or 262 percent more than in 1971. Master's degrees in engineering awarded in 1996 were 28,566.

The picture overseas is quite different. The sons and daughters of families abroad flock to U.S. engineering schools, then return to their native lands to apply their knowledge to industrial buildups in those countries. So many have come, in fact, that our engineering schools have come to depend heavily on them to maintain enrollments. The United States grants about 26,000 science and engineering doctoral degrees every year, roughly 10,000 of them to citizens from other countries. Approximately 36 percent of the engineering faculty members in higher education in the United States are foreign-born.

FIGURE 13.1   Percentage Share of U.S. College Degrees

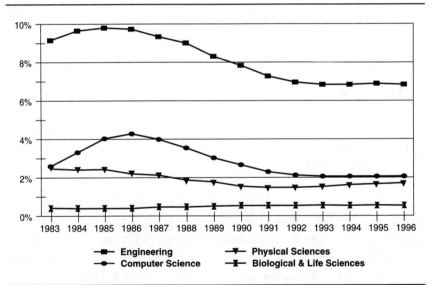

SOURCE: U.S. Statistical Abstract, 2000

SNUBBED

Manufacturing typically gets the equivalent of a blank stare, at best, in much of academia. Yet, while campus-based research has often led to important commercial applications, far more often the useful products come primarily from within companies. The National Science Foundation cites a landmark multi-industry study, done in 1975–1985, that found the percentage of new products particularly dependent on academic research never exceeded 29 percent in a single industry. Jeffrey Pfeffer, a Stanford University professor, argues that most industrial advances are fueled by "firm-special skills" that companies nurture internally. Often, when universities do play a significant research role in bringing on a new product or process, success comes only after steady interaction between the campus, the company, and the customers.

Similarly, today's mantra from public officials and members of the press is that industry urgently needs college-educated, white-collar workers who can participate meaningfully in the so-called new economy. This need was not expressed as a grave concern by the industrial professionals with whom we talked. Instead, they cite a need for tool and die makers, welders, moldmakers, machinists, competent assemblers, and, above all, dependable workers. Often, a two-year degree from a good technical college is enough to land many good jobs in industry. Managers at company after company repeated a singular refrain: It's been difficult, in a time when so much hype has been heaped onto finance, consulting, and fields related to the Internet, to attract young talent to manufacturing.

Remarkably, manufacturing was all but invisible in the presidential campaign of 2000, despite the now-established fact that a factory-led economic downturn was brewing as the election approached. Instead, both of the major parties' candidates were busily taking credit for a generally robust economy. Virtually no debate surfaced about U.S. trade policies or the informal barriers to entry faced by companies. Nor was there mention of the waves of corporate mergers that, some people believe, could create significant new concentrations of economic power. Energy policy failed to get any serious attention. The 2000 political campaign may be one of the few in more than a century where the nation's industrial condition received almost no attention at all.

AGING INDUSTRIAL PROFESSIONALS

Over time, this lack of concern raises an unsettling question: Are we replacing our cadre of aging industrial professionals with a new crop of competent and enthusiastic managers who can carry on? Some history is appropriate here. After World War II, veterans flocked to engineering schools and then to jobs in industry. They were supported by the GI Bill, and eager to find better jobs than their parents had. Veterans who were born in 1923, came out of the service in 1945, and graduated in 1950 can still be found actively engaged in their chosen field.

Bob Johnson, Honeywell's retired director of manufacturing, is among them. After completing his tour of duty as a Navy pilot, Johnson finished school and remained at Honeywell until he retired in 1985. Then he carved out a new career in manufacturing. Johnson took a turn as international president of the Society of Manufacturing Engineers (SME), a professional organization for which he still serves as a director. He visited plants and universities throughout the world on behalf of SME. Now, he teaches manufacturing engineering at the University of St. Thomas in St. Paul where, at age 77, he still chairs the school's laboratory committee.

Today, engineers and technicians more skilled in computer-based engineering software and proficient with automated equipment work side-by-side with the older professionals. We may be replenishing this aging cadre with successors who will carry manufacturing to new heights. M. Eugene Merchant, a research scientist for the Institute of Manufacturing Sciences in Cincinnati, has long been a champion of modern methods of manufacturing. At 87, he remains active in research. Merchant is an optimist. "My impression is that we are getting an adequate number of new people," he says. "The universities are improving their curricula and industrial and mechanical engineering programs are incorporating more manufacturing concepts."

Still, one wonders. Many of today's prominent manufacturing suppliers were started as companies around the time of World War II. Some of the founders are still on the scene. The U.S. engineering faculty is also getting older. Twenty-six percent were 55 years of age or older in 1997—twice the 13 percent in 1973.

FACTORIES—GOOD PLACES TO WORK

The irony is that even as factories are often looked on with disdain, many of them are good places to work. Remmele Engineering's plants in Minnesota are marvels of cleanliness and order. Ford's Lincoln assembly plant in Wixom, Michigan, is another immaculate plant. Nucor's steel mill in Crawfordsville, Indiana, exudes modernization and safety. Toolmakers at H.S. Die and Mold in Grand Rapids, Michigan, ably manipulate precision equipment to make some of the largest molds used by the auto industry. As in agriculture, mining, and other fields, life has generally become less arduous for manufacturing workers. Just as almost nobody farms with horses anymore, few U.S. factory workers face sweatshop conditions. The surroundings are mostly good, the equipment fast and efficient. The opportunities to apply technical expertise are as great or greater than in many "knowledge industries." In the highest-paying industries—autos, paper mills, aircraft, pharmaceuticals, and others—the wages are very good. Even average manufacturing wages remain well above average pay for the entire workforce.

Perhaps the glamour of a desk job was instilled by our parents who toiled strenuously to provide for the education and training of their sons and daughters. Who would want to work in a mine, or in the dingier factories of old? Yet, 21st century manufacturing has become a good place to work.

CHAPTER 14

The Darker Side of Merger Mania

On the last day of 1998, the *Los Angeles Times* put the magnitude of that year's mergers and acquisitions into perspective. The value was $1.2 trillion—enough to pay for 78 million new Volkswagen Beetles or 13,483 baseball teams with the payroll of the Baltimore Orioles. Another $360 billion in deals involving U.S. and foreign companies brought the grand total up to more than $1.5 trillion. In 1999, global merger and acquisition activity was estimated at a record $2.2 trillion, and it continued at a frenetic pace until finally tailing off in 2001. Among the larger manufacturing mergers since 1998 were Pfizer's acquisition of Warner-Lambert ($82 billion), Exxon's purchase of Mobil ($77 billion), Daimler's acquisition of Chrysler ($44 billion), and AlliedSignal's purchase of Honeywell ($15 billion).

Despite this ferocious activity, skepticism is widespread about the strategic effectiveness of mergers—except, not surprisingly, for dealmakers or their immediate subordinates. A 1999 study by KPMG International suggested that more than 80 percent of deals failed to enhance shareholder value, yet 82 percent of executives at the merged firms believe their deals were successful.

Another study, reported in the April 2001 issue of *Bloomberg Markets* magazine, found that the festival of late-1990s international deals didn't deliver on the promises of the merger-makers. *Bloomberg*'s researchers found that of the 30 biggest international mergers done in 1998 and 1999, the deals involving U.S. acquirers produced an average annualized return for shareholders of just .3 percent. That anemic return lagged far behind those of the major stock market indexes. Nine of these deals involved American manufacturers as buyers or sellers, with the Daimler-Benz acquisition of Chrysler being one of the biggest and best-known of the transactions. DaimlerChrysler stock was one of the worst performers, with a −12.1 percent return. Nonetheless, cross-border deals proliferated, more than quadrupling from 2,100 in 1997 to 9,200 in 2000, according to *Bloomberg* data.

Bloomberg cites several factors that drove the deal boom. Regulations that previously had blocked them were eased or dropped. Trade barriers fell, opening up new markets. The advent of the eurodollar gave European companies access to more capital. Investment bankers and other intermediaries, who could make enormous fees by bringing companies together, pushed hard for the consolidations. Still, as the magazine article and others note, many obstacles hinder the integration of the companies once they have been merged. Among them: conflicting cultures; loss of key executives; unrealistic expectations; language barriers; unworkable "power-sharing" arrangements among executives; sharp differences in executive pay levels at the companies being merged; employee confusion; and pricey deals that forced the combined company to trim or sell off critical operations in order to pay for the merger.

Invariably, executives from the companies involved in mergers announce them with great fanfare. Typically, they pepper their speeches, interviews, and press releases with words like "synergy," which means the combined companies will fare better together than they could as separate companies. One and one will make three, they say, extolling economies of scale that they will realize as a result of the deal; bigger, they contend, is always better.

Mark Sirower, a professor at New York University's Stern School of Business, argues in his 1997 book, *The Synergy Trap*, that most major acquisitions are predictably dead on arrival no matter how well managed they are after the deals close. In great part, that's because the premiums the acquirers pay are too high, sometimes in excess of 100 percent of the acquired firm's market value. Sirower cites one study showing that shareholders of acquiring firms in 1993–1995 deals lost an average of 10 percent of their investment on announcement of the deal. He points to a McKinsey & Co. study that found 61 percent of acquisition strategies failed because they didn't produce a sufficient rate of return. A common problem: Once the deal closes and companies begin integrating, the costs of getting out of a failed merger can climb very high. Undoing combined salesforces, information systems, or distribution networks is a difficult task. "And in the process,"

Sirower writes, "acquirers may run the risk of taking their eyes off competitors or losing their ability to respond to changes in the competitive environment."

Among the manufacturing deals that didn't pan out, Sirower cites Anheuser-Busch's 1979 acquisition of snack-maker Campbell Taggert; AT&T's 1991 purchase of NCR; Quaker Oats' 1994 acquisition of Snapple; and the 1986 Burroughs-Sperry merger to form Unisys.

> *Once the deal closes and companies begin integrating, the costs of getting out of a failed merger can climb very high. Undoing combined salesforces, information systems, or distribution networks is a difficult task.*

Anheuser-Busch tried to combine its Eagle Snacks line with Campbell Taggert's snacks, but market leader Frito-Lay counterattacked with a new line of snack foods. Anheuser-Busch ended up selling four Eagle snack plants, after 17 years of losses at Eagle, to Frito-Lay and spinning off Campbell Taggert. AT&T, which had lost $2 billion in its own computing business between 1985 and 1990, coughed up $7.6 billion to buy computer-maker NCR. The price was a 125 percent premium over NCR's preacquisition price, yet NCR lost $4 billion before AT&T decided to spin it off five years later. The $1.7 billion Quaker Oats-Snapple deal was the largest in Quaker Oats' history. Quaker touted Snapple's strong position in ice teas and juice drinks, but PepsiCo and Coca-Cola promptly launched competing brands. By mid-1996, Quaker found itself giving away $40 million worth of Snapple products to ease losses of market share to Pepsi and Coke. At Unisys, the two merger partners failed to integrate their distribution systems well. Equipment orders were late. Parts were often missing. Service was slow. By 1990, the price of Unisys stock had fallen below $3 a share, a decline of more than 90 percent from its preacquisition price.

Only a quarter of the recent mergers involving U.S. companies have involved manufacturers. Banks, communications companies, utilities, media companies, and insurers have all been big players. But some of the manufacturing-related mergers have eroded the nation's industrial expertise, a precious asset that can be more difficult to replace than what gets lost when banks or entertainment companies are merged. Chrysler's leading sellers of today—the PT Cruiser, the Ram pickup, the Durango Sport Utility, the 300 Sedan, and, of course, the minivan—were developed before its 1998 acquisition by Daimler-Benz. In the years just before the merger, Chrysler, the third-largest U.S. auto producer, was riding high in sales, profit, and product innovation. The theory behind the Daimler-Chrysler deal was that Daimler's reputation for high quality would blend with Chrysler's ability to bring forth a steady stream of well-designed, innovative vehicles that could be produced at costs low enough to ensure sales. The marriage of Daimler and Chrysler was presented as a "win-win" merger of equals, with each partner retaining its independent management, design philosophies, and financial measurements. Since this deal closed, though, two presidents and many top designers and marketing executives have left the company. Chrysler's share of the U.S. auto market fell from 8.6 percent in 1999 to 7.3 percent in 2000. The company has been losing money and slashing jobs. The value of DaimlerChrysler stock has been cut in half. "It's been a calamity, an absolute calamity," Chris Will, an analyst at Lehman Brothers, told *Bloomberg* in describing the deal. Critics fear that over the longer term, what remains of Chrysler Corp. will be a demoralized, unprofitable, and disorganized operation in the hands of an authoritarian culture unfamiliar with either local markets or how to build a good vehicle at low cost. The responsibility for maintaining an independent U.S. presence in the auto industry now rests exclusively with Ford and General Motors.

Honeywell's acquisition by AlliedSignal was not pretty, either. Burdened with huge debt, low margins, a weak balance sheet, and slow-moving inventory, AlliedSignal was a poor partner for the more conservative and technically competent Honeywell. After the acquisition, AlliedSignal took Honeywell International as its name, but moved the headquarters from lower-cost Minneapolis to higher-cost New Jersey. The deal quickly fell short of its promise. Less than a year later, Honeywell's directors agreed to sell the company to General Electric. Then, as GE prepared to slash thousands of jobs once it absorbed Honeywell, the European Commission blocked aspects of the deal. GE pulled out, after its executives and their counterparts from Honeywell had devoted long hours to merger integration. Suddenly, an unprepared Honeywell International was back on its own.

Waves of mergers have occurred throughout U.S. history with mixed results. An active merger boom in the early 1900s created such combinations as International Merchant Marine, U.S. Steel, International Harvester, and General Motors. The conglomerate era of the 1960s featured goliaths built on rapid-fire acquisitions—LTV, Lionel, ITT, Gulf & Western Industries—all of which turned out to be houses of cards. Even the most successful of these consolidations did not achieve continuously favorable results. GM had to be rescued in 1910 and again in 1920. U.S. Steel enjoyed success due largely to the heavy investments of its main predecessor, Carnegie Steel, but eventually encountered competitive pressures that led to a long decline. International Harvester was an amalgamation of more than 15 major agricultural equipment producers that failed to attain the internal efficiencies of Deere, initially a much smaller stand-alone company that grew largely through internal expansion.

The performance of the conglomerates generally fell somewhere between unsatisfactory and disastrous. LTV entered bankruptcy, finally emerging after trying unsuccessfully to get the federal government to take over its unfunded pension obligations. The price of Litton Industries stock reached $140 per share in the late 1960s, but fell to $15 a few years later. AMF dropped from $66 to $10, Lionel from $38 to $4.50. Robert Sobel chronicled the problems of overambitious consolidations of the 1960s and 1970s in his classic book, *The Rise and Fall of Conglomerate Kings*.

Different circumstances surrounded the mergers of earlier times. Many smaller and midsize producers existed in earlier times, so the case for consolidation did hold out at least some promise for capturing better economies of scale. Today, the sizes of the companies involved are frequently much larger than before. Combining huge entities such as Exxon and Mobil might offer further efficiencies, but it is hard to make the case that companies of such vast size were too small to achieve scale economies on their own.

TODAY'S MERGERS—BIGGER AND MORE DISPARATE THAN EVER

Today's mergers often span huge geographic areas and frequently cross international boundaries. Many are so large as to raise the specter of new problems potentially more difficult to solve: Will these gargantuan combinations be so big that they will be less efficient, less innovative in product development, and less responsive to the needs of the marketplace than the parts were as stand-alone companies? Questions are already surfacing. Many operating units of large companies are now quite distant from the corporate epicenters where strategies get shaped and resources allocated. These distances, often vast in both geography and organizational structure, may be so immense that overall competitiveness becomes harder to achieve and perhaps even more difficult to sustain.

Still, Wall Street loves mergers—especially if costs are being cut. Cost reductions are important, of course. When mergers remove bureaucratic waste, they can lead to higher output and better products. Sometimes, though, merger-triggered cost reductions reduce more muscle than fat. Talented and dedicated employees can become demoralized when they sense that their company's mission, capability, and purposes are being thoughtlessly degraded. In some instances, the voids created by the disruption and demoralization of acquired U.S. producers have been filled by enterprising overseas competitors.

The ticker tape has proven to be an unconvincing indicator of what happens to a firm's competitive position as it acquires, divests, restructures, and consolidates. AT&T's stock price rose at various times when it acquired NCR, spun off both Lucent and NCR, bought several media companies, and then decided to break itself into four parts. Yet, after so many multibillion-dollar transactions, AT&T has transformed itself from one of the world's best-known and most successful companies into a disjointed amalgamation of unrelated activities, with a stock price lower than it was before.

Very few of these vast mergers have turned out satisfactorily for the acquirer's shareholders, but their impact on communities and the nation has, in some cases, been even more adverse. LTV greatly worsened Republic Steel—a key supplier of high alloy steel—hurting the regions where Republic had mills. In Wisconsin, Allis-Chalmers, once the state's largest employer, was a highly technical company known not only for its farm equipment, but for its electrical generating equipment and for its research in fuel cells. Rather than concentrating on its core business, the company focused on acquisitions, buying 20 companies from 1968 to 1985. It sold or closed 29 plants. Its employment fell by roughly two-thirds, to 12,000. In 1987, Allis-Chalmers filed for bankruptcy.

There have been successful mergers, of course. Few, however, have taken on overwhelming debt loads and managerial challenges that we are seeing today.

TWO KINDS OF MERGERS

Two kinds of mergers merit special attention: investment-driven deals and cost-driven deals. Investment-driven acquisitions are like those done by Pentair or Medtronic, where one company acquires another and then invests to improve the competitive position of its newly acquired property. These acquisitions often work, enhancing wealth in typically friendly deals followed by welcoming affiliation and heavy investment. The acquiring companies provide resources and encourage fruitful cooperation to accomplish a clearly defined purpose. Good mergers recognize past accomplishments of the acquired companies.

Cost-driven deals, on the other hand, are often made by companies not particularly successful financially. Cost savings, often justified by illusory economies of scale, become necessary for the acquisition to pay for itself—right away. Costs must be quickly reduced to show that the merger has the "synergistic" potential promised to Wall Street. Managers downgrade the idea of investing in a valued property, or building new capabilities. Instead, they concentrate on reducing the cost of what was done before in order to pay for the acquisition. They do little to build up their companies' technical strengths and product offerings. They place relatively less value on their workers as a part of the company, despite rhetoric to the contrary. Cost-driven acquisitions show less promise and are often wealth-destroying rather than wealth-enhancing.

The Sartell Mill

AFL-CIO officials recommended the Champion Paper mill in Sartell, Minnesota, to us as an example of a workplace where labor and management had cooperated extensively to improve both working conditions and competitiveness. Indeed, we were impressed with the general atmosphere of the mill, which had well-equipped training facilities and was in near-spotless condition. The mill, located on the Mississippi River, employs about 550 workers. They transform huge logs into the paper used to make some of America's most familiar magazines, catalogs, and newspaper inserts.

Labor-management relations were rocky in the late 1980s, when competitive conditions led to cost reductions borne by both the company and its employees. In 1990, after new leaders came into power at the union and in management, both sides agreed to a "Joint Statement of Commitment and Cooperation" that precipitated widespread improvements in safety, productivity, profitability, and product quality. In 1997, the company won the coveted Shingo Prize for Excellence in Manufacturing. That year, mill employees worked more than 3 million hours without a lost-time accident, an achievement claimed by only five other U.S. mills in any year. Union grievances plunged. Outlays for training soared. Profitability and production rose. Union and management representatives went to Washington, to testify about the success of their labor-management compact before a workforce panel of Congress.

Then a new merger wave, sweeping through the paper industry, reached Champion. In February of 2000, the company's directors accepted a $6.5 billion bid by Finnish-based UPM-Kymmene for the company, and integration teams at UPM and Champion set about the task of merging the two companies. Two months later, mammoth International Paper (IP)—almost five times larger than Champion—came along with a richer offer. UPM trumped that bid. Then IP, which had been quietly eyeing Champion for a year, raised the ante again. In May, Champion accepted IP's bid valued at $9.5 billion in cash, stock, and debt.

Union members at the mill were rattled by the news that they would become a part of International Paper, which fell out of grace with organized labor when it knocked out a union local after a bitter battle in the early 1980s at a mill in Jay, Maine. Tom Cusciotta, president of the Sartell paper workers' local at the time of the merger, says members feared IP management would not be as committed to working closely with the union as Champion was. Cusciotta says that fear eased during the year after the merger. Soon after the deal, IP CEO John Dillon met with the Sartell workers and told them the company was trying to soften its hard-edged image. The workers were reassured when Dillon sent in a new plant manager from a Champion mill, rather than an executive who had been with IP. No union members had been laid off as of the fall of 2001, though some management jobs had been trimmed.

On the surface, the merger makes sense. Champion's top executives hailed it as a way to gain access to the resources of the world's largest paper and forest products company. Product lines of the two companies complement one another. The merger gives the combined company the opportunity to optimize production at the 115 paper mills now part of IP, plus prospects for further cost savings. On the other hand, IP headed into the merger barely profitable. And as the merged corporation began life, it found itself facing a slowing economy and overcapacity in its industry—with a heavily leveraged balance sheet.

Meanwhile, foreign paper producers had been entering the U.S. market with strong infrastructures behind them. Twenty years ago, there were six major manufacturers of paper-making machinery in the United States. Today, there are none. Three companies—from Germany, Finland, and Japan—make most of today's equipment, which is faster and more productive. The Sartell mill has three paper machines. Two, which were built in 1905, produce paper in 140-inch widths at 1,800 feet per minute, resulting in 50,000 tons of paper annually for each machine. The third machine, installed in 1983, is much larger, at 280 inches in width, and faster, at 4,000 feet per minute, resulting in 200,000 tons of paper per year. Today, new paper machines coming onto the market typically have a 350-inch web, run at 6,500 feet per minute, and produce 400,000 tons of paper. Some competing mills have several of the newer machines.

Still, when rumors of yet another huge deal—IP buying Finnish-based Stora Enso—surfaced in a Swedish newspaper in late summer of 2001, workers were unsettled. "It's scary," says Cusciotta. "The first thing they do in a merger is downsize." Workers worry that with overcapacity in the industry and older equipment in a debt-laden company, the mill is vulnerable to better-equipped, rapidly emerging foreign rivals. The equipment is expensive—the paper and pulp business is one of the most capital-intensive industries in the world. Can the Sartell mill, with its slower and older equipment, survive and prosper under these circumstances? Will the excellent labor relations continue? Will the mill win the investment it needs to update its equipment, or will it slowly be harvested? Will this merger work, for the managers and workers who did so well at Sartell in the 1990s?

The Divisions of SPX

Owatonna Tool Co., in Owatonna, Minnesota, was once a well-run specialized manufacturer of excellent products—wheel pullers and other tools used by auto, truck, and agricultural equipment mechanics. In 1991, the OTC Power Team plant was named one of the top ten manufacturing plants in the United States by *Industry Week* magazine. The Kaplan family, viewed as devoted to the community, active in the business, popular with employees, and adamantly against layoffs, ran the company until 1985.

Then the Kaplans sold it to SPX Corp. from Muskegon, Michigan. SPX was the old Sealed Power Piston Ring Co., which supplied auto parts and aspired to become a large-scale industrial conglomerate. SPX's strategy, however, did not unfold quickly. After a flurry of acquisitions, divestitures, and mergers, the company lost money annually from 1995 to 1998. In 1999, when it finally got back into the black, much of the reported profits came from the reverse acquisition of General Signal in 1998. General Signal had formally acquired SPX, but the SPX name and management was retained. Then, in 2000, SPX began rearranging the 20 or so diverse businesses of General Signal and SPX. These consolidations raised concerns in communities where SPX operated. Plants were closed in Wayland, Michigan, in Europe, and in Owatonna. Plants in Philadelphia and McMinnville, Tennessee, were closed and then merged into SPX's DeZurik operation in St. Cloud, Minnesota.

Employees who left to join other companies said SPX DeZurik was a confusing place to work. Like many factories across the country, DeZurik went through several owners as it was dealt from one conglomerate to another. First, there was Colorado Gas, then General Signal, now SPX. First came big cutbacks and then the merger with two other out-of-state plants. "It was a numbers game," said one 15-year former employee.

Similar stories came out of Owatonna, where the once-renowned Power Team plant was closed, and its business transferred to another

SPX plant in Illinois. A Power Team employee lamented that the company went through four presidents in four years. "There are four plant moves going on within SPX at the moment," he said. Another person very familiar with SPX complained that the company was letting people with valuable skills leave. "It is no way to build the business in the long term."

Many of the nation's best producers have gotten wrapped up in the merger buzz saw. Onan, a manufacturer of both midrange and smaller generators, had four owners in a few years before becoming part of Cummins Engine. Electronic components manufacturer Amp fought off a hostile takeover by AlliedSignal, only to be acquired by Tyco International a few months later.

The jury on the hyperactive merger and acquisition activity of recent years remains out. The evidence suggesting that these deals destroy shareholder value more often than they create it is not the only concern. They have disrupted the lives of hundreds of thousands of production workers and others who depend in various ways on manufacturing jobs. Even if they don't lose their jobs, the parade of ownership changes adds to the uncertainty and lack of loyalty that make working conditions more difficult. Perhaps more importantly for the long run, poorly thought-out mergers and acquisitions may have seriously weakened the competitive position of the United States.

THE SEARCH FOR A MANAGERIAL MODEL

Some major companies, most notably General Electric, have had an immense influence on the evolution of manufacturing in the United States. GE grew during the 20-year reign of CEO Jack Welch to become the world's most valuable company. The company, widely perceived to be well managed, has served as a training ground for prospective CEOs who go on to take top spots at other companies. As CEO, Welch oversaw 993 acquisitions and sold 408 businesses. His deal-making was a key part of a strategy that featured steady cost-cutting, massive layoffs, involuntary retirements, global expansion, and the movement of jobs to nonunion locales. GE has practiced the strategic selection style of management—buying, dismembering, and selling companies in order to end up only in fields where it ranks number one or number two. Responding to the pressures to perform well or be sold, many GE divisions have done well—especially during the prosperous 1990s. One problem, though, was $230 billion in debt.

It is far less clear if the acquire-sell–slash-and-burn model will work to fix problems in more difficult times. To a great extent, the acquisitive strategy has been helped by the availability of willing buyers in a hot market. It was not so difficult, in the 1990s, to sell off unwanted industrial pieces for more than was paid. Selling may prove to be both more difficult and less rewarding in the more subdued market that has emerged since.

It is also unclear whether exiting from all difficult industries is an appropriate strategy for the long-term competitive position of the nation. As Columbia University Professor Donald Hambrick has pointed out, a large fraction of U.S. businesses have small-to-medium market shares in important but slow-growth industries. Among them, though, are outstanding companies that consistently do well financially, provide good jobs to employees, and create wealth for their communities. A managerial model that essentially writes off this important group of companies may not be nearly as useful in the long run as it seems over the short term.

The strategic selection paradigm is not the only one. There are other templates—more remedial if you like. Instead of emphasizing the selection of the winning business, these models show how to improve existing businesses. Given today's high levels of international competition, these approaches may prove more useful over time. Even Jack Welch admits that the final verdict is out on the GE model. "You should measure my success eventually by how well GE does in the next five years," he told the *Wall Street Journal* in fall of 2001.

Companies like Nucor, Paccar, Parker-Hannifin, and Winnebago have learned to survive, excel, and prosper over time, often with key ratios and debt structures that look superior to those of some of the more acquisitive companies such as Tyco International, International Paper, SPX, and, quite often, General Electric.

The acquisitive model could come under greater scrutiny in the years ahead, particularly if the economy grows more slowly. The wild ride of the past few years has created companies capable of outstanding growth in some markets, but are their more acquisitive managerial styles applicable to all times and all markets?

What percentage of the many mergers and acquisitions of recent times will stand the test of time? The KPMG study found that only 45 percent of the merged companies even bothered to carry out formal reviews of how well or poorly the deals had worked. Executives at many of the surviving companies perhaps do not want to know. As Samuel Hayes, professor emeritus of finance at the Harvard Business School, puts it: "Whenever you buy another firm, you're buying a pig in a poke; you never know what you're buying until you open the bag and see the animal."

The larger question, for this inquiry, is: What are we doing to the essential industrial structure of the United States?

The KPMG study found that only 45 percent of the merged companies even bothered to carry out formal reviews of how well or poorly the deals had worked.

CHAPTER 15

Wanted:
Better Leaders

 In his book, *Plain Talk,* steel entrepreneur Ken Iverson articulates the easily understandable philosophy he used to build Nucor into the fastest-growing and most profitable steel company in the United States. Even as he did this, much of the rest of the U.S. steel industry was in decline. Iverson's winning strategy: investment, efficiency, innovation, and a strong appreciation for the contributions of individual employees. Modest overhead was part of the prescription, too. Nucor's headquarters is in an unassuming office on the fourth floor of an unpretentious building in Charlotte, North Carolina.

Iverson's record at Nucor shows how leadership is crucial for American manufacturers.

Leadership can be defined in countless ways, but sometimes events speak more clearly than words could ever do. After the end of the Cold War, many Americans became more apprehensive as terrorism mounted and resentment of America's culture, values, and power grew. In 1999, the United States Commission on National Security/ 21st Century published a report that lent substance to their concerns. The report warned that over the next 25 years, "America will become increasingly vulnerable to hostile attack on our homeland . . . Americans will likely die on American soil, possibly in large numbers." Similar warnings came from the Bremer Commission. Leaders did not react. Antiterrorism initiatives, recommended time and again, weren't the kind of thing people wanted to talk about, let alone pay for. Airport security remained almost a joke. Just two years later, terrorists slipped through porous airport security systems to carry out the catastrophic attacks on the World Trade Center and the Pentagon.

In the weeks before the attacks, the Pew Research Center posed this question to U.S. leadership elites and to the general public: "It has been ten years since the end of the Cold War. In your opinion, is the world now more dangerous, less dangerous, or about the same compared to ten years ago?" Nearly all of the leadership elites—scientists and engineers, business/finance and labor leaders, news media, religious leaders, state and local government officials—replied overwhelmingly that the perils had receded. The general public, however, responded by a 53-to-14 margin that the world had become a more dangerous place. As Andrew Kohut, director of the Pew Center, put it in a memo to his staff two days after the attacks: "I thought you might be interested in seeing how prescient the public was versus the elites. In our line of work, we hear so much criticism of how little the public knows." The public, he concluded, is often right in its judgments.

THE NEED FOR A NOBLE PURPOSE

Similarly, the workers in American corporations often have more sensible ideas than their leaders. On the factory floor, leadership takes diverse forms and requires many skills. Managers must be able to understand how informal networks within their organizations operate. They must take responsibility for their workers. They must achieve and maintain a reputation for fairness with their suppliers. They must help their customers solve problems. Frequently, good leadership goes beyond best practices to take on almost spiritual qualities. Profits are a factor in the leadership equation. Often, though, long-term success on the bottom line results more from sound management practices than from the CEO barking out orders to make the next quarter's earnings.

In 2000, Medtronic enjoyed an after-tax profit margin of 21.9 percent. Yet, you find little mention of either profit or shareholder value in the company's mission statement, which has been virtually unchanged for 40 years. Instead, the statement is all about applying medical technology to save or extend lives. Every December, at its employee holiday party, Medtronic invites as honored guests people whose lives have been saved by its medical devices. They tell their stories, often with emotions that move the crowd to tears.

Most notably, Medtronic's financial success in recent years has been the rule, not the exception. Among the Fortune 500 companies, Medtronic ranked 22nd, with an average return to stockholders of 34.2 percent over the decade that ended in 1999. Clearly, Medtronic's noble mission and its long-term business performance are inextricably linked.

Nucor's 1999 annual report rarely spoke of boosting shareholder value or, for that matter, profits. Instead, it stressed the accomplishments of individual employees. Yet, Nucor made $245 million that year, more than five times as much as larger rival U.S. Steel. The third and fourth largest U.S.-based steel producers, Bethlehem Steel and LTV, both of which were formerly much larger than Nucor, lost money and ultimately filed for bankruptcy.

Organizations look to their leaders for examples. Employees at companies struggling to compete tend to be street savvy. They recognize the importance of the task at hand, and they expect their managers to behave professionally. Sometimes, managers do accept responsibility and behave professionally, but sometimes, they do not. Managers often blame external forces when their companies fall into crisis, but sometimes, the managers themselves bear much of the blame. They are the principal culprits when they have neglected fundamentals such as ideals, believability, and purpose. It is not enough for leaders to merely espouse ideals. To be credible, they must operate in accordance with those ideals. Particularly in competitive situations, managers must be perceived as fair, honest, and appreciative of the need to integrate the goals of the organization with those of its workers.

This particular thought is hardly a new observation. While many of today's management specialists strive to leave the impression that they and their contemporaries are the new disciples of management wisdom, their predecessors also knew a thing or two.

In 1938, Chester Barnard recognized the link between ideals and the personal credibility of leaders in his book, *The Functions of the Executive.* Barnard theorized that the more workers trust their managers, the more support they will give the bosses. Barnard advanced another thought, often overlooked by human relations professionals. He concluded that how managers treat other workers can be as important to an individual as how they treat that individual. People use how others are treated as an index of how they will be treated. The more managers are seen as opportunistic, the less they'll be able to mobilize their organizations.

People use how others are treated as an index of how they will be treated.

In 1941, social worker turned management consultant Mary Parker Follett suggested in her book, *Dynamic Administration,* that "the cause" is important to the rank and file in instances where a company is struggling to compete. Workers aren't likely to think much of their leaders if they perceive them to be interested primarily in "managing upward"— buttering up their own bosses—or hooked on big offices, sky-high paydays, and cushy perquisites.

MANAGERS PEOPLE CAN READ

Another shortcoming of today's leadership is the rise of "beige wallpaper managers"—bosses who are seen not as antagonists but as neutrals who do not count for much. They look, talk, and act like the captains of industry they profess to be. They aren't disliked. They are, however, difficult to read. They are perceived as colorless by their workers. They have no readily discernible character traits, no quirks that send out signals about what they deem important. Cadillac founder Henry Leland crashed bad castings onto the concrete to emphasize the need to make good castings. Though Ford's Lew Veraldi was a great people person with a big heart, he pounded on the table to stress the importance of making a higher-quality Taurus. A fellow Ford executive remarked: "I can never remember people being confused about what Veraldi wanted." Beige wallpaper managers fail to convey the sense of an identifiable higher purpose.

The recognition of good leadership is yet another sore spot. Internal politics can plague manufacturers, just as it does other organizations. Industry's most innovative leaders have not always been popular within their own companies. Veraldi might have been able to create the world's best-selling car at Ford, but that did not mean that he won popularity contests with other Ford executives. Bob Lutz, famed product development leader, struggled against bureaucracies at both Ford and Chrysler.

Unfortunately, manufacturing has had its share of poor leaders. No studies exist to suggest whether the manufacturing sector has a greater or lesser allocation of such leadership. Surely, though, the icon-like image that Albert J. Dunlap built up for his supposed feats at Florida-based Sunbeam Corp. and other manufacturers stands as one of the most brazen examples of illusory management in modern times. Dunlap, of course, became known far and wide as "Chainsaw Al," a nickname that reflected his practice of slashing jobs wherever he went. Just the news of his arrival as CEO at Scott Paper drove the company's stock price up 41 percent. Investors continued to hail him for cutting 11,200 jobs at Scott. After Kimberly-Clark acquired Scott, Dunlap bragged that the deal generated $100 million for him. "Did I earn that?" he asked in his 1996 autobiography, *Mean Business*. "Damn right I did. I'm a superstar in my field. . . ." Then, when he moved on to become CEO at Sunbeam, Sunbeam's stock soared on the news of his arrival. Dunlap lived up to his reputation; four months later, he announced plans to cut 6,000 jobs. A few investors and several prominent business journalists—John Byrne, in *Business Week;* Roger Lowenstein, in the *Wall Street Journal;* Joe Nocera and Herb Greenberg, in *Fortune*— had warned that all was not quite as it seemed with Dunlap. No matter. The stock, which was trading for $12.50 a share the day before his hiring was announced, soared to a high of $52 early in 1998.

Then Sunbeam jolted stockholders by reporting a first-quarter loss. *Barron's* published charges that Sunbeam had engaged in creative accounting techniques to fatten up its earnings. Directors investigated, then fired Dunlap. The Securities & Exchange Commission (SEC) launched its own investigation. Early in 2001, the company filed for protection under bankruptcy laws. Three months later, the SEC charged in a civil lawsuit that Dunlap had directed a massive accounting fraud "to create the illusion of a successful restructuring of Sunbeam and facilitate the sale of the company at an inflated price." At the very time that Dunlap was tossing thousands of employees out of work and calling 1997 an "amazing year," the SEC said the company was claiming sales it never made. By then, the stock had fallen below 10 cents a share.

In July of 2001, the *New York Times* published a front-page investigative piece on Dunlap. The *Times* reported that the rosy portrait Dunlap had painted of himself in his book failed to mention that he had been fired from two top jobs early in his career. In one case, the *Times* reported, he was fired after the company's board accused him of overseeing an accounting fraud "remarkably similar" to the one the SEC alleged at Sunbeam. "We were shocked when we heard about this," Jerry Levin, Dunlap's successor at Sunbeam, told the newspaper. "I find it unusual that anyone could be hired as a chief executive of a major company without having their background thoroughly checked. This seems to have escaped everyone's attention."

Unusual, but not unprecedented. In 1999, *Barron's* found that Jeffrey T. Grade, CEO at Harnischfeger Industries in Milwaukee, had falsely claimed in his official corporate biography that he had "served in Vietnam as a pilot in the United States Navy." He wowed the company's employees with stories of his dangerous night landings in the South China Sea. He described how he had fought his way to freedom after being shot down in enemy territory. He said he had a synthetic elbow because of an injury in Vietnam. Yet, *Barron's* discovered that the Navy was unable to find any record of a Vietnam-era Navy veteran with either Grade's name or his Social Security number. Confronted with that finding, Grade admitted that he hadn't been in the regular Navy or flown combat missions in Vietnam.

Meanwhile, Grade was leading the company in the wrong direction. Debt soared during his six years as CEO, a bad strategy for a company facing a cyclical downturn. The company borrowed heavily to make expensive, questionable acquisitions. One deal, buying Asia Pulp & Paper, led to cost overruns and write-downs totaling $237 million. Grade loaded up on pay and perquisites, while 3,400 workers lost their jobs in cost-cutting moves. Harnischfeger spent millions of dollars to build a lavish headquarters. The stock fell from $50 a share to about $1. And Harnischfeger, long famed for its production of heavy equipment, turned to the bankruptcy court for protection.

Today, Harnischfeger has emerged from bankruptcy as Joy Global. The company still makes mining equipment. It has survived, mostly because it has large shares of the market for its mining equipment. Yet, it has suffered grievously from Grade's illusory leadership. As Salomon Smith Barney analyst Tobias Lefkovich said shortly after Harnischfeger turned up in bankruptcy court: "The company's Chapter 11 filing last month was not a death by natural causes."

Two once-proud manufacturers, two bankruptcies. Did they suffer such indignities because their markets were maturing? Were they simply victims of what economist Joseph Schumpeter called "creative destruction?" Or were they mugged, in each case, by a CEO whose leadership qualities turned out to be largely a mirage?

In other cases, CEOs in recent years have become more interested in basking in the limelight than nurturing productive team atmospheres in their companies. Writing in the *Wall Street Journal*, Jim Collins, author of *Good to Great*, cited as a case in point the publicity-seeking activities of Carly Fiorina, CEO of Hewlett-Packard. Collins noted that Fiorina had been on the job for less than six months when she posed for a cover article in *Forbes*. The extensive publicity did not seem to help Hewlett-Packard, which suffered reduced profitability and market presence. In fall of 2001, announcements were made by both the Hewlett and Packard families that they would vote their own shares and those of their foundations against the Fiorina proposed acquisition of Compaq.

In the same article, Collins also criticized AT&T CEO Michael Armstrong's penchant for attention. Both companies, Collins observed, were suffering financially at the very time their CEOs were busily publicizing themselves. Collins noted that his researchers had just wrapped up a five-year project analyzing leaders who took good companies and made them great. "All of the good-to-great leaders were the complete opposite of Ms. Fiorina and Mr. Armstrong," he wrote. "They deflected attention away from themselves, shunned the limelight, and quietly focused on the tasks at hand."

Perhaps we put too many expectations on our CEOs. That's what Harvard Business School professor Rakesh Khurana thinks. Khurana argues that corporate boards, the investment community, the media, and others are searching for silver bullets when they elevate the CEO position to almost exalted status. "I think it's very much out of hand, and essentially dysfunctional for the long-term competitive advantage of companies," he says. "Large organizations are too complex to be easily affected by a single personality."

| *They deflected attention away from themselves, shunned the limelight, and quietly focused on the tasks at hand.*

THE IMPORTANCE OF STEWARDSHIP

Good leadership becomes paramount in tough times. Even the best-managed companies suffer economic adversity. Stock markets fall off. Customers become cautious. World events can change our priorities. Some excellent managers find success elusive under such conditions, and no one is immune.

Yet, in good times or bad, managerial stewardship is a potent factor in the success of companies and, ultimately, in the success of the communities that house these companies. The chief difference does not seem to be raw talent, because many people in all ranks have talent and many people in all ranks do not. Neither does success seem to hinge on where the managers went to school, because successful executives come from a variety of educational backgrounds, if they went to college at all. What counts most is the sense of managerial responsibility—the executive's view of the stewardship role. Good managers feel for their organizations and they often hope and pray that they will be up to tasks laid before them. Then, when something good happens, they look around to see who helped.

PART FIVE

Staying on the Edge

Part Five looks at American industry's many bright spots. Its 17 million workers, who include untold numbers of top performers, provide the backbone for its many successes. Private sector innovation in the United States is centered in manufacturing. Constructive partnerships between manufacturers and other groups are flourishing. We'll look closely at this sector's strengths, and how they can be perpetuated, in this section:

Chapter 16 explores the technology stock crash from the perspective of manufacturing, examining how the bubble in these stocks diverted investment away from production and into speculation. The run-ups in the tech stocks put more pressure on manufacturers to come up with outsized returns, and many manufacturers were unable to do so. Some reacted by embracing or exploring new opportunities such as being acquired by buyout groups, or going private on their own. Yet, the bursting of the tech stock bubble could signal a back-to-basics trend favoring manufacturers.

Chapter 17 shows how manufacturing drives private sector innovation in the United States, focusing on North Carolina's Research Triangle Park. Both startups and established companies are sparking manufacturing successes there.

Chapter 18 explains how partnerships help industries, focusing on how they helped Jackson, Tennessee, to become a successful manufacturing community.

Chapter 19 summarizes the main points of the book overall, and looks back at the implications of the discoveries—the achievements of the workers, the jolts that change job levels almost overnight, and the highs and the lows of this important sector. Finally, we offer our recommendations for strengthening this critical part of the American economy.

CHAPTER 16

Wall Street: Return to Sanity?

 Early in 1999, as the mania about technology stocks was driving them into the stratosphere, we met Stephen Cohen at an academic gathering. In the mid-1980s, Cohen and his colleague, John Zysman, at the Berkeley Roundtable on the International Economy, had written a widely acclaimed book, *Manufacturing Matters.* Their book, like this one, underscored the importance of the manufacturing sector to the U.S. economy.

When asked what he had done on this topic since his book, Cohen served up a surprising response. "I haven't written anything new, researched that line of inquiry . . . zip," he replied. Why not? "All debates are on ice, with the Nasdaq Index representing the only idea of truth. . . ."

Indeed, the tech bubble of the late 1990s had become the only game in town for a while. Everyone from cab drivers to day traders became glued to the latest stock tip. Hordes of first-time investors were venturing into the market, lured by the prospect that they could strike it rich overnight simply by sinking their money into soaring Internet or communications stocks.

Generally, the euphoria for tech stocks in the 1990s affected manufacturers in two ways. First, Wall Street paid less attention to many manufacturing stocks, which were often dismissed as boring in contrast to glitzy Internet, telecommunications, and software issues. Second, the sky-high price gains on tech stocks inflated investors' expectations for all kinds of companies. These greater demands, in turn, put more pressure on manufacturers to boost profits or revenues by contracting work out, acquiring other companies, cutting employees, or squeezing suppliers.

The UBS PaineWebber-Gallup Organization's monthly Index of Investor Optimism shows how heady the expectations became. Survey researchers established the Index at a baseline of 100 in October of 1996. By February of 1999, the Index hit its peak at 184. Five months later, with the Nasdaq Composite Average racing up to its all-time high, pollsters found that the least-experienced investors—those in the market 5 years or less—expected annual returns of 22.6 percent over the next decade. Even investors with more than 20 years of experience envisioned annual returns of nearly 13 percent over this stretch.

Legendary investor Warren Buffett, writing in *Fortune* magazine's November 1999 issue, described such rosy prospects as sheer fantasy. Buffett analyzed past trends in profits, interest rates, and stock prices, then concluded: "I think it's very hard to come up with a persuasive case that equities over the next 17 years will perform anything like—*anything* like—they've performed in the last 17." After working through the math to take apart the case for such a bullish outlook, he put the more likely return at 4 percent in real terms.

Meanwhile, growth stock advocates were deriding Buffett for refusing to line the portfolio of his company, Berkshire Hathaway, with soaring technology issues. Buffett had said he avoided these stocks because he couldn't understand their long-term prospects, but in 1999, that kind of thinking was not acceptable. Berkshire's stock fell sharply. "I'll tell you what Warren Buffett should say when he releases his statement to shareholders—'I'm sorry!'—that's what,'" declared Harry Newton, publisher of *Technology Investor* magazine. "I can't understand it. How did Buffett miss the silicon, wireless, DSL, cable, and biotech revolutions?" Buffett did apologize, in Berkshire's annual report for 1999. In his annual letter to shareholders, released almost exactly as the Nasdaq average pierced through the 5000 level, he wrote that the company had "the worst absolute performance" in his many years at its helm. "My grade for 1999 most assuredly is a D," he told shareholders. "Even Inspector Clouseau could find last year's guilty party: your chairman." Yet, Buffett stuck with his practice of avoiding tech stocks. Soon, his followers were rewarded. Berkshire Hathaway stock climbed back up near its high; tech stocks crashed.

The rebound of Berkshire Hathaway stock might seem representative of a renaissance for manufacturing stocks, because Berkshire has a very industrial composite. More than half of its businesses are manufacturers. Buffett's late-2000 acquisition of Shaw Industries boosted manufacturing's share of Berkshire noninsurance revenues to roughly 60 percent. Shaw, which has annual sales of about $4 billion, is the world's largest producer of tufted carpets. Thus, the headline above the story about the Berkshire comeback, coupled with the tech stock crash, might well say something like "The Revenge of the Manufacturers." Yet, the stunning tech stock bubble and its equally stunning aftermath are, from manufacturing's perspective, a more complicated story.

The breadth of this sector makes it impossible for the stock movements of any single stock, or any one industry, to reflect the market performance of the overall sector. The Leuthold Group, an investment firm known for its big-picture analyses of the stock market, divided the manufacturing sector into five subsectors in order to examine its stock market performance during and after the bubble. It is interesting to note that these respected analysts avoided using the term "technology" to describe these groups. That was a wise decision, because certainly a great deal of real technology exists in the companies that did not participate in the speculative runups of the 1990s.

The categories used were:

- Stable—Producers of consumer staples, household products, packaged goods, pharmaceuticals
- Cyclical—Auto and steel industries, machinery producers, other more traditional industries
- Growth Cyclical—Producers of consumer electronics goods, medical device makers, wineries, electrical instrumentation manufacturers
- Cyclical Non-economic—Oil and gas producers, agricultural goods
- Growth-Turned-Cyclical—Internet-related companies, telecommunications, and networking equipment producers

Many of the companies in this last sector do not like to be viewed as manufacturers. They contract out much of their assembly work, and often position themselves with investors as information technology companies. Nonetheless, they are manufacturers.

While the price movements of stocks in these subsectors showed many differing patterns in the aftermath of the bubble, one trend stands out: The growth-turned-cyclical stocks plunged. Companies in this category experienced a mammoth overall rise in valuation as frenzied speculators piled into Internet-related stocks. Prices soared on stocks ranging from established companies such as Cisco Systems to scores of newly public startups. Investors, enthralled by the siren call of the so-called new economy, made huge bets that these were growth stocks destined to climb up, up, and away. Analysts came up with exotic rationales to explain why the old rules of stock valuation no longer held. Nonetheless, the excitement of the Internet and new technology soon gave way to the reality that tech stocks were, after all, still cyclical stocks. The more they had climbed during the rise of the bubble, the more they would wilt as their sales and earnings faltered.

And wilt they did. Brothers Anthony and Michael Perkins documented the crash of the newly public Internet stocks in the second edition of their book, *The Internet Bubble*. At the peak of the bubble, on March 9, 2000, 378 newly public Internet companies had a combined market value of $1.5 trillion. "This number was truly amazing when you consider it was supported by a meager $40 billion in total annual sales, most of which were concentrated in the hands of a few companies such as Qwest, AOL, and Amazon.com," they wrote. "And most incredibly, 87 percent of those 378 companies had yet to even show a quarterly profit." By December of 2000, their value had plunged 75 percent.

But did manufacturers whose stocks were never in the bubble benefit after it popped? Based on their stock prices, the answer is barely, if at all, according to our analysis. We compared the performance of stocks in various industries from March of 2000, when the Nasdaq Composite peaked, to May of 2001 (Figure 16.1). We avoided using frequently cited price-to-earnings multiples, because earnings vary greatly with the state of the economy. Instead, we looked at the price-to-sales ratios. We found that three "bubble" stock fields—telecommunications equipment, networking equipment, and semiconductors—experienced massive declines in their once bloated price-to-sales ratios. Meanwhile, comparable ratios in a wide range of traditional industries rose only minimally. Among the six shown in the table, only the ratios for the pharmaceutical and packaged foods industries showed significant rises. Using another well-regarded measure of stock performance, the price-to-cash flow ratio, we found similar patterns.

FIGURE 16.1   Price-to-Sales Ratios During and After the Bubble

SECTOR	DURING MARCH 2000	AFTER MAY 2001	% NET CHANGE	MAY 2001 MARKET VALUE ($ BILLIONS)
Telecom Equipment	48.91	3.30	−93.3%	$357.9
Networking Equipment	91.01	5.53	−93.9	31.4
Semiconductors	35.21	4.92	−86.0	476.0
Steel	0.44	0.47	6.8	16.9
Auto Parts	0.78	0.66	−15.4	40.7
Auto	0.39	0.40	2.6	161.7
Defense & Aerospace	1.07	1.33	24.3	253.0
Pharmaceuticals	4.92	6.89	40.0	773.3
Industrial Machinery	0.90	0.99	10.0	73.1
Packaged Foods	1.04	1.43	37.5	94.7

SOURCE: Data supplied by Leuthold & Associates, June of 2001

It is worthy to note that, except for pharmaceuticals, the ratios for the three bubble stock fields remained far above the more traditional industries in price-to-sales ratios as of May 2001. Telecommunications equipment maker Qualcomm was still valued at $45 billion—almost three times the worth of the entire steel industry. Intel's $182 billion value topped that of the entire auto industry. Systems software maker Oracle's $85 billion capitalization exceeded that of all of the makers of industrial machinery.

These comparisons, of course, were much more pitched toward the tech stocks when the bubble was at its peak 14 months earlier. Even after the stock market declines of 2000 and 2001, several computer, Internet, and communications stocks continued to carry very high market capitalizations.

After 18 months of declining prices among communications, Internet, and computer-related stocks, there were considerable differences noted in the important stock valuation ratios such as price-to-sales and price-to-cash flow. Figure 16.2 shows that seven technology stocks had a combined market value of $328 billion—25 percent more than eight pillars of American industry—*long after the bubble popped*. This raises the question of whether the tech stock bubble represented a massive misallocation of resources.

FIGURE 16.2   Communications, Computer, and Traditional Manufacturing Stocks

COMPANY	ANNUALIZED REVENUE ($ MILLIONS)	ANNUALIZED EARNINGS ($ MILLIONS)	MARKET CAP. 11-19-01 ($BILLIONS)	PRICE-EARNINGS RATIO 11-19-01	PRICE-TO-SALES RATIO 11-19-01	PRICE-TO-CASH FLOW 11-19-01	EMPLOYEES
Communications, Internet, and Computer stocks							
Qualcomm	$2,570.0	$(777.2)	$47.5	N/A	17.12	−214.60	6,500
Yahoo Inc.	664.4	(96.4)	9.3	N/A	10.52	−128.80	3,259
Cisco Systems	17,792.0	(1,072.0)	151.9	N/A	7.25	117.80	38,000
Dell Computer	30,444.0	(404.0)	70.3	61.18	2.18	40.20	40,000
ADC Telecommunications	2,190.0	(232.0)	3.9	N/A	1.23	−4.60	22,450
Worldcom Inc.	13,936.0	132.0	43.4	13.22	1.15	5.80	71,200
Amazon.com	2,556.8	(679.2)	3.4	N/A	1.12	−4.30	9,000
Hewlett-Packard	43,504.0	388.0	41.9	67.34	0.92	67.10	88,500
Traditional Manufacturers							
Merck & Co.	$47,678.0	$7,792.4	$147.9	20.97	3.17	17.20	69,300
Du Pont de Nemours	22,564.0	568.0	46.3	70.54	1.78	18.50	93,000
Nucor Corp.	4,212.0	82.0	3.5	20.91	0.86	8.10	7,900
Caterpillar Inc.	20,224.0	820.0	17.2	19.16	0.82	8.30	68,440
Parker-Hannifin	5,903.6	242.0	4.8	16.76	0.78	9.40	46,300
Deere & Co.	14,198.0	287.2	9.8	29.90	0.73	9.90	43,700
Eaton Corporation	7,000.0	160.0	4.8	21.79	0.68	7.70	59,000
Boeing Co.	54,748.0	2,600.0	28.0	9.21	0.49	5.90	198,100

SOURCE: Thomson Financial Solutions, <http://thomsoninvest.netscape.com/>, November 19–20, 2001, and University of St. Thomas

THE COST OF THE NATIONAL CRAP SHOOT

David Tice, who heads an investment firm in Dallas, answered that question affirmatively at a congressional hearing called in mid-2001 to air testimony about securities analysts' conflicts of interest. Here's how Tice put it: "Do you wonder why our country does not have enough power plants and oil refineries, yet we have a reported 80 percent to 90 percent overcapacity in fiber optic cable? There is a consequence to keeping stock prices artificially high for extended periods while extending credit recklessly in the midst of a mania. The overpriced sectors sucked capital away from other vital areas of the economy. For years, refinery stocks sold at low multiples of earnings and book value, and received comparatively little coverage for companies of their size. It is not surprising that companies in this industry were unable to increase capacity."

> There is a consequence to keeping stock prices artificially high for extended periods while extending credit recklessly in the midst of a mania.

Tice cited research his firm's analysts had done to turn up nearly 1,000 U.S. companies that had fewer than three "buy" recommendations and, usually, sparse coverage from analysts. Each of these firms had more than $250 million in market capitalization. He identified 48 of the companies, many of them manufacturers, in his testimony.

The Internet bubble was not a new phenomenon. In an earlier age, railroad stocks, many of them fraudulent, were fashionable speculations. In his excellent history of the U.S. railroad industry, historian John Stover suggested that "most of the post–Civil War railroads suffered from the evils of inflated construction costs, fraudulent stock manipulations, and incompetent management." The railroads contributed mightily to the nation's development, but not all of them were investment winners.

Steel was the stock market darling following railroads, not only in the United States but elsewhere. Countries with even minimal industry seemed to lose face unless there was a prominent national steel company. In the United States, companies such as U.S. Steel reached prominence in the 1920s, partly due to the acquisitive activities of J.P. Morgan.

The stock values of these companies, and of the conglomerates of the 1960s, escalated for a while, and then plummeted before the companies themselves drifted into obscurity.

Good companies and exciting new technologies were present in each of these industries just as exciting new companies are emerging today. The question is, How long will the speculative bubble last?

In a landmark article from the *Journal of Political Economy* (1994), researchers Javonovich and MacDonald tracked the tire industry from 1900 to 1972. Tires are useful. The average U.S. family owns about 20 tires (cars, trailers, lawn mowers, etc.), so it would be hard to argue that it was not a growth industry at some time during its history. In their study, researchers followed the number of tires sold, tire company revenues, and share prices, along with the number of companies active in the industry. In 1922, there were 275 tire companies operating in the United States. The researchers' conclusion was interesting. Share prices turned out to be related not to the number of tires sold, industry revenue, or the selling prices of the tires sold; share prices were related to the number of companies entering and leaving the industry. Share prices rose steeply as more companies entered the industry, and then fell steeply as companies began to withdraw.

As David Tice infers, the principal concern with hyperinflated stock values is the opportunity cost. Maybe it is to our benefit to be in on the ground floor of exciting new industries, and clearly, there are opportunities. However, as we divert resources to adventures not well understood, we are losing our position in some of the best wealth-creating industries we have had in the past. In many critical industrial components such as switches, encoders, bearings, compressors, pumps, ships, motors, and generators, the United States is no longer the leader, and, in some cases, not even a major player. More recently, we have begun to see erosion in the high-value products made from these critical components such as airplanes, machine tools, instruments, diagnostic equipment, and even medical devices.

IS GOING PRIVATE THE ANSWER?

One option for publicly held companies unable to attract investors, of course, is to go private. Seagate, the world's largest disk drive producer, went private in 2001. A growing number of other manufacturers have done so in recent years, often working with buyout groups that have become more active. These investors are on the prowl for companies that have more value than the stock market has recognized. In many cases, the jury is still out on how well these deals will work out. Going private, however, is not easy. Just ask Vince Martin, chairman of Jason Inc., a diversified manufacturer based in Milwaukee. Martin, other senior managers at the company, and Saw Mill Capital, a New York–based buyout firm, took Jason private in 2000. The company had sales of $459 million in 2000, three times what they were a decade earlier. It employed 3,500 workers at 20 plants in the United States and another 15 abroad. Jason's earnings per share grew at an annual average of 17 percent from 1987 to 1999, a pace few companies could match. Yet, Wall Street was not impressed. The stock had slipped to little more than $7 a share, from $12 in the mid-1990s. The company had a market value of just $150 million. Only one analyst was covering Jason. Unproven dot-coms were going public with stunning valuations. Martin was frustrated, but he knew why investors cared little about his company.

They didn't understand Jason. About a third of its business was automotive, but the rest of it came from a number of different industries. Jason was viewed as "low tech" or, as Martin put it: "We had no buzz to us." Perhaps worst of all, Jason stock was not broadly traded. Martin and his principal partner, Mark Train, held about 40 percent of the stock. Other insiders and a handful of institutions owned much of the rest, and they tended to sit on the stock.

Yet, getting away from Wall Street was no easy matter. One potential trouble spot was that once the word got out, the stock could go into play. A hostile buyer might surface overnight. This didn't become a problem at Jason, because Martin and Train were large shareholders. Financing the deal was tough, though. Top company officials went on a road show to borrow money publicly, but their campaign fizzled. Instead, Jason got debt financing from the private market. Then the price of the deal ended up higher than Martin had expected, but lower than the company's outside directors thought it should have been. Martin and Train had to agree to sell their stock at a lower price, $10.90 a share, than the $11.25 that public shareholders got. "The tension in reaching that price was very high," says Martin.

All the travail was worth it, though. First, says Martin: "We don't have to deal with quarterly earnings reports and all the pressure that being public puts on short-term earnings." Second, when the company was public, directors and stockholders were extremely worried about its low stock price. That concern, says Martin, tended to drive the management into decisions that weren't in the best long-term interest of shareholders. Third, managers now have more time to spend with employees and customers. Finally, it's less expensive, because the company no longer needs to spend time producing the financial reports required of a publicly held concern.

Concludes Martin: "I certainly have a lot of friends in publicly held companies who are saying, 'Boy, would I like to do that.'"

For many companies, though, going private is not a practical alternative. It is disruptive, time-consuming, and fraught with potentially devastating conflicts of interest. Yet, the impact of low stock evaluations could bear heavily on our competitiveness in years ahead. Many of our most respected international competitors did gain their enviable positions solely because of expertise, which is widely distributed geographically and available to many companies. These large companies have succeeded, in part, because it was easy for them to raise money in their home markets. Toyota has excellent technical knowledge, but having the money to build brand new auto plants fully equipped with the most modern state-of-the-art equipment has been helpful as well. The United States had the money too, but we did not use it in the same way: We bought into Amazon.com at $100 per share.

The end of the Internet mania that virtually took the stock market hostage should provide us with an opportunity to consider more fundamental sources of national prosperity than mere speculation. If the collapse of the tech stocks injects at least a modest form of sanity into the stock market, it could signal an easing of the intense pressures for short-term speculative returns that led so many companies to make moves not in their best long-term interests. Also, the swift and stunning collapse of Enron late in 2001 could have a positive effect on the investment climate for manufacturing stocks over the longer haul. Growing investor concern over accounting abuses, which allowed Enron to hide its debt in off-the-books partnerships, now reaches far beyond Enron. Indeed, some investors have become so skeptical of accounting practices that they are avoiding the market altogether. Only a sweeping overhaul of securities regulations will win them back. Such a situation would seem tailor-made for solid, back-to-basics manufacturing companies that have avoided slick accounting moves all along. Wall Street has had a return to sanity, though we are not sure how long it will last, nor are we sure if the return is fully accomplished. Still, greater investor appreciation of solid companies with established earnings recipes should bode well for solid manufacturers, their employees and communities, and, ultimately, for their shareholders.

> *If the collapse of the tech stocks injects at least a modest form of sanity into the stock market, it could signal an easing of the intense pressures for short-term speculative returns that led so many companies to make moves not in their best long-term interests.*

CHAPTER 17

Driving Innovation: Manufacturing and Research

 The magic moment finally arrived, minutes after Joe De-Simone tossed his sports jacket into a dry cleaning machine as big as a hotel room and as heavy as four minivans. All summer long, a frustrated team of engineers had struggled for months to work the kinks out of this huge steel box, an environmentally friendly invention designed to revolutionize the dry cleaning industry. At first, they thought it would take weeks. Instead, the crew had been holed up for months at the Fairfield Inn in Midland, Michigan, nearly a thousand miles from their wives, families, and friends in North Carolina. The team had filled a van with secondhand clothes collected from the local Goodwill outlet, and fed them into the machine day after day. Time and again, the clothes had come out frozen, wrinkled, or fouled in some other way. Now, for the first time, DeSimone, chairman of Micell Technologies and chief executive visionary for the project, had flown up from his base of operations in North Carolina's Research Triangle region to see if the machine would work. Everyone was nervous. The future of Micell and its "Hangers" dry cleaning subsidiary was riding on this machine.

Micell represents one of the many scientific triumphs of the Research Triangle Park area. The company's machine, which uses a carbon dioxide–based fluid to clean clothes, is the linchpin for a fast-growing chain of "green" dry cleaning outlets. Micell has attracted more than $52 million in venture capital, much of it for Hangers, from global investor George Soros and Home Depot cofounder Ken Langone. The machine, dubbed Wilma, has ushered in a new process that DeSimone touts as the first significant technological change seen by the dry cleaning industry in half a century. Micell is applying the carbon dioxide (CO_2) research initiated by DeSimone and his colleagues. DeSimone, a chemistry professor, oversees the labors of these researchers—nearly

100 students, faculty members and corporate specialists working at four universities—from a third-floor nest of laboratories at University of North Carolina (UNC) in Chapel Hill.

"We're doing things you couldn't imagine doing with other solvents or water," he declares. "We're changing peoples' lives."

CONSTRUCTING RESEARCH TRIANGLE PARK

DeSimone's work benefits immensely from the talent, infrastructure, and innovation that have sprung up at, and spread out from, Research Triangle Park. The Park, dotted with richly landscaped corporate campuses, covers an area almost as large as the city of San Francisco. Driving through it on Interstate 40 is like heading across a national park, with signs telling motorists when they are "entering Research Triangle Park" and when they are exiting. This is not a scene that a passing observer would readily associate with factories and production. Thus, it may seem surprising that most of the Park's 40,000-plus employees work for manufacturers. Five large manufacturers—IBM, Nortel Networks, GlaxoSmithKline, Cisco Systems, and Ericsson—account for three-fourths of the Park's jobs. Research Triangle Park stands as a monument to one of the most important contributions of American manufacturers: innovation.

The scope of their commitment, relative to other sectors of the economy, is impressive. According to the National Science Foundation, manufacturers account for close to 75 percent of the private outlays for research and development in the United States. The *International Science Yearbook* estimates that just six U.S. manufacturers—Ford, Lucent Technologies, General Motors, IBM, DuPont, and Intel—spent $35.4 billion for research and development (R&D) in 2000. That's about as much as all nonmanufacturing companies in the United States spend on R&D. Globally, the publication predicted, five of the top ten R&D spenders in 2001 would be U.S.-based manufacturers. Figure 17.1 shows how the yearbook envisioned the rankings for 2001.

> *According to the National Science Foundation, manufacturers account for close to 75 percent of the private outlays for research and development in the United States.*

FIGURE 17.1   Research Spending by Corporations

WORLD RANK	COMPANY	COUNTRY	EST. R&D SPENDING, 2001 ($ BILLIONS)
1	DaimlerChrysler	Germany/United States	$7.26
2	Ford Motor	United States	7.23
3	Lucent Technologies	United States	6.43
4	General Motors	United States	6.33
5	Siemens	Germany	6.05
6	IBM	United States	4.84
7	DuPont	United States	4.58
8	Nortel Networks	Canada	4.51
9	Ericsson	Sweden	4.39
10	Toyota	Japan	4.37

SOURCE: The International Science Yearbook estimate, 2001

One lesson learned from poring over such lists is that Wall Street traders, media gurus, and shopping mall tenants are not in the vanguard of innovation. Manufacturers are. Nowhere is manufacturing-led innovation more concentrated than at research parks—most of all at Research Triangle Park. "Everybody's heard of the Triangle Park and what it's done for North Carolina," says Katie Burns, a publications editor for the Association of University-Related Research Parks, which represents 300 planned technology developments around the world. "I always try to warn them, 'You're not going to be able to duplicate what they did.'" The next largest of the U.S. parks—Cummings Research Park in Huntsville, Alabama, and the Stanford Research Park in Palo Alto, California—rank far below the Triangle Park both by physical size and by employment.

Raleigh-Durham was unable to escape the economic downturn that stormed across the country in 2001. Nortel closed all of its Triangle operations for a week. Lucent scrapped plans for a research center at North Carolina State's Centennial campus in Raleigh. Cisco, IBM, JDS/Cronos, Triangle Pharmaceuticals, and a long list of other employers in and around the Triangle Park laid off workers. Yet, the region still stands tall as one of the nation's leading enclaves of science and technology.

The Triangle Park was conceived in the mid-1950s, with the late Governor Luther Hodges taking the lead. Top officials from business, government, and academe recognized they had a precious asset: Raleigh-Durham was the smallest metropolitan area in the country with three large research universities—University of North Carolina at Chapel Hill, North Carolina State University at Raleigh, and Duke University at Durham. The physical locations of the three schools formed the triangle that gave the Park its identity. The project grew out of a concern, eventually proven correct, that North Carolina's then-ascendant "Big Three" industries—tobacco, furniture, and textiles—were headed for trouble and, thus, the state needed a more diverse economy.

The Park's founders have been successful in reversing the tendency of the state to lose its best and brightest up-and-comers to other parts of the country. Today, the Raleigh-Durham region keeps much of its most promising talent, and has become the land of opportunity for job hunters from far afield as well.

"We've stemmed the brain drain, and we've become a brain draw," declares Michael Luger, a public policy analyst at UNC. "The success of the Park stemmed from a realistic strategy, building on a manufacturing culture that was heavily embedded here."

Mike Walden, an economist at North Carolina State University, has tracked the shift. Walden notes that the old Big Three industries accounted for only 10 percent of the state's economy in 1996, down from 20 percent in 1977. He says the slide in these industries would have been devastating to North Carolina but for the fact that the state expanded in other fields, often higher-value manufacturing.

In 1999, Hammer Siler George Associates published a history of the Park and its role in influencing regional change. The consulting firm classified Triangle area jobs into two groups of industries—old-line manufacturing, such as tobacco, furniture, and textiles; and technology-related new-line manufacturing, including electronics, computers, and communications. They found that in 1956, only 15 percent of the jobs were in new-line industries. The region was barely ahead of the state, slightly behind the Southeast, and far behind the nation. Thus, despite the presence of three major research universities, the area lagged badly in creating the kinds of jobs that count for so much. By 1995, however, new-line jobs in the area had risen to 47 percent of the total, leapfrogging past the Southeast and the United States. (See Figure 17.2.)

FIGURE 17.2   The Metamorphosis of Raleigh-Durham's New-Line Industries*

	1956	1966	1977	1986	1995
Raleigh-Durham	14.9%	27.3%	35.6%	42.2%	46.9%
North Carolina	11.8	17.5	22.7	26.1	32.9
Southeast	16.9	22.3	27.2	30.3	36.9
United States	26.0	31.3	34.3	36.6	40.6

* New-line industries as a share of new-line and old-line industries

SOURCE: Hammer Siler George Associates, 1999

In the 1950s, a risk-averse, Tobacco Road culture prevailed in Raleigh-Durham. Many who have studied the region's history or grew up there in that era say a tradition of entrepreneurship was almost totally lacking. Portions of this ethos endured into the 1980s, with Luger noting that a "branch office mode" still prevailed.

Today, all of the five big manufacturers with operations located in the Park have their headquarters elsewhere. More of their Triangle workers do research or research-supporting work that eventually leads to products, rather than actually making the products. For the most part, these companies have prospered. IBM went through a massive worldwide downsizing from 1993 to 1995, but its Raleigh-Durham workforce survived almost unscathed. Dick Daugherty, the retired IBM executive who headed the company's North Carolina operations from 1982 to 1995, says that's because the Park had become the central location for IBM's growing personal computer and networking operations. Many of the company's other sites were saddled with more mature products and services less in demand. "We were lucky," says Daugherty. At the turn of the century, IBM had 14,000 people working in or near the Park, more than at any of the company's other sites. Fewer than 10 percent of them were in assembly jobs. Others worked in research, consulting, and marketing.

Cisco Systems arrived at the Park in 1995. By 2000, Cisco had 3,000 employees in the Park at nine buildings on its 313-acre campus, with three more buildings under construction. The company's fortunes suddenly soured early in 2001, forcing it to shelve its expansion plans. Still, major expansion at the Park remains in its long-term business plan.

IBM, Cisco, and Nortel, like many other high-tech producers, do not view themselves as pure manufacturers. Instead, they prefer to be known primarily as information technology companies. That makes it easy for the public to believe manufacturers don't have much of a presence in the Triangle Park or, for that matter, many other places. These companies' practices of farming out assembly work strengthen this perception. Consider Nortel. The company came to the Park in the early 1980s. Since then, its Triangle payroll has grown to about 8,000 workers, nearly one-third of them in manufacturing. The employees, however, concentrate on research, test equipment, and order fulfillment, and send out assembly work to contract manufacturers. In 2000, Nortel sold a telecommunications equipment plant in the Park to Solectron, the large, California-based contract manufacturer.

Nearby, at GlaxoSmithKline, Larry Miller arrived at work every day motivated by a singular passion: to discover a drug that can effectively treat osteoporosis. Finding a new drug can cost as much as $500 million and take up to 15 years. The odds of success are slim. Researchers choose a disease and study it intensely enough to target the point at which a drug could intervene to arrest or control the illness. Typically, they screen more than 500,000 potential compounds at the outset, seeking to find a few that provide the ideas to begin a chemistry program. On those rare occasions when they formulate a drug promising enough to reach clinical trials, typically after about a decade of work, they end up filing up to 80,000 pages of documentation with federal regulators. Only pharmaceutical giants such as Glaxo can afford such enormous risks.

Miller has grown accustomed to working in the research laboratories of large institutions, where broad networks of specialists and administrators can support towering achievements. Before joining Glaxo in 1991, he earned his doctorate in biochemistry from UCLA in 1987, and did postdoctoral research at the federal government's sprawling National Institutes of Health (NIH). Two of Glaxo's icons, Gertrude Elion and George Hitchings, won the Nobel Prize for medicine in 1988 for their work in developing AIDS-fighting drugs at the company's labs in the Triangle Park. Often, Elion would eat lunch alone in the company cafeteria. Employees, in awe of Elion, avoided her.

"The people here in R&D have decided they want to spend their lives finding medicines," says Miller. "I could have decided to take my

Ph.D. and become a professor at a university. In this way, I could have probably advanced science per se more. However, I could not have the potential direct impact on people's lives that I might have if drugs are developed here. I think most people in R&D share some form of this vision and have thus decided to spend their scientific careers in pharmaceuticals."

At the NIH, Miller figured out the structure of the protein that triggers allergy attacks. Several academic publications published his findings, which led to screening for new medicines to treat allergies. He started out at Glaxo, searching for medicine to treat rheumatoid arthritis. After a year and a half at the company, he was named to lead the search for an osteoporosis drug.

Osteoporosis is characterized by low bone mass and structural deterioration of bone tissue, leading to bone fragility and a heightened vulnerability to fractures primarily of the hip, spine, and wrist. More than 13 million Americans, mostly women, are afflicted with this disease. Another 15 million have low bone mass and, thus, are susceptible to osteoporosis. The World Health Organization has declared osteoporosis the second leading threat to health, after cardiovascular disease.

Miller likened his quest for an osteoporosis treatment to the tinkering mechanics do with cars. The trick, he said, is to formulate a drug, without adverse side effects, able to mimic the biological signals that form the bone, arresting the bone's degradation so it can resume its growth. Then, once again, the bone can handle stress much as the chassis of a car does.

Miller and his associates worked within a time line, which serves as a roadmap to their goal. The team hit prearranged benchmarks and milestones to survive in the rugged intracompany competition for the resources needed to pursue discovery.

The idea for the osteoporosis project came from Miller. He outlined the scientific rationale and the potential benefits of the effort, along with a proposed research plan, to a high-powered "Targets Committee" made up of 40 top managers from the company's entire research division. "I had to sell them on my idea," he said. "They gave me the green light." Miller started with a 4-member team. After six years, it had grown to 36 members tapping into the expertise of 20 different specialists from throughout the company—chemists, biologists, toxicologists, geneticists, automation scientists, and others.

Progress was uneven, and marked by joy, frustration, and intensity. Once, Miller's team discovered a gene present only in bone. "We were very happy," said Miller. "It was scientifically very exciting." Then the team quickly learned that the technology needed to make medicine from its discovery didn't exist. Other times, approaching deadlines raised the urgency to hit a certain benchmark or milestone. Miller sometimes worked night after night, and on weekends.

By early 2001, the team faced new uncertainties. Glaxo Wellcome merged into Smith-Kline-Beecham, which had its own osteoporosis research team working on a treatment for the disease. The merged company, GlaxoSmithKline, blended the work of the two teams into a single research effort at a research lab near Philadelphia. Miller moved up into a division-wide management role, but he remains excited about his work. "I came here to find new medicines," he said. "I wanted to be involved in treating disease. It's like a big detective story. Every time you discover something, you find ten new questions."

The ultimate prize of having responsibility for making tangible products, in this case new medicines, continues to motivate him. "After the merger," he said, "there will certainly be changes that will affect us all. However, we are still here to find new medicines. Someday, if I get one bottle of pills out there, that would do it."

In the 1990s, entrepreneurism—spurred in part by the 1995 merger of Burroughs Wellcome into Glaxo—turned the Triangle Park's branch plant reputation on its head. Talented managers and researchers left the merged pharmaceutical giant to pursue new careers with startups. Many of the new entrepreneurs were in software and biotech fields, but some launched manufacturing companies.

Triangle Pharmaceuticals was among 15 companies started by former Glaxo managers and scientists. David Barry, who had led research and development for Glaxo, took nearly half a million dollars from his personal savings to found this startup. The company, which promptly went public, seeks to formulate medicines that can treat viral diseases.

Cronos Integrated Microsystems, based in the Park, grew out of a state-backed technology consortium early in 1999. The company makes microelectromechanical systems, or MEMS—tiny switches on a semiconductor chip.

Ziptronix was born late in 2000 at the nonprofit Research Triangle Institute (RTI), one of the country's largest independent research centers. Its creation reflects a strategic shift at the institute, long heavily dependent on government contracts. Victoria Franchetti Haynes, RTI's new president, has been encouraging the institute's specialists to commercialize their research, which could direct significant new revenues to RTI from licensing and from sale of equity stakes in the spinoffs. Ziptronix, a semiconductor integration firm, was only the second spinoff from the institute in 41 years. The company's technology enables manufacturers to bond silicon wafers together, combining many chips into one that is smaller and more efficient.

Recognizing the potential of such companies, venture capitalists began pouring money into the Raleigh-Durham area—$126 million in 1997, $252 million in 1998, $577 million in 1999—according to the PricewaterhouseCoopers Money Tree Survey. Late in 2000, the Council for Entrepreneurial Development, based in the Triangle Park, formed an "emerging technology industrial roundtable" to support start-ups that make a product or have developed processes used in manufacturing.

The entrepreneurism spawned in the Park and at the three universities has spilled out to satellite office and industrial centers beyond the Park's borders. William Little, a retired chemistry professor at UNC, has become the unofficial scorekeeper in charting this activity. He estimates that the Park has helped to spawn 50 smaller parks nearby, with office space approaching twice that within the Park. He argues that many of these projects wouldn't exist but for the park.

The rapid-fire chain of events at Cronos offers a glimpse into the heady pace at some of the region's high-tech manufacturing startups. When the technology consortium sent this company off on its own, it had 30 employees. Among them was Karen Markus, dubbed by her colleagues as "the queen mother of MEMS." A few months before the spin-off, *Science* magazine published an article describing MEMS as a step toward "a new sub-Lilliputian species that not only can think like Pentium chips but also can sense the world and act upon it." The magazine cited estimates that 10,000 scientists and engineers at 600 university, government, and private laboratories around the world were working on MEMS devices. Markus described these tiny systems as a throwback to last century's machine age, when you could see how something worked simply by looking at it. When you examine MEMS under a microscope, "you can see motors driving shafts, turning gears that turn other gears, push plungers, and so on," Markus told the publication. "MEMS are enablers. They'll be all over, like plastic. They're viral. They will infiltrate everything."

That kind of attention won believers. Late in 1999, Cronos attracted venture capital from Intel and other investors. The company was on track to go public but a few months later, just as it was about to seek more venture money, JDS Uniphase turned up as a potential buyer. JDS, on the prowl for acquisitions and then armed with a towering stock price (which later fell by more than two-thirds after the tech bubble popped), bought Cronos for $750 million. The price was the highest ever paid for an emerging high-tech company in the state. The deal stirred controversy, because the technology consortium, which owned nearly a third of Cronos, had received $280 million in state funds over the previous 20 years. Legislators, saying a return on their investment was long overdue, demanded that the state get a hefty cut of the windfall. Meanwhile, JDS moved quickly to expand, taking over a large site that had been vacated by Motorola and hiring rapidly. Markus became chief technology officer at the company, renamed Cronos/JDS.

Other small manufacturers nearby offer sharp contrasts to the Cronos experience. Troxler Electronic Laboratories, a family firm founded in 1958, was for many years the only homegrown company in the Triangle Park. Unlike Cronos, Troxler has never had any intention of going public or selling out. The company makes measuring devices, using radioactive isotopes and other technologies. It does almost everything for itself, instead of contracting out work as so many other high-tech companies do. William Troxler Jr., president, says the firm's best-selling product today has been its top seller for more than 35 years. The product, a portable measuring device well known to engineers as "The Troxler," is used the world over to test the moisture content of soil. Troxler is modestly expanding its facilities in the Park, but its workforce remains at just 150 employees.

A few miles beyond the Park, research initiated in the mid-1980s has put Shelia Dunigan on a promising career path at 3Tex, a high-tech textile industry start-up, after years of a hardscrabble life. Dunigan began working a minimum wage job in a sewing plant in 1980, when she was 20 years old. Two years later, she moved on to the Spanco textile mill in Sanford, North Carolina, where she inched up to $7.70 an hour before being laid off in 1992. Using dislocated worker benefits, she went back to school, earning a two-year degree in industrial plant maintenance from Central Carolina Community College in Sanford. Then, she took a job at another textile producer, the Polymer Group. There, her hourly pay climbed to $16.56 from $7.25, but not much else was good about that job. Dunigan, a single mom raising three daughters, was working weeknights and weekends, sometimes for 11 days in a row. She couldn't go to conferences with her daughters' teachers without having the time count as an absence, raising the risk she could be fired. She had to drive 100 miles in her bedraggled 1986 Chevy Cavalier every workday, to get to the mill and back home. "I've always owned pieces of cars that you had to hold together by rubber bands," she quips.

Dunigan had built up a solid résumé, so she went shopping for a better job. She could drive a forklift truck, and was familiar with how textile machines got built. She had sewing and weaving experience, and had done stints in handling and shipping departments. She knew how to weld, and she could train other workers how to run weaving machines. "I like training," says Dunigan. "I've got three children, and I'm the oldest of five. I probably baby-sat for 100 different kids." 3Tex hired her in May of 1999 and, by early 2001, she was making $19.05 an hour in an 8-to-5 job with far better benefits than Spanco had offered. Her new employer is picking up the tab for her to get another two-year degree in electronics engineering at Wake Technical Community College. Her job is a 20-minute drive from home.

Shelia Dunigan quickly became, as she puts it, "a Jacqueline of all trades" at 3Tex. When an engineer drew a design, she would turn the design into a piece of equipment. When a machine stopped working, she would fix it. About a year after she joined 3Tex, she was assigned to a special project—development of "circular weaving." Workers can use this process to weave tubular or conical structures. The company has patents on this technology and is building a prototype machine to help commercialize the process. Later, 3Tex sent her to Rutherford County to train machine operators. Soon after she arrived at the company, she gave away her Cavalier—it had clocked enough miles to go around the world eight times—and bought a 1996 Jeep Cherokee with 35,000 miles on it.

3Tex took root in 1987, when North Carolina State's Mohamed Mansour became convinced that if only he could weave fibers in three dimensions rather than two, he could create "preforms" that, when reinforced with resin, would produce strong, lightweight materials—composites. Then the composites, stronger than steel, lighter than aluminum, and less costly than these and other materials, could be used to make a striking variety of products—bulletproof vests, engine parts, prosthetic joints, missile nose cones, bridge decking—for many industries. Mansour pursued the idea off and on for nearly a decade, even as he headed North Carolina State's Textile Engineering Department. Often, this was a frustrating experience. Finally, he incorporated the company, retired from the school, and recruited former Dow Chemical executive Brad Lienhart to run the firm. The University retained patent rights to the technology, licensing it to 3Tex in exchange for a stake in the company.

TEFLON AND GREEN CLEAN

Back at the UNC's Chapel Hill campus, Joe DeSimone holds forth at the blackboard, racing through an explanation of his ever-broadening effort to find commercial applications for CO_2. At 36, DeSimone has become a legendary figure in the Triangle Park—a rare combination of prodigious researcher, energetic marketer, and persistent entrepreneur. He reeled in $18 million from the National Science Foundation (NSF) for a prestigious NSF center that he and his colleagues created to pursue CO_2 research. He found a new way to make Teflon, helping to convince DuPont to build a $270 million plant in eastern North Carolina. DeSimone became the first holder of an endowed chair shared by UNC and North Carolina State. He received the Presidential Green Chemistry Challenge Award for discovering a carbon dioxide compound.

Jim McClain and Tim Romack, cofounders at Micell, were graduate students in DeSimone's group when his CO_2 research was in its early stages. "One of the things that was probably the toughest was making the leap from academic proof of the concept to the real world, where people would buy it," says Romack. "A lot of people didn't believe Joe." In 1995, however, the three men had persuaded investors of the value of their process, which combines liquid CO_2 with agents known as surfactants to clean clothes. They formed Micell to commercialize their idea. McClain, Romack, and other former students of DeSimone hail him. "I used to have a fear of speaking in front of people," says

Terri Carson, a researcher for Dow Chemical in Texas who studied under DeSimone for four years. Her anxiety vanished, she says, after she learned how to give presentations to his research groups.

So far, Micell's Hangers unit, with 60 dry cleaning stores in eight states, represents the most visible application to come out of De-Simone's growing CO_2 research empire. The chain arose only after DeSimone's troops created Wilma during their grueling encampment in Midland, Michigan. This cube-shaped machine—11 feet on a side, built with 10-inch squares of structural steel and weighing 10 tons—houses chambers that can clean up to 70 pounds of clothes at a time. It uses a new carbon dioxide compound that replaces environmentally damaging solvents such as perchloroethylene, or "perc," still employed by most of the nation's 35,000 dry cleaning outlets.

Breathing life into Wilma wasn't easy. "All the stuff we didn't know and didn't think about reared its ugly head," recalls McClain, a member of the team sent to Michigan. "Pipes needed to be redone. Things got in the way of each other." Every morning, the team members, all avowed "nonmorning people," would begin their day with breakfast at 7 AM. "We had an agreement that we wouldn't speak to one another until after breakfast, because we'd be talking to each other all day." Their workdays typically lasted at least 12 hours, running from 7:30 in the morning to 8 at night, sometimes even longer. Mike Cole, a process engineer, worked eight weeks in a row with only two days off. The project looked shaky from day one, early in February. "We had a very depressing day," says McClain. "We took the design we had on paper, balled it up, and threw it in the trash." Team members thought they could build the machines for about $100,000 apiece, but the cost turned out to be more than $300,000. Says McClain, "The question of the day was starting to become, 'Is it going to work?' not when." As fall approached, members of the Midland team, resigned to being stuck there for months, were giving away their coveted tickets to the games of the UNC's men's basketball team. "It was blood, sweat, and tears from about March until October," says McClain. "We stopped shaving. We looked like mountain men." By late September, the tension had finally eased. "We were playing whiffleball in the parking lot. We were starting to have fun."

Two months later, after more debugging, workers shrink-wrapped the machine and sealed it onto a flatbed truck headed for its first customer, Williams Cleaners in Wilmington, North Carolina. McClain, Micell's vice president of technology development, followed the truck for the first ten miles of its journey. A second machine, a prototype called Snafu, went separately to Micell's shop in Raleigh, where engineers could tinker with it. Then, in February of 1999, Ted Williams Sr. flung open the doors to the first of the Hangers stores. Congressman David Price was there. So was Mayor Hamilton Hicks, who marked the occasion by declaring it "Clean Water Day."

Months earlier, DeSimone's sports jacket had emerged perfectly clean, and in impeccable condition, eight minutes after he had flung it into Wilma. Hangers, conceived in the fertile manufacturing climate of the Research Triangle, was off to the races.

Nurturing the hothouses that give rise to ventures as promising as Hangers calls for an elusive blend of intelligence, passion, resilience, creativity, and practicality. Andrew Van de Ven, a respected Professor of Management at the University of Minnesota who has studied innovation for years, describes the process as an unpredictable and delicate balancing act. Van de Ven says managers must give their researchers the opportunity to break away from existing ways of doing things (divergence). At the same time, he stresses that managers must find ways to channel their innovators' talents into marketable products (convergence).

That is precisely what has been happening in the Research Triangle region. Here, producers are reinventing themselves and their varied industries, enabling the region to prosper by emphasizing a core strength of manufacturing: research that leads to the creation of good jobs, income, and wealth.

CHAPTER 18

Partnerships
That Work

 In heavily Protestant Jackson, Tennessee, Sister Immaculata is happy. Her Catholic school has doubled in enrollment over the past few years, and is on the verge of another expansion. According to Father Parham, the pastor of St. Mary's, the reason is simple: "Industry keeps moving here and they bring in Catholics."

Jackson and the rest of Madison County have attracted manufacturers from traditional industrial centers such as Cincinnati, Pittsburgh, and upstate New York in recent times. Yet, much of the growth is internal. Companies have moved to the area, liked it, and then expanded. Madison County is a Gradual Grower—consistent, forward-leaning, and home to the leading production facilities of some very fine companies.

Porter-Cable, which makes high-grade power tools, illustrates these marks of distinction. Different owners have made its tools over the years, at different locations, but Jackson is now the company's only production site. Porter-Cable, now part of Pentair Corp., employs 1,222 employees at 1.2 million square feet of manufacturing and distribution space in Jackson.

Pentair has worked closely with the community in Jackson, a city whose partnerships point up one of the bright spots for American manufacturing. Alliances have taken many shapes in U.S. manufacturing. In many parts of the country, organized labor and management, so often in pitched battles with one another, have in fact worked closely to train employees through joint programs. So have industries and educational institutions, particularly community colleges.

One of the most extensive of these alliances is the Manufacturing Extension Partnership. This loosely knit web of more than 400 independent centers, organized into a national network in 1989, helps small manufacturers become more productive through the application of new technologies and best management practices. Sometimes these businesses must scramble to find the resources they need to remain competitive. Larger manufacturers often take such resources for granted. Many of the partnership's centers were established in the 1980s, after concerns intensified about strong competitive challenges from manufacturers in Japan, Germany, and other lands. It can be argued that the manufacturing extension network was long overdue, considering that the nation has had a widespread extension system providing many services to the agricultural sector since the 19th Century.

In Jackson, Russell Toone acts as a one-man ambassador to manufacturing, covering a 23-county region of western Tennessee. He works for the state's Manufacturing Extension Partnership and the University of Tennessee's Center for Industrial Services, and shares an office with the state's agricultural extension service. Since he joined the center in 1996, Toone has logged thousands of miles driving to and from the 200 or so companies, almost all with fewer than 500 workers, that are on his calling list. He spends much of his time on the factory floor, working with companies to figure out creative ways to improve the competitiveness of Tennessee manufacturing.

Toone helped Reitter & Schefenacker (R&S) improve its performance at the company's plant in Selmer, Tennessee. R&S, which makes parts for General Motors' Saturn unit, had invested in new robotics equipment for its first Saturn line. Yet, its managers hadn't trained anyone to use the equipment. "At the time," Toone recalls, "they didn't even have a training coordinator." Toone turned to the McWherter Center of Advanced Industrial Technologies at Jackson State Community College. There, he found ready assistance from Richard Skelton, a one-time engineer for Ford and Johnson Controls who heads the school's department of electromechanical engineering. R&S and Skelton cut a deal that sent Skelton to Ohio to learn how to run programmable logic controllers, then called for him to set up training for employees at the plant. It turned out that R&S didn't have adequate training space. Toone discovered the necessary space right around the corner from R&S, at Spectrum Acquisitions. Spectrum's workers, too, needed to learn how to run the controllers. So, in the fall of 1998, the two companies agreed to share the cost of training—two nights a week for six weeks—for workers from both firms.

These and other creative initiatives seem to typify Madison County's approach to industrial development: practical help, coupled with effective coordination of municipal affairs, rather than massive subsidies.

Porter-Cable's success reflects the hospitable environment for doing business in Jackson. The company started out in 1906, in Syracuse, New York, manufacturing portable electric tools, then grew as the demand for its tools rose. In 1960, Rockwell International acquired the company. Five years later, Rockwell built a plant in Jackson. By 1979, it had consolidated all of Porter-Cable's manufacturing into its Tennessee facilities. Then, Rockwell lost interest in what had become a highly competitive market for portable tools and, in 1981, sold the operation to Pentair.

"It was tough to get any money out of Rockwell," recalls Gary Gateley, Porter-Cable's vice president of operations, who started during the Rockwell years. "Both companies listened to what we needed but the Pentair people delivered." Pentair has expanded its Jackson factory several times.

The portable power-tool market is highly competitive. Cheaper foreign tools are pouring in from Taiwan, Mexico, and China. Reputable quality products continue to arrive from Germany (Bosch) and Japan (Makita). Several U.S. producers (Black & Decker/DeWalt, Skil, Milwaukee) remain active with good products. To stay in the game and grow, Porter-Cable had to invest heavily in facilities, equipment, and people. Its capital expenditures average about $13,000 per employee, roughly twice the average for U.S. manufacturing. Training is thorough, widespread, and continuous. While annual sales per employee grew by 69 percent from 1993 to 1998, defects plummeted, costs fell, and on-time deliveries approached 100 percent. These attributes of high-quality, low-cost, and dependable performance enabled Porter-Cable to earn, for four years in a row, the coveted "Supplier of the Year" award from Home Depot. No other company has won this award more than twice. In 1999, *Industry Week* magazine named Porter-Cable's Jackson factory as one of its "Ten Best Plants."

Yet, even the attainment of customer appreciation in a competitive industry is not at the top of Porter-Cable's list of objectives. The top goal is employee safety, an area where company performance is roughly four times better than the average for the industry. Employees, organized into teams, work closely with managers. The workers run their teams as if they were their own businesses. They have the power to hire and fire, conduct training, and make other key decisions. Management oversees an incentive system and provides the resources workers need to meet goals on safety, quality, cost, delivery, and inventory.

Beyond Pentair, a drive through Madison County shows how fervently the region has embraced manufacturing and nurtured the skills to compete internationally. Signs along the roads read like pages from the *Thomas Register of American Manufacturing:* Maytag, Procter & Gamble, Murray, Delta Faucet, Pillsbury, Bruce Hardwood Floors, Kaiser Aluminum, Intermet Corp., Van de Kamps Foods, AEMP, International Paper, Sonoco, AmeriSteel, and Purodenso, which is a joint venture of Purolator and Denso of Japan. Oil filters stamped with the Pennzoil, Motorcraft, Quaker State, Toyota, or Purolator name may seem different, but all are likely to be made at Purodenso's factory in Jackson. So are air filters, housings, and fuel filter systems made for a variety of U.S. and Japanese vehicles. Most of the plants are relatively new and have international ties. In 1998, Jackson's 44 percent growth in exports was the 13th fastest for any area in the country.

Clearly, something special has been happening in Madison County. From 1977 to 1988, manufacturing employment in the county grew by only 6 percent, to just over 8,800 jobs. From 1988 to 1997, however, it shot up 43 percent to almost 12,600. Specifically, the 3,772 jobs gained in this county over the latter stretch accounted for 25 percent of the total statewide growth of 15,017 jobs. This, despite the fact that Jackson County claimed only 2.5 percent of all of the state's manufacturing jobs in 1997. Since 1997, manufacturers have continued to announce relocations and expansions in Jackson. Heating supplier Hart & Cooley unveiled a 275-employee expansion in 1999. Later that year, diecaster Tool Products, now a division of Intermet, announced a $20 million expansion.

Jackson's biggest industrial workforce is at Procter & Gamble's (P&G) Pringles factory, which employs 1,400 workers. The plant ships about a third of its production abroad, to 53 countries in Asia, Europe, North America, and Latin America. "It's P&G's largest plant in export volume," says Randy Kennedy, public affairs manager. It takes a lot of heat, electricity, and water to make Pringles. These services are available reliably and at reasonable cost in Jackson.

The presence of healthy manufacturing has strengthened the quality of life in Jackson, which claims an unusually large collection of community assets for a city with a population of little more than 50,000. Jackson sports a symphony orchestra, a ballet company, a spacious auditorium and convention hall, and a 6,000-seat stadium—Pringles Park—partially funded by P&G. Industry supports and interacts with the programs of the five four-year colleges and the McWherter Center. Jackson saw a 69 percent increase in per capita income from 1990 to 1998 and ranked in the top 50 of *Industry Week's* "World Class Communities" in both 1997 and 1998.

Two partnerships work particularly well to strengthen manufacturing in Madison County. The State of Tennessee plays an aggressive role in employee training, far beyond instances such as the help that Toone gave to R&S and Spectrum. Tennessee provides training equipment, facilities, and full-time staff support, and matches manufacturers' training needs with the technical capabilities of the McWherter Center. Jeff Thomas, human resources manager for Delta Faucet, says that after the company opened a plant in Jackson in 1995, two full-time training specialists from the state helped Delta for three years.

Other companies readily endorse Tennessee's approach to employee training. They hail the state for helpful stances on other issues—reasonable environmental regulations, efficient permit procedures, and well-coordinated utility services—that frequently impede industrial expansion elsewhere.

Jackson's second important partnership is with its utility. While industry in much of the rest of the nation grapples with the uncertainties of utility deregulation, environmental activism, and the cost of energy, Madison County has streamlined its approach. All utility services have been consolidated into a single, municipally owned utility, the Jackson Utility Division, which sells electricity, natural gas, propane, water, and sewer in one package. The utility works closely with the Jackson Area Chamber of Commerce to cut through the myriad of permits, environmental rules, and other issues that can slow a new plant.

Jackson Utility buys its electricity from the Tennessee Valley Authority (TVA). Established by Congress in 1933 to provide flood control, navigation, electricity, and development in the Tennessee River

Valley, TVA is the nation's largest public utility system. Only 6 percent of TVA's generating capacity comes from its 29 hydroelectric plants, 31 percent comes from 3 nuclear plants, and the remainder from 11 fossil fuel plants. This mix has allowed TVA to hold down its rates while providing reliable power. Average revenue per kilowatt hour barely rose in the 1990s, only increasing to 4.18 cents in 2000, from 4.15 cents in 1990.

Jackson Utility relies heavily on the expertise, generating capability, and dependability of the TVA. Commercial electrical rates are never easy to describe, given complex demand, energy, and facility charges, but Jackson Utility's incremental cost of one more kilowatt hour usually runs under three cents for larger customers—an advantage promoted by economic developers trying to attract industry. Manufacturers expanding in the Jackson area have benefited from reasonably priced, reliable power. That is particularly meaningful in Jackson, home to energy-intensive customers such as P&G, Intermet, AmeriSteel, and Kaiser Aluminum.

Jackson is not at the top of the list in everything. The city's daily newspaper, the *Jackson Sun*, often runs stories chronicling the need for better schools—a concern often echoed in other communities. Workers are uneasy about the constant shuffling of ownership and products at the region's larger employers. Purodenso is controlled by the Japanese, Hart & Cooley by the British, and AmeriSteel by the Brazilians. Chinese-owned Murray, which, in 2000, had expanded to 1,000 employees from 750 at Jackson, closed its plant there in mid-2001. Alcoa would have shut down its Alumax plant in Jackson but for an eleventh hour leveraged buyout by management and employees. Porter-Cable and Delta contract out some of their production to manufacturers in Asia, but so do many U.S. producers.

> *The region's formula for industrial progress is not complex: dependable services delivered at reasonable cost, energetic employees, sympathetic governments, and a favorable reputation among some very good companies. A single, commonsense theme courses through this mix: Practical, well-coordinated services at reasonable cost and people working together make manufacturing work.*

For generations, Jim Bregi and his family have run Doppler Gear, a Minneapolis supplier of key gear components for small machinery, and Murray, Inc. of Jackson, Tennessee, has been a customer. After the Chinese company purchased Murray and then closed a relatively new plant, Bregi worried that many of the components that Doppler and other U.S. manufacturers produce would soon be supplied from within China. This is what happened with several U.S. manufacturing operations acquired by another Chinese company, Foxcon.

A few weeks after Murray closed its Jackson factory, the city went back on the expansion trail as Johnson Controls and a unit of Toyota announced a joint venture to make auto parts. The project means another 150 jobs by 2002 for Jackson, and possibly more later. The region's formula for industrial progress is not complex: dependable services delivered at reasonable cost, energetic employees, sympathetic governments, and a favorable reputation among some very good companies. A single, commonsense theme courses through this mix: Practical, well-coordinated services at reasonable cost and people working together make manufacturing work.

CHAPTER 19

Raising the Odds for a Better Tomorrow

American manufacturing is rich with material for both optimists and pessimists. If you want good news, you can find it. If you're looking for bad news, there's plenty of that, too. In scores of interviews and reams of reports and data, we found reason for reassurance as well as concern. The country's manufacturing sector has been imperiled in so many ways, in so many places. Yet, it has also developed almost stealthily in some locales, and occasionally in industries where more established companies have failed. Given the stresses and strains pounding in on so many manufacturers, it is in many ways remarkable how resilient so many of them have been. Yet, to keep going, they need more people to understand the importance of what they do. We don't think the country's elites should dial up big-picture policy changes to preserve and strengthen this crucial part of the economy. Instead, it's up to countless individuals in many locales to turn many small knobs.

There is much to cheer. In a part of the American economy that has been dismissed by so many as a fading old economy niche, provocative and creative thinking abounds:

- In North Carolina, Shelia Dunigan has moved up to a better life. She works for 3Tex, a promising high-technology startup. The company benefits from her commitment and competence at everything from fixing machines to training new workers.
- At Red Wing Shoe in Minnesota, Jim Nash cut shoe leather for 46 years—same job, same shift—before retiring. He did well enough to send his two sons to college.
- In Philadelphia, Ed Hook left his job as a short-order cook in 1965. Ever since, he's been running machines at Messinger Bearings. Hook has made a good living, enough to raise five children.

Millions of Americans work for manufacturers, making an amazing array of products. While endless experts hailed the wonders of the Internet, the "synergism" of mergers, and the marvels of knowledge workers in sectors other than manufacturing, the employees of American industry just kept on working.

SUDDEN CHANGES CAN JOLT COUNTIES

Sometimes, employees get jolted out of their jobs. Our examination of U.S. manufacturing illustrates how quickly things can change, right down to the county level, particularly when volatile international conditions come into play. In north central Wisconsin, Price County has been a stronghold of manufacturing. Then the Asian economic crisis slammed into Marquip, a big producer there. Scores of skilled workers, who had been making the machines used to produce cardboard boxes, lost their jobs. Other producers in the county's paper industry faced cutbacks. Price County's unemployment rate went from being one of the lowest in the state to one of the highest.

Changes in employment levels at Boeing still matter most in the Seattle area, despite all of the ink spilled on Microsoft, Amazon.com, and other software or Internet-related companies there. Boeing's commercial aircraft division employed 60,000 workers in the area in the fall of 2001. The company's payroll there remains one of the largest for an industrial employer in any urban area of the world. Its sprawling plant in Everett, just north of Seattle, stands as a symbol of American technological achievement. Workers turn out 747, 767, and 777 jetliners in an 11-story structure covering the equivalent of 89 football fields—the world's largest building by volume. Yet, for all of the advantages it bestows on the Seattle area, Boeing operates in a highly cyclical industry. Just as residents cheer when the company's business is good, their hearts sink when things turn down. In the deep downturn of 1969–1970, Boeing laid off 5,000 workers in the Puget Sound area in one week; in October of 2001, with sales shrinking rapidly, the company laid off 5,000 Seattle area workers in one day.

In Kansas's Sedgwick County, Wichita's dominant aircraft industry drove a boom for years. In mid-summer of 2001, Boeing, Cessna Aircraft, Raytheon, Bombardier Aerospace, and several other aircraft-related producers accounted for 60,000 of the area's 74,000 manufacturing jobs. The unemployment rate was still only 3.5 percent. When commercial airline orders began plunging, the region's manufacturers were forced to turn to layoffs. The mood changed almost overnight.

Our geographic database also shows dramatic differences in the strength and direction of manufacturing in counties next door to one another. This is most evident in larger metropolitan areas. As we noted in Part Two, suburban areas often do well and central cities poorly. The pattern of such contrasts is also apparent in many other locales. In Indiana, for example, factory troubles have hurt economic growth in South Bend and St. Joseph County for decades, while manufacturing successes made neighboring Elkhart County a star of the state's economy. Now, with increasing competition from RV manufacturers in other regions and difficulties at one of Elkhart's major employers, that may change.

In the big cities of the Northeast and Midwest, steep industrial declines led to weaker economies. Competition from abroad, changing technology, and other factors may have made much of this decline inevitable, but there is no denying the effect of losses. At many companies, the strains are apparent. Sometimes they lead managements to put heavy pressure on their workers, raising tensions in the workplace.

Stark differences within states suggest that state policies to pump aid of one form or another to lagging manufacturers might not help much. Mostly, what counts is the quality of the companies, the strength of their competition, and the condition of their industries. Other versions of these contrasts turn up within the same industries, in the same states. In economically troubled northwestern Indiana, integrated steelmakers have been losing jobs for years. In more vibrant northeastern Indiana, new minimills have strengthened the economy.

The problems that plague such regions often are reflected in the nation's trade deficit, a key barometer of manufacturing performance that has reached record levels in recent years. Part of the reason for the deficit is the loss of great companies that were once world leaders, employing thousands of well-paid workers in technologically sophisticated jobs. Less attention has been given to the losses of suppliers and skills that have accompanied or, in some cases, foretold declines in industries such as computing and optics. Some of the forces at work here are beyond America's control. The development of strong support networks for manufacturing in Singapore, Shanghai, and other cities is not to be disdained. Their citizens cannot be blamed for seeking the keys to material wealth. Growing commitments to education are strengthening manufacturing in these regions. But Americans need to be more aware of the gains being made in these lands, and the fragility of their own industrial-driven prosperity as a consequence.

A WARNING ON COMPETITIVENESS

The United States, by some measures, is slipping in education. In 1999, the Council on Competitiveness, an alliance of leaders from business, organized labor, and academe, concluded that the United States had regained its position as the world's leader in innovation per capita in 1995. Then, however, the council's 94-page report said this: "Despite eight consecutive years of economic expansion, the United States could lose its status as the world's preeminent innovator nation in the next decade if current national policy and investment choices continue unchanged. At a time when U.S. competitiveness is the envy of the world, it may seem like an alarmist message, yet, the moment of greatest apparent success can be a nation's moment of greatest vulnerability. A concerted effort is needed now to renew the foundation for long-term U.S. competitiveness and prosperity."

Some of the problems cited by the council include falling or flat spending on basic research; a declining number of college degrees being awarded in the physical sciences and engineering; foreign nationals who return to their native lands after earning advanced engineering and science degrees at U.S. schools; weak scores on high school math and science tests; and falling investment in high school and college education. The report predicted that if current trends continue, the country will slip to sixth place in its innovation ranking by 2005.

A concerted effort is needed now to renew the foundation for long-term U.S. competitiveness and prosperity.

Part of the problem has been a get-rich-now culture that all but took over the stock market and spurred a long run of mergers. The merger wave eased considerably when the market turned bearish. Critics say it was driven as much by big fees on Wall Street and investors' desires for large capital gains as by good fits that promised better performance. First and foremost, the markets should act as capital-raising mechanisms for sound, steady economic growth. That function seemed to recede in the late-1990s, as the imperatives for quarterly earnings gains or presence in Internet-related sectors prevailed.

We found shortcomings of leadership. In certain cases, managements and shareholders failed to invest in equipment and innovation. Sometimes, top executives became too focused on lucrative pay and benefits. In a few instances, they joined forces with the media, using magazine covers and TV interviews to stress their own importance above that of their companies.

It became clear to us that in many quarters, manufacturing has fallen out of fashion. NIMBY-like opposition has curbed expansion of factories, power plants, and other industrially-related projects. Engineering and related curriculums have fallen out of favor on college campuses, and as a result, fewer graduates are heading for the manufacturing sector. This has compounded a generational issue for manufacturing—aging management. A sense that manufacturing is declining has raised recruiting concerns at many companies.

MANY BRIGHT SPOTS

We found much evidence of innovation. Often, companies are applying existing technologies in creative ways, rather than bringing on entirely new technologies. The innovation process is inherently unpredictable; there is no assurance that anything will come of research endeavors. Sometimes, researchers turn up results more useful than what was intended. For example, 3M's failed experiments in making toner for copiers led to the discovery of Thinsulate, advanced filtration materials, and the highly absorbent material that mops up oil spills. Size, money, education, and reputation are not an automatic ticket to creative success. The same company that assigned 15,000 people to develop one of the market's most memorable flops, the Edsel, put just 220 to work on a notable success of that era, the Lincoln Continental. Success or failure, most of the privately funded research outlays continue to be made by manufacturers, rather than by companies in other parts of the economy.

Consider the partnerships. We found customized training programs growing in state after state as community colleges and manufacturers forged closer ties. Organized labor and management have embarked on many cooperative efforts as they have gained each others' respect. A new system of outreach programs, similar to the agricultural extension programs that universities have run for many decades, grew up in the 1990s to give technical and management advice to smaller and midsized producers. Increasingly, these efforts are drawing dedicated people who are deeply committed to the importance of maintaining strong production capacity.

> *Success or failure, most of the privately funded research outlays continue to be made by manufacturers, rather than by companies in other parts of the economy.*

Heroes have emerged, working behind the scenes to lead difficult battles for survival and supremacy. Often, they are managers whose main expertise seems to be to laud credit on other people in their organizations. Many of the heroes are workers who perform excellent work without fanfare and take pride in it.

We found that many cities have made progress in keeping and attracting manufacturing jobs through land banking, innovative pollution cleanups, one-stop permit shopping, and other programs.

And with the dot-com era history, there is a reasonable prospect that more investors will rediscover the intrinsic value that rests within so many American manufacturers.

Manufacturing, we discovered time and again, still drives American productivity. Despite its decline in jobs as a share of the workforce, this sector has held its own when measured by output.

IDENTIFYING THE SMALL KNOBS

What kinds of "small knobs" could be turned to boost manufacturing over the long haul?

- Politicians and economists should debate the causes of the nation's trade deficit, an important accounting measure that reflects declining competitiveness in key industries. This does not mean adopting protectionist policies that could precipitate counterproductive international trade wars.
- Policymakers can learn from the successes of emerging lands in thickening their manufacturing networks. These countries are building up the skills and supplier systems that support production, while in some cases our networks are becoming less robust.
- City officials should try harder to replicate the successes of some municipalities in retaining and attracting manufacturers, and they should realistically appraise where their local economies stand.
- Leaders could do more to heed the recommendations of the Council on Competitiveness. To stay on top in the innovation sweepstakes, the council urges more long-term spending for private research; more public investment in basic research; a rebuilding of the pool of scientists and engineers; and an easing of the regulatory burden on innovators without lowering standards.
- The public should do more to hold elected officials and regulators more accountable for assuring the nation of adequate power plant and refining capacity. This is of critical importance to U.S. manufacturers and their communities.
- Government officials should constantly review regulations and bureaucratic procedures that hamper factory expansions. Such restrictions helped to chase manufacturers out of New York City and other built-up areas over the years.
- Investors should stop accepting so readily the assumptions of securities analysts about what constitutes good corporate performance and pay more attention to business associates, employees, journalists, and accounting watchdogs who might be raising serious questions about stewardship.
- Public officials should monitor tax burdens more closely. In Philadelphia, and other places, there is widespread agreement that high levels of taxes have been a factor in deterring retention and expansion of manufacturers.
- Various parties should continue the debate about the advisability of providing public subsidies for plants and, more particularly,

nonmanufacturing developments such as stadiums, other entertainment projects, and shopping centers.

- Managements and their workers should strive harder to improve labor relations in the factories. Workers who feel good about their managers are likely to be more productive than workers who don't. And, managers who feel good about their employees are almost always more effective.
- Public and private educational institutions should strengthen their programs and extension partnerships to provide technical and managerial assistance to manufacturers.
- Manufacturers should consider whether they need to become more self-sufficient in order to develop and sustain key competitive skills. In some cases, this may mean contracting out less work. In other cases, new concerns about Canadian and Mexican border security may force U.S. producers to stock more inventory on-site rather than rely on just-in-time inventory strategies.
- States should remain open to foreign investment—and domestic investment.
- Americans should cast a skeptical eye on the argument that we have reached some sort of "postindustrial state," wherein manufacturing will give way to a higher order that calls for other nations to do the producing while the United States enjoys the fruits of that production. There is little evidence that this vision is practical.
- Mergers and acquisitions should be scrutinized more carefully. Too often, they lead to high debt loads, dispirited employees, and reduced presence in important markets.
- The media and investors should analyze more thoughtfully the fundamental differences between investment and speculative excesses as they are occurring, instead of afterward.
- Public officials in the executive branch of government should take care that trade negotiators are experienced in industry and familiar with problems in local economies due to the uneven application of the worthy principles of fair trade.
- Economists should direct more of their inquiries away from eulogizing the principle of comparative advantage and instead conduct more solid research into how comparative advantage is created and lost.

The concept of the postindustrial state has won widespread acceptance among intellectual and technology elites. This idea expands on the "creative destruction" theory formulated by economist Joseph Schumpeter in the 1930s. Schumpeter argued that businesses failing to adapt to emerging technologies and new ways of producing and distributing goods would be destroyed by more innovative rivals. Embracing his theory, however, does not require us to write off the losses of once-great companies and vital industries simply by etching "victim of creative destruction" on their gravestones. The causes of death weren't always invisible or inevitable forces utterly beyond the control of failed companies. Sometimes, real people make bad decisions that bring companies down. Consider American Optical of Southbridge, Massachusetts. William Beecher founded this company in 1833, to make frames for eyeglasses. Innovative optical products flowed steadily from the company—precision lenses of all sorts, ophthalmoscopes for examining the eye, otoscopes for examining the ear, bombsights for the military in World War II, optical lasers, ultra-high-speed cameras, wide-screen motion picture projection, the contact lens, the surgical microscope, and early work on fiber optics. In the late 1960s, the company employed 17,000 workers worldwide, a third of them at its main plant in Southbridge.

After Warner-Lambert acquired American Optical in 1967, the company seemed to lose its edge. A former employee, noting this shift, suggests that managers of the acquiring company were often acting without a clue. "Warner-Lambert brought in people who did not appreciate what there was to the business," he said. In 1982, Warner-Lambert sold American Optical to two venture capitalists lampooned by the locals as "Mo and Rudy." Then, the company was systemically harvested. Parts of American Optical are scattered about as subunits of other companies, blurring the final outcome of this saga. For Southbridge, though, the picture is crystal clear: Where there were once 5,800 workers, now there are 60.

There is little assurance, in a volatile world economy, that something won't happen tomorrow to foul up the best plans of today's leading companies.

Similar stories abound in the machine tool industry, suggesting that American Optical's demise was not an isolated case. Japanese, German, Swiss, and Italian machine tool makers have become global leaders. Meanwhile, many once-significant U.S. rivals—Cincinnati Milicron, Kearney & Trecker, Warner & Swasey, and others—have been acquired or gone out of business.

Others have accepted too readily facile assumptions about the principle of comparative advantage—the idea that each country will be best off by concentrating on producing what it makes best. Many Wall Street analysts and corporate strategists have taken this to mean that if a company is not No. 1 or No. 2 in its industry, it should exit the field. That kind of thinking can be a recipe for failure. Enron, seemingly on top of its industry as 2001 began, was in Chapter 11 bankruptcy by year's end. There is little assurance, in a volatile world economy, that something won't happen tomorrow to foul up the best plans of today's leading companies.

AN AMERICA WITHOUT MANUFACTURING

Try this exercise to get a better sense of manufacturing's continuing importance to the nation. Imagine what would happen if this sector suddenly disappeared. Nearly 17 million jobs would be lost. The country would immediately fall into a deep and long-lasting economic depression. Tax revenues would plunge, forcing schools to close and governments to slash services. All kinds of government jobs, including many that carry ample health care and pension benefits, would be eliminated. Income to charities would shrink. The dignity of our people, the opportunities for our youths, and the quality of higher education would come under sustained pressure.

Drive through the once-predominant industrial centers of America in the Northeast and the Midwest, and you'll see many signs of deterioration and decay. Look at the social structure of these communities and examine their fiscal condition. Even in the core counties of these areas, manufacturers retain huge investments in plants, equipment, and payrolls.

Visit the faster-growing counties where manufacturing is thriving. In many metropolitan areas, manufacturing acts as a principal force fueling growth in jobs and income.

Turn off the freeways that wrap around our major cities. There, in the often-hidden industrial parks near the interchanges, light manufacturers and suppliers generate much of the economic activity that powers the growth of whole communities.

A common view has been that the action has swung to the services sector. Certainly, from an employment standpoint, that's true. As the 21st Century began, there were roughly 51 million jobs officially defined as services, three times the number 30 years ago. Then, the manufacturing sector employed about 19.6 million workers, slightly more than service jobs. Today, the manufacturing workforce is somewhat smaller. Still, while manufacturers now account for less than 15 percent of the overall employment, their workers bring home 18 percent of the earnings. In contrast, the service sector accounts for 32 percent of the jobs, but only 29 percent of earnings. Put another way, the average manufacturing job pays $41,293 annually, the average service job, $26,533.

Plus, manufacturing jobs support many of the jobs in services and other sectors. This is still evident in Indiana's Lake County, home of U.S. Steel's huge Gary Works. A ride through the region on the Indiana Toll Road seems like a journey back to the past. Mile after mile of shuttered factories, abandoned rail sidings, and overgrown weeds have become the signatures of this once-mighty part of the country. Gary was a boomtown a century ago, when freighters moving down the Great Lakes first began shipping ore from Minnesota's Iron Range to the fiery blast furnaces at the southern tip of Lake Michigan. Workers at the mammoth integrated mills melted and reshaped the ore into steel that manufacturers elsewhere used to build the cars, trucks, skyscrapers, and stadiums that became the hallmarks of 20th Century America. Today, newer operators, using more efficient technologies, have built minimills elsewhere in the United States and overseas. Back in Lake County, where many steelworkers have lost their jobs, casinos are often cited as the salvation for the region's ailing economy. It won't work.

Even now, though, steel remains a critical part of the Lake County economy. U.S. Steel has poured investment into its Gary Works. Employment there is far below what it was a decade ago, but the workers are more productive. The steel industry still employs nearly half of the manufacturing workforce there. Steelworkers take home almost a fourth of the county's wages, even though they hold only an eighth of the jobs. If manufacturing were to suddenly disappear from this part of the country, Lake County would spiral into a paralyzing depression.

Then there's Pittsburgh. Known for most of the 20th Century as the heart and soul of the steel industry, this region fell into a steep economic decline starting in 1979. Big Steel, the primary source of the travail, lost roughly 100,000 jobs over the decade that ended in 1988. Pittsburgh's leading producers limped through relentless downsizing and shutdowns, with their difficulties triggering similar cutbacks at many support companies. Today, U.S. Steel's Mon Valley Works, with about 4,000 workers, is the area's only remaining integrated producer.

As a result, the Pittsburgh area has lagged behind most of its peers, by the measures of both population and job growth. Since 1970, the region has fallen from the 10th to the 19th most populous metropolitan area of the country. Its manufacturing employment over that same stretch skidded from 306,000 to 135,000. The area has replaced much of the lost manufacturing work with new jobs. Some are "hamburger flipper" jobs, paying little more than minimum wages. Others are in better-paying fields—banking, software, consulting. Pittsburgh is frequently hailed for being a city that has made the transition to the service economy from one based on old-line manufacturing. Yet, manufacturing has not vanished from this area. This sector still employs 10 percent of the metropolitan area's workforce, and its jobs account for 17 percent of the region's earnings. In fact, new arrivals and expansions in advanced manufacturing are part of the reason why Pittsburgh has morphed from an old-line manufacturing economy into one with a newer look. Thus, scrubbing this sector off the books would do serious damage to the region.

In the Detroit area, manufacturing carries more than twice the weight it has around Pittsburgh. Detroit still reigns as the world capital of the auto industry. Manufacturers account for a fourth of Wayne County's 751,000 jobs and 37 percent of its payroll. Transportation equipment workers, making mostly cars and trucks, hold a fourth of the industrial jobs and, again, a disproportionately large share of the payroll. Employees in the metal-working and machinery industries, important suppliers to the vehicle manufacturers, account for as many jobs again as the auto industry. The *New York Times* has profiled Ford's huge River Rouge plant near Detroit as one of the most profitable factories in the world.

Imagine the economic devastation that taking all this out would bring to the Detroit area. Much of the rest of Michigan and the Midwest, also dependent on the auto industry, would not be spared.

High-tech boosters typically describe California's Silicon Valley as the epicenter of the information economy. Listening to them, you'd never know that much of the region's reputation is rooted in its manufacturers—Cisco Systems, Intel, Hewlett-Packard, and others. Economists and consultants are fond of telling us that intellectual capital has replaced manual labor as America moves up to a higher stage of development, but Silicon Valley's successes provide powerful evidence that these two elements work best when they work together.

Manufacturers employ 256,000 workers, or nearly 30 percent of the workforce, in Santa Clara County, where Silicon Valley is located. They account for almost 40 percent of the county's earnings. Twice as many employees work in the electronic equipment subsector of manufacturing as in computer and data processing services, which is part of the services sector. Taking the manufacturers out of Silicon Valley would cut out its heart.

Even in the fastest-growing areas, where manufacturing accounts for far less of the workforce than around San Jose or Detroit, the industrial sector looms large.

In the Atlanta area, while manufacturers now account for only one of every ten jobs versus one of every five in 1970, their total job count has risen to 236,000 from 171,000 over this stretch. Only a fourth of these jobs are in Atlanta's core county, Fulton; the rest are widely dispersed throughout the other 19 counties of the metro area. This scattering over such a large region makes the manufacturing sector almost invisible, but its presence remains important. A similar pattern has developed around Phoenix.

In one area after another where manufacturing has taken it on the chin in recent years, this sector still endures as an anchor for the regional economy.

In Ohio's Mahoning County, the population of Youngstown skidded from 115,000 to 95,000 over the 1980s as the steel industry retrenched. Yet, today, manufacturing workers still make up 14 percent of the county's workforce and 19 percent of its earnings. Industrial employment in the county stabilized in the 1990s. Now, roughly 13,000 workers there make auto parts, aluminum products, metal stampings, machinery, hydraulic components, and other industrial goods.

In downstate Illinois, Peoria and Tazewell Counties have been hammered by job losses at Caterpillar, long that region's dominant employer. Despite these losses, manufacturing still employs 21 percent of the workforce and 34 percent of the payroll in the two counties. The average manufacturing job there pays about $45,000 annually.

Other areas, noted for their university-linked high-tech successes, would be flattened by the sudden disappearance of manufacturing. In the Raleigh-Durham area, manufacturers in Research Triangle Park provide a pivotal underpinning for the region's economy. They account for one of every six jobs in Durham and Wake Counties, and nearly one of every four dollars earned. Manufacturers play a similar role in Travis County, Texas. There, high-tech producers, attracted by the region's amenities and the main campus of the University of Texas, have flocked to Austin. A similar story is unfolding in Dane County, Wisconsin, home of the University of Wisconsin at Madison. There, manufacturers now account for 15 percent of the county's workforce and 20 percent of its payroll. In all three of these areas, manufacturing jobs rose sharply in the 1990s.

Of course, manufacturing would never fall silent at once, all across the country. Even in the worst possible circumstances, only a gradual decline would occur. Yet, as the dust settles on an era when so many of us were rushing into tomorrow's economy without much regard for what remains today, thinking the unthinkable drives home an often-forgotten reality: America still needs manufacturing.

Industrial-driven prosperity is always a temporary condition. Retaining the edge in manufacturing takes dedication, investment, and the cooperation of the entire community, not just those directly employed in the industrial sector. The most formidable enemy is not precipitous decline, which might promote action, but gradual drift, which usually does not.

We hope, too, that the reader will not detect partisan rhetoric in this report. The problems discussed here are of crucial importance to the social tranquility of the United States. Many of these problems gradually unfolded over decades, and they are unlikely to be solved by broad ideological platitudes. Specificity, investment blended with practicality and good will, is needed to maintain the industrial prominence of the United States. We need to work together.

> *The most formidable enemy is not precipitous decline, which might promote action, but gradual drift, which usually does not.*

Much of what makes the country great rides on the expertise and vigor of its industry. From Phoenix to Raleigh-Durham, from Pittsburgh and Detroit on out to San Jose, manufacturing remains a critical part of America. By coming to a better understanding of how and where manufacturing works best today, we can enhance the chances that it will work well tomorrow. That, in turn, will go a long way toward guaranteeing the nation a more prosperous future.

APPENDIX A

Methodology for Choosing the County Groups

First, we identified 704 counties with more than 4,800 manufacturing employees in 1995. Next, we tabulated percentage changes in manufacturing employment and payroll for these counties from 1977 to 1999. We used five time periods to examine both employment changes and manufacturing employment changes, and manufacturing payroll changes, to identify the counties with the greatest growth or shrinkage in their manufacturing sectors relative to the norm. Changes in employment for each county were compared to the mean for the initial 704 counties for the time periods 1977–1997, 1986–1997, 1995–1997, 1977–1999, and 1986–1999. Changes in payroll relative to the mean were examined for the time periods 1979–1997, 1986–1997, 1995–1997, 1979–1999, and 1986–1999. We repeated this process several times, occasionally considering some subjective information usually related to special circumstances for a few communities. We next identified an equal number of counties performing above average and below average—116 in each of these two groups. These 232 counties represented approximately the top sixth and the bottom sixth of the sample. We then divided these two groups into four categories achieving greater growth than the mean and three groups achieving slow or negative growth versus the mean during the time periods we considered.

COUNTIES GAINING MOMENTUM

Each of the four above-average groups was chosen on the basis of geographic characteristics:

- **Hinterland Highspots**—Counties where manufacturing is growing rapidly, without an interstate highway, and not part of a metropolitan area
- **Metro Movers**—Counties part of a metropolitan area where manufacturing is growing rapidly
- **Freeway Flyers**—Counties where manufacturing is growing rapidly, with an interstate, and not part of a metropolitan area
- **Gradual Growers**—Counties where manufacturing is growing modestly that may or may not be part of a metropolitan area

COUNTIES LOSING MOMENTUM

Each of the three below-average categories was classified by size only:

- **Smaller Sliders**—Counties with the greatest manufacturing shrinkage and 1995 manufacturing employment of between 4,800 and 9,999
- **Midrange Sliders**—Counties with the greatest manufacturing shrinkage and 1995 manufacturing employment of between 10,000 and 34,999
- **Sliding Goliaths**—Counties with the greatest manufacturing shrinkage and 1995 manufacturing employment of 35,000 or more

Our intent was not to create lists of winners and losers. The expansion or contraction of manufacturing within a particular county is often dependent on the performance of an individual company or industry. Also, a few counties with the most notable shrinkage had to be excluded from consideration because of missing or peculiar data. And, in some cases, payroll or job trends have shifted notably in the later years of the comparisons or since 1999, the latest year for which comparable information is available. Thus, we resisted the temptation to unhesitatingly judge these counties "good" or "bad." Rather, our intent was to identify the two ends of the normal curve—roughly the top sixth and the bottom sixth of the 704 counties in manufacturing growth—and then to see what can be learned by looking more closely at these counties.

We could have chosen 5 percent, 25 percent, or some other number. We feel that our methodology has yielded a good-sized and defensible sample, but we caution readers to avoid branding any county with a lasting designation. Companies, industries, and economic conditions all change over time—sometimes rapidly.

CENSUS BUREAU SHIFT FROM THE SIC SYSTEM TO THE NAICS METHODOLOGY

Effective with the data collected for the year 1998, the U.S. Bureau of the Census dropped the Standard Industry Classification (SIC) system for data at the county level in favor of the newly developed North American Industry Classification System (NAICS). The changes are quite minor except for the shifting of the publishing industry from the "Manufacturing" category to the newly formed "Information" category. Overall, the new system is better than the old one, but it requires both caution and knowledge of individual communities to make comparisons in manufacturing growth over some time periods.

The authors wish to point out that the 1998 change in classification of publishing from manufacturing (under the SIC system) to the information category (NAICS system) resulted in a significant reduction in the number of people classified as working in manufacturing in some cities. The total number of employees reclassified in this manner was slightly over 700,000 in 1998. Because newspaper publishing was part of this reclassification, and because many major newspapers are located in large cities, as well as much book and periodical publishing, the reported changes in manufacturing in major cities was no doubt disproportionately worsened by this change. However, we do not feel that these changes materially impacted our analysis, because we used the ten separate time and data periods (as described on page 247) in making our selections for the various categories. The Sliding Goliath counties were among those most affected by the SIC to NAICS change, and the facts are that these counties showed very appreciable declines before 1998, when the new system went into effect. The authors wish that the Census Bureau would have continued coreporting employment, payroll, and establishments under the SIC system for two more years, but it did not.

Detailed Statistics
on Sample Counties

Figure B.1   Manufacturing Employment History—Hinterland Highspots

STATE #	COUNTY #	COUNTY NAME	METROPOLITAN AREA	MFG. EMPLOYMENT 1977	MFG. EMPLOYMENT 1999	% EMPLOYMENT CHANGE 1977–1999	% MFG. PAYROLL CHANGE 1979–1999
1	59	Franklin, AL		2,400	5,188	116.2%	328.3%
1	95	Marshall, AL		7,400	13,599	83.8%	273.2%
1	133	Winston, AL		4,200	6,931	65.0%	207.2%
5	55	Greene, AR		4,400	5,991	36.2%	247.1%
13	69	Coffee, GA		2,800	6,110	118.2%	397.3%
18	85	Kosciusko, IN		10,400	14,924	43.5%	306.7%
18	113	Noble, IN		5,500	11,501	109.1%	401.0%
19	125	Marion, IA		3,100	7,796	151.5%	418.2%
19	167	Sioux, IA		1,800	4,711	161.7%	325.8%
26	55	Grand Traverse, MI		3,700	5,892	59.2%	270.5%
27	85	McLeod, MN		4,800	8,990	87.3%	296.6%
29	9	Barry, MO		3,000	6,943	131.4%	438.6%
29	159	Pettis, MO		3,200	5,544	73.3%	340.1%
31	141	Platte, NE		4,600	5,937	29.1%	157.9%
41	3	Benton, OR		2,800	8,712	211.1%	474.3%
		Hinterland Highspots	Totals =	64,100	118,769	85.3%	307.7%
			Count =	15			

Figure B.2 Manufacturing Employment History—Metro Movers

STATE #	COUNTY #	COUNTY NAME	METROPOLITAN AREA	MFG. EMPLOYMENT 1977	MFG. EMPLOYMENT 1999	% EMPLOYMENT CHANGE 1977–1999	% MFG. PAYROLL CHANGE 1979–1999
5	143	Washington, AR	Fayetteville-Springfield-Rogers, AR	7,900	15,014	90.1%	399.9%
6	61	Placer, CA	Sacramento-Yolo, CA	2,400	8,131	238.8%	834.4%
6	65	Riverside, CA	Los Angeles-Riverside-Orange County, CA	23,400	49,509	111.6%	307.7%
6	67	Sacramento, CA	Sacramento-Yolo, CA	17,700	31,865	80.0%	232.6%
6	97	Sonoma, CA	San Francisco-Oakland-San Jose, CA	11,000	26,391	139.9%	470.4%
8	69	Larimer, CO	Fort Collins-Loveland, CO	9,800	12,718	29.8%	303.5%
12	81	Manatee, FL	Sarasota-Bradenton, FL	4,100	10,995	168.2%	468.8%
12	83	Marion, FL	Ocala, FL	3,400	9,420	177.1%	390.0%
13	135	Gwinnett, GA	Atlanta, GA	8,300	27,468	230.9%	534.1%
16	1	Ada, ID	Boise City, ID	6,800	19,169	181.9%	456.3%
16	27	Canyon, ID	Boise City, ID	6,500	10,790	66.0%	319.8%
18	33	De Kalb, IN	Fort Wayne, IN	5,100	13,706	168.7%	464.1%
18	57	Hamilton, IN	Indianapolis, IN	4,100	6,604	61.1%	210.5%
18	81	Johnson, IN	Indianapolis, IN	3,700	6,551	77.1%	260.9%
21	15	Boone, KY	Cincinnati-Hamilton, OH-KY-IN	4,600	9,387	104.1%	286.8%
21	117	Kenton, KY	Cincinnati-Hamilton, OH-KY-IN	4,000	7,777	94.4%	460.3%
21	151	Madison, KY	Lexington, KY	3,600	6,331	75.9%	298.0%
21	209	Scott, KY	Lexington, KY	2,600	10,318	296.8%	1524.1%
26	87	Lapeer, MI	Detroit-Ann Arbor-Flint, MI	2,900	6,420	121.4%	442.4%
26	93	Livingston, MI	Detroit-Ann Arbor-Flint, MI	4,100	10,047	145.0%	494.9%
27	19	Carver, MN	Minneapolis-Saint Paul, MN-WI	2,100	9,309	343.3%	787.8%
29	183	St. Charles, MO	Saint Louis, MO-IL	5,000	14,387	187.7%	458.6%
32	3	Clark, NV	Las Vegas, NV-AZ	5,400	18,430	241.3%	499.6%
37	63	Durham, NC	Raleigh-Durham-Chapel Hill, NC	16,000	30,780	92.4%	284.8%
38	17	Cass, ND	Fargo-Moorhead, ND-MN	3,800	6,745	77.5%	282.5%
39	165	Warren, OH	Cincinnati-Hamilton, OH-KY-IN	3,800	13,018	242.6%	723.3%
41	67	Washington, OR	Portland-Salem, OR-WA	23,100	37,147	60.8%	258.8%
46	99	Minnehaha, SD	Sioux Falls, SD	7,600	12,725	67.4%	172.1%
48	85	Collin, TX	Dallas-Fort Worth, TX	4,700	24,208	415.1%	1828.9%
48	121	Denton, TX	Dallas-Fort Worth, TX	5,700	13,277	132.9%	452.8%

(Continued)

Figure B.2   Manufacturing Employment History—Metro Movers, *continued*

STATE #	COUNTY #	COUNTY NAME	METROPOLITAN AREA	MFG. EMPLOYMENT 1977	MFG. EMPLOYMENT 1999	% EMPLOYMENT CHANGE 1977–1999	% MFG. PAYROLL CHANGE 1979–1999
48	157	Fort Bend, TX	Houston-Galveston-Brazoria, TX	6,600	11,091	68.0%	159.8%
48	251	Johnson, TX	Dallas-Fort Worth, TX	3,700	6,437	74.0%	345.1%
48	339	Montgomery, TX	Houston-Galveston-Brazoria, TX	2,100	7,280	246.7%	616.5%
48	453	Travis, TX	Austin-San Marcos, TX	17,800	53,728	201.8%	826.7%
48	491	Williamson, TX	Austin-San Marcos, TX	2,000	9,685	384.3%	1136.3%
49	11	Davis, UT	Salt Lake City-Ogden, UT	3,200	8,144	154.5%	386.1%
51	41	Chesterfield, VA	Richmond-Petersburg, VA	7,400	10,357	40.0%	239.7%
51	59	Fairfax, VA	Washington-Baltimore, DC-MD-VA-WV	7,600	13,050	71.7%	284.1%
53	61	Snohomish, WA	Seattle-Tacoma-Bremerton, WA	21,400	62,102	190.2%	377.6%
55	109	St. Croix, WI	Minneapolis-Saint Paul, MN-WI	2,100	5,965	184.0%	460.1%
		Metro Movers	Totals =	287,100	666,476	132.1%	445.2%
			Count =	40			

Figure B.3   Manufacturing Employment History—Freeway Flyers

STATE #	COUNTY #	COUNTY NAME	METROPOLITAN AREA	MFG. EMPLOYMENT 1977	MFG. EMPLOYMENT 1999	% EMPLOYMENT CHANGE 1977–1999	% MFG. PAYROLL CHANGE 1979–1999
5	93	Mississippi, AR		6,400	7,115	11.2%	218.7%
5	115	Pope, AR		3,300	4,642	40.7%	172.6%
13	139	Hall, GA		10,000	18,294	82.9%	338.5%
18	37	Dubois, IN		7,400	14,715	98.9%	314.7%
18	71	Jackson, IN		4,100	6,375	55.5%	312.6%
18	151	Steuben, IN		2,100	7,890	275.7%	592.8%
20	169	Saline, KS		4,000	6,921	73.0%	236.6%
21	93	Hardin, KY		3,700	7,231	95.4%	408.3%
27	147	Steele, MN		4,500	8,309	84.6%	317.4%
28	115	Pontotoc, MS		3,200	6,455	101.7%	420.0%
37	77	Granville, NC		3,200	6,525	103.9%	344.0%
37	89	Henderson, NC		4,800	8,000	66.7%	306.9%
39	91	Logan, OH		3,800	6,575	73.0%	439.5%
47	31	Coffee, TN		4,500	5,682	26.3%	288.7%

Figure B.3   Manufacturing Employment History—Freeway Flyers, *continued*

STATE #	COUNTY #	COUNTY NAME	METROPOLITAN AREA	MFG. EMPLOYMENT 1977	MFG. EMPLOYMENT 1999	% EMPLOYMENT CHANGE 1977–1999	% MFG. PAYROLL CHANGE 1979–1999
47	119	Maury, TN		6,200	11,355	83.1%	650.8%
47	123	Monroe, TN		2,300	5,530	140.4%	752.7%
51	165	Rockingham, VA		5,200	9,927	90.9%	373.7%
55	27	Dodge, WI		8,700	13,432	54.4%	220.1%
55	97	Portage, WI		3,500	5,313	51.8%	222.6%
55	127	Walworth, WI		6,300	10,970	74.1%	272.1%
		Freeway Flyers	Totals =	97,200	171,256	76.2%	293.2%
			Count =	20			

Figure B.4   Manufacturing Employment History—Gradual Growers

STATE #	COUNTY #	COUNTY NAME	METROPOLITAN AREA	MFG. EMPLOYMENT 1977	MFG. EMPLOYMENT 1999	% EMPLOYMENT CHANGE 1977–1999	% MFG. PAYROLL CHANGE 1979–1999
1	77	Lauderdale, AL	Florence, AL	4,200	7,037	67.5%	313.9%
1	117	Shelby, AL	Birmingham, AL	5,000	6,021	20.4%	214.6%
1	125	Tuscaloosa, AL	Tuscaloosa, AL	10,100	12,460	23.4%	318.2%
4	19	Pima, AZ	Tucson, AZ	11,100	29,214	163.2%	375.1%
6	47	Merced, CA	Merced, CA	4,500	8,322	84.9%	290.2%
6	71	San Bernardino, CA	Los Angeles-Riverside-Orange County, CA	36,200	68,909	90.4%	211.7%
6	79	San Luis Obispo, CA	San Luis Obispo-Atascadero-Paso Robles, CA	2,400	6,894	187.3%	447.9%
12	71	Lee, FL	Fort Myers-Cape Coral, FL	3,000	5,293	76.4%	266.2%
13	247	Rockdale, GA	Atlanta, GA	3,100	6,912	123.0%	368.9%
17	97	Lake, IL	Chicago-Gary-Kenosha, IL-IN-WI	50,400	59,746	18.5%	206.4%
18	145	Shelby, IN	Indianapolis, IN	4,200	7,349	75.0%	328.1%
18	157	Tippecanoe, IN	Lafayette, IN	10,900	17,213	57.9%	235.5%
21	101	Henderson, KY	Evansville-Henderson, IN-KY	4,300	7,237	68.3%	240.6%
24	25	Harford, MD	Washington-Baltimore, DC-MD-VA-WV	4,200	6,484	54.4%	376.9%
26	5	Allegan, MI	Grand Rapids-Muskegon-Holland, MI	9,100	17,959	97.4%	374.5%

(Continued)

Figure B.4   Manufacturing Employment History—Gradual Growers, *continued*

STATE #	COUNTY #	COUNTY NAME	METROPOLITAN AREA	MFG. EMPLOYMENT 1977	MFG. EMPLOYMENT 1999	% EMPLOYMENT CHANGE 1977–1999	% MFG. PAYROLL CHANGE 1979–1999
26	139	Ottawa, MI	Grand Rapids-Muskegon-Holland, MI	20,100	41,072	104.3%	354.7%
27	37	Dakota, MN	Minneapolis-Saint Paul, MN-WI	15,100	17,319	14.7%	149.0%
27	145	Stearns, MN	Saint Cloud, MN	7,200	13,170	82.9%	281.6%
27	163	Washington, MN	Minneapolis-Saint Paul, MN-WI	6,200	11,034	78.0%	331.6%
28	33	DeSoto, MS	Memphis, TN-AR-MS	3,400	6,385	87.8%	249.4%
29	19	Boone, MO	Columbia, MO	3,100	5,757	85.7%	239.5%
29	71	Franklin, MO	Saint Louis, MO-IL	6,400	10,857	69.6%	267.9%
32	31	Washoe, NV	Reno, NV	6,800	11,773	73.1%	221.8%
33	15	Rockingham, NH	Boston-Worcester-Lawrence-Lowell-Brockton, MA-NH	10,700	17,033	59.2%	231.2%
37	179	Union, NC	Charlotte-Gastonia-Rock Hill, NC-SC	8,800	13,239	50.4%	284.8%
39	55	Geauga, OH	Cleveland-Akron, OH	6,500	11,018	69.5%	337.3%
39	103	Medina, OH	Cleveland-Akron, OH	7,800	11,317	45.1%	257.0%
39	133	Portage, OH	Cleveland-Akron, OH	8,000	13,775	72.2%	256.0%
47	45	Dyer, TN		4,600	6,473	40.7%	225.5%
47	113	Madison, TN	Jackson, TN	8,300	12,734	53.4%	259.4%
47	125	Montgomery, TN	Clarksville-Hopkinsville, TN-KY	5,600	7,401	32.2%	272.8%
47	165	Sumner, TN	Nashville, TN	5,000	10,447	108.9%	368.6%
48	139	Ellis, TX	Dallas-Fort Worth, TX	5,700	9,854	72.9%	268.2%
48	187	Guadalupe, TX	San Antonio, TX	3,100	5,787	86.7%	426.0%
48	215	Hidalgo, TX	McAllen-Edinburg-Mission, TX	5,500	11,865	115.7%	265.3%
51	87	Henrico, VA	Richmond-Petersburg, VA	9,200	10,768	17.0%	144.3%
53	73	Whatcom, WA	Bellingham, WA	6,400	9,495	48.4%	175.2%
55	25	Dane, WI	Madison, WI	18,200	26,681	46.6%	217.2%
55	73	Marathon, WI	Wausau, WI	13,200	18,368	39.2%	184.4%
55	87	Outagamie, WI	Appleton-Oshkosh-Neenah, WI	16,700	21,422	28.3%	184.6%
55	131	Washington, WI	Milwaukee-Racine, WI	10,900	15,333	40.7%	227.1%
		Gradual Growers	Totals =	385,200	617,427	60.3%	252.3%
			Count =	41			

Figure B.5   Manufacturing Employment History—Smaller Sliders

STATE #	COUNTY #	COUNTY NAME	METROPOLITAN AREA	MFG. EMPLOYMENT 1977	MFG. EMPLOYMENT 1999	% EMPLOYMENT CHANGE 1977–1999	% MFG. PAYROLL CHANGE 1979–1999
1	33	Colbert, AL	Florence, AL	9,800	4,832	−50.7%	−15.5%
1	121	Talladega, AL		9,400	7,017	−25.4%	63.4%
6	23	Humboldt, CA		8,800	5,262	−40.2%	27.8%
17	1	Adams, IL		8,500	6,224	−26.8%	25.5%
17	99	La Salle, IL		14,300	6,215	−56.5%	2.3%
17	179	Tazewell, IL	Peoria-Pekin, IL	18,100	6,944	−61.6%	−11.0%
17	183	Vermilion, IL		14,100	6,980	−50.5%	−1.0%
18	169	Wabash, IN		6,600	5,322	−19.4%	89.2%
23	1	Androscoggin, ME	Lewiston-Auburn, ME NECMA	12,900	8,387	−35.0%	91.3%
23	11	Kennebec, ME		9,900	4,491	−54.6%	4.1%
28	3	Alcorn, MS		6,200	4,647	−25.0%	86.1%
28	47	Harrison, MS	Biloxi-Gulfport-Pascagoula, MS	4,900	4,435	−9.5%	116.9%
34	1	Atlantic, NJ	Philadelphia-Wilmington-Atlantic City, PA-NJ-DE-MD	8,700	4,656	−46.5%	19.7%
34	41	Warren, NJ	New York-Northern New Jersey-Long Island, NY-NJ-CT	12,600	7,076	−43.8%	52.1%
36	9	Cattaraugus, NY		9,100	5,094	−44.0%	18.0%
36	57	Montgomery, NY	Albany-Schenectady-Troy, NY	7,700	4,775	−38.0%	53.1%
36	75	Oswego, NY	Syracuse, NY	8,400	5,279	−37.2%	23.9%
36	83	Rensselaer, NY	Albany-Schenectady-Troy, NY	7,100	4,872	−31.4%	81.9%
36	93	Schenectady, NY	Albany-Schenectady-Troy, NY	24,400	5,209	−78.7%	−48.9%
36	111	Ulster, NY		7,900	6,414	−18.8%	−20.7%
37	47	Columbus, NC		5,200	4,269	−17.9%	69.8%
37	83	Halifax, NC		5,900	2,912	−50.6%	45.2%
37	153	Richmond, NC		6,300	4,800	−23.8%	80.3%
37	181	Vance, NC		6,800	4,411	−35.1%	65.2%
42	21	Cambria, PA	Johnstown, PA	16,600	7,937	−52.2%	−24.1%
42	73	Lawrence, PA		9,700	5,778	−40.4%	5.1%
42	97	Northumberland, PA		13,200	7,652	−42.0%	47.8%
44	9	Washington, RI	Providence-Warwick-Pawtucket, RI NECMA	10,100	6,804	−32.6%	93.8%
45	55	Kershaw, SC		7,900	4,699	−40.5%	41.4%

(Continued)

Figure B.5   Manufacturing Employment History—Smaller Sliders, *continued*

STATE #	COUNTY #	COUNTY NAME	METROPOLITAN AREA	MFG. EMPLOYMENT 1977	MFG. EMPLOYMENT 1999	% EMPLOYMENT CHANGE 1977–1999	% MFG. PAYROLL CHANGE 1979–1999
45	57	Lancaster, SC		9,800	4,756	−51.5%	29.0%
45	87	Union, SC		7,500	3,393	−54.8%	7.7%
51	89	Henry, VA		11,200	7,614	−32.0%	102.6%
54	11	Cabell, WV	Hurlington-Ashland, WV-KY-OH	13,100	5,871	−55.2%	−11.9%
54	39	Kanawha, WV	Charleston, WV	14,300	6,447	−54.9%	2.7%
		Smaller Sliders	Totals =	347,000	191,474	−44.8%	23.8%
			Count =	34			

Figure B.6   Manufacturing Employment History—Mid-Range Sliders

STATE #	COUNTY #	COUNTY NAME	METROPOLITAN AREA	MFG. EMPLOYMENT 1977	MFG. EMPLOYMENT 1999	% EMPLOYMENT CHANGE 1977–1999	% MFG. PAYROLL CHANGE 1979–1999
1	55	Etowah, AL	Gadsden, AL	11,800	8,066	−31.6%	9.0%
6	13	Contra Costa, CA	San Francisco-Oakland-San Jose, CA	27,300	18,890	−30.8%	63.1%
8	31	Denver, CO	Denver-Boulder-Greeley, CO	42,400	24,640	−41.9%	9.2%
9	11	New London, CT	New London-Norwich, CT NECMA	39,200	18,805	−52.0%	95.3%
13	59	Clarke, GA	Athens, GA	10,200	7,464	−26.8%	70.1%
13	89	De Kalb, GA	Atlanta, GA	25,600	23,495	−8.2%	88.2%
17	119	Madison, IL	Saint Louis, MO-IL	29,300	17,379	−40.7%	24.9%
17	143	Peoria, IL	Peoria-Pekin, IL	32,900	13,519	−58.9%	−17.2%
17	161	Rock Island, IL	Davenport-Moline-Rock Island, IA-IL	26,700	9,676	−63.8%	−32.6%
18	35	Delaware, IN	Muncie, IN	14,200	9,391	−33.9%	34.7%
18	91	La Porte, IN		16,800	9,973	−40.6%	39.1%
18	95	Madison, IN	Indianapolis, IN	25,600	10,279	−59.8%	−2.2%
22	17	Caddo, LA	Shreveport-Bossier City, LA	22,200	12,647	−43.0%	44.3%
22	33	East Baton Rouge, LA	Baton Rouge, LA	17,800	11,574	−35.0%	44.5%
22	71	Orleans, LA	New Orleans, LA	21,400	9,366	−56.2%	−1.8%
23	19	Penobscot, ME	Bangor, ME NECMA	14,300	8,931	−37.5%	47.1%
25	3	Berkshire, MA	Pittsfield, MA NECMA	18,800	8,447	−55.1%	−2.2%

Figure B.6   Manufacturing Employment History—Mid-Range Sliders, *continued*

STATE #	COUNTY #	COUNTY NAME	METROPOLITAN AREA	MFG. EMPLOYMENT 1977	MFG. EMPLOYMENT 1999	% EMPLOYMENT CHANGE 1977–1999	% MFG. PAYROLL CHANGE 1979–1999
26	77	Kalamazoo, MI	Kalamazoo-Battle Creek, MI	30,000	20,619	−31.3%	34.5%
28	49	Hinds, MS	Jackson, MS	14,200	8,991	−36.7%	44.3%
28	59	Jackson, MS	Biloxi-Gulfport-Pascagoula, MS	30,100	16,660	−44.7%	57.0%
34	17	Hudson, NJ	New York-Northern New Jersey-Long Island, NY-NJ-CT	72,200	20,840	−71.1%	−25.8%
34	21	Mercer, NJ	New York-Northern New Jersey-Long Island, NY-NJ-CT	35,900	9,805	−72.7%	−32.8%
34	25	Monmouth, NJ	New York-Northern New Jersey-Long Island, NY-NJ-CT	26,600	11,280	−57.6%	−4.0%
36	5	Bronx, NY	New York-Northern New Jersey-Long Island, NY-NJ-CT	33,100	11,675	−64.7%	−18.6%
36	7	Broome, NY	Binghamton, NY	30,700	18,378	−40.1%	30.8%
36	27	Dutchess, NY	New York-Northern New Jersey-Long Island, NY-NJ-CT	27,400	13,491	−50.8%	1.4%
36	71	Orange, NY	New York-Northern New Jersey-Long Island, NY-NJ-CT	15,200	9,373	−38.3%	64.0%
36	87	Rockland, NY	New York-Northern New Jersey-Long Island, NY-NJ-CT	14,800	9,731	−34.3%	52.5%
36	101	Steuben, NY		14,200	7,467	−47.4%	13.8%
37	127	Nash, NC	Rocky Mount, NC	12,400	9,899	−20.2%	130.3%
37	157	Rockingham, NC		16,700	13,164	−21.2%	63.4%
39	3	Allen, OH	Lima, OH	16,800	10,330	−38.5%	48.1%
39	93	Lorain, OH	Cleveland-Akron, OH	39,800	26,239	−34.1%	33.9%
42	45	Delaware, PA	Philadelphia-Wilmington-Atlantic City, PA-NJ-DE-MD	44,800	19,613	−56.2%	11.1%
42	69	Lackawanna, PA	Scranton—Wilkes-Barre—Hazleton, PA	26,100	15,753	−39.6%	55.8%
42	77	Lehigh, PA	Allentown-Bethlehem-Easton, PA	47,800	22,722	−52.5%	14.6%
42	79	Luzerne, PA	Scranton—Wilkes-Barre—Hazleton, PA	40,500	22,159	−45.3%	52.0%
42	95	Northampton, PA	Allentown-Bethlehem-Easton, PA	39,300	16,996	−56.8%	−10.4%

(Continued)

Figure B.6   Manufacturing Employment History—Mid-Range Sliders, *continued*

STATE #	COUNTY #	COUNTY NAME	METROPOLITAN AREA	MFG. EMPLOYMENT 1977	MFG. EMPLOYMENT 1999	% EMPLOYMENT CHANGE 1977–1999	% MFG. PAYROLL CHANGE 1979–1999
45	77	Pickens, SC	Greenville-Spartanburg-Anderson, SC	17,500	10,909	−37.7%	66.7%
47	93	Knox, TN	Knoxville, TN	25,400	17,654	−30.5%	70.5%
47	163	Sullivan, TN	Johnson City-Kingsport-Bristol, TN-VA	25,500	17,568	−31.1%	81.3%
48	245	Jefferson, TX	Beaumont-Port Arthur, TX	28,400	14,540	−48.8%	18.5%
48	423	Smith, TX	Tyler, TX	12,100	9,908	−18.1%	88.3%
51	680	Lynchburg, VA	Lynchburg, VA	19,900	12,634	−36.5%	92.7%
51	760	Richmond, VA	Richmond-Petersburg, VA	34,800	20,727	−40.4%	44.9%
55	101	Racine, WI	Milwaukee-Racine, WI	27,200	20,032	−26.4%	33.7%
		Mid-range Sliders	Totals =	1,215,900	661,699	−45.6%	54.2%
			Count =	46			

Figure B.7   Manufacturing Employment History—Sliding Goliaths

STATE #	COUNTY #	COUNTY NAME	METROPOLITAN AREA	MFG. EMPLOYMENT 1977	MFG. EMPLOYMENT 1999	% EMPLOYMENT CHANGE 1977–1999	% MFG. PAYROLL CHANGE 1979–1999
6	75	San Francisco, CA	San Francisco-Oakland-San Jose, CA	42,900	21,725	−49.4%	−33.3%
9	1	Fairfield, CT	New Haven-Bridgeport-Stamford-Danbury-Waterbury, CT	117,300	51,975	−55.7%	8.6%
9	3	Hartford, CT	Hartford, CT NECMA	116,700	70,243	−39.8%	43.3%
10	3	New Castle, DE	Philadelphia-Wilmington-Atlantic City, PA-NJ-DE-MD	50,700	24,058	−52.5%	3.3%
12	25	Dade, FL	Miami-Fort Lauderdale, FL	85,100	58,699	−31.0%	41.0%
17	31	Cook, IL	Chicago-Gary-Kenosha, IL-IN-WI	687,500	345,873	−49.7%	12.8%
18	89	Lake, IN	Chicago-Gary-Kenosha, IL-IN-WI	85,600	35,019	−59.1%	−15.7%
24	5	Baltimore, MD	Washington-Baltimore, DC-MD-VA-WV	57,900	29,243	−49.5%	2.3%
24	510	Baltimore city, MD	Washington-Baltimore, DC-MD-VA-WV	72,900	25,803	−64.6%	−16.4%
25	13	Hampden, MA	Springfield, MA NECMA	55,700	31,710	−43.1%	45.2%

Figure B.7 Manufacturing Employment History—Sliding Goliaths, *continued*

STATE #	COUNTY #	COUNTY NAME	METROPOLITAN AREA	MFG. EMPLOYMENT 1977	MFG. EMPLOYMENT 1999	% EMPLOYMENT CHANGE 1977–1999	% MFG. PAYROLL CHANGE 1979–1999
25	21	Norfolk, MA	Boston-Worcester-Lawrence-Lowell-Brockton, MA-NH N	54,900	33,781	−38.5%	81.1%
25	25	Suffolk, MA	Boston-Worcester-Lawrence-Lowell-Brockton, MA-NH N	54,700	19,108	−65.1%	−5.5%
26	163	Wayne, MI	Detroit-Ann Arbor-Flint, MI	334,500	128,741	−61.5%	−11.6%
29	95	Jackson, MO	Kansas City, MO-KS	64,600	36,320	−43.8%	6.8%
29	510	St. Louis City, MO	Saint Louis, MO-IL	92,600	30,792	−66.7%	−28.5%
34	3	Bergen, NJ	New York-Northern New Jersey-Long Island, NY-NJ-CT	109,100	55,157	−49.4%	23.1%
34	13	Essex, NJ	New York-Northern New Jersey-Long Island, NY-NJ-CT	86,100	34,015	−60.5%	−6.4%
34	23	Middlesex, NJ	New York-Northern New Jersey-Long Island, NY-NJ-CT	80,500	50,359	−37.4%	42.5%
34	31	Passaic, NJ	New York-Northern New Jersey-Long Island, NY-NJ-CT	65,300	31,029	−52.5%	15.3%
34	39	Union, NJ	New York-Northern New Jersey-Long Island, NY-NJ-CT	92,600	37,648	−59.3%	3.6%
36	29	Erie, NY	Buffalo-Niagara Falls, NY	108,800	62,301	−42.7%	26.7%
36	47	Kings, NY	New York-Northern New Jersey-Long Island, NY-NJ-CT	118,400	44,679	−62.3%	−15.3%
36	55	Monroe, NY	Rochester, NY	126,200	72,961	−42.2%	22.0%
36	59	Nassau, NY	New York-Northern New Jersey-Long Island, NY-NJ-CT	92,100	36,787	−60.1%	1.2%
36	61	New York, NY	New York-Northern New Jersey-Long Island, NY-NJ-CT	359,400	70,559	−80.4%	−57.0%
36	67	Onondaga, NY	Syracuse, NY	47,800	33,015	−30.9%	45.3%
36	81	Queens, NY	New York-Northern New Jersey-Long Island, NY-NJ-CT	94,100	47,671	−49.3%	15.7%
36	119	Westchester, NY	New York-Northern New Jersey-Long Island, NY-NJ-CT	62,200	18,355	−70.5%	−48.3%

(Continued)

Figure B.7   Manufacturing Employment History—Sliding Goliaths, *continued*

STATE #	COUNTY #	COUNTY NAME	METROPOLITAN AREA	MFG. EMPLOYMENT 1977	MFG. EMPLOYMENT 1999	% EMPLOYMENT CHANGE 1977–1999	% MFG. PAYROLL CHANGE 1979–1999
37	67	Forsyth, NC	Greensboro-Winston-Salem—High Point, NC	41,700	26,819	−35.7%	23.1%
39	35	Cuyahoga, OH	Cleveland-Akron, OH	226,100	114,898	−49.2%	8.6%
39	61	Hamilton, OH	Cincinnati-Hamilton, OH-KY-IN	139,600	71,679	−48.7%	15.9%
39	95	Lucas, OH	Toledo, OH	59,900	30,757	−48.7%	23.7%
39	153	Summit, OH	Cleveland-Akron, OH	75,600	41,784	−44.7%	15.3%
42	3	Allegheny, PA	Pittsburgh, PA	150,300	55,384	−63.2%	−20.7%
42	101	Philadelphia, PA	Philadelphia-Wilmington-Atlantic City, PA-NJ-DE-MD	157,500	44,023	−72.0%	−33.3%
44	7	Providence, RI	Providence-Warwick-Pawtucket, RI NECMA	91,100	48,213	−47.1%	33.3%
		Sliding Goliaths	Totals =	4,358,000	1,971,183	−54.8%	38.8%
			Count =	36			

Manufacturing Organizations

 Scores of organizations offer resources to help American manufacturing. Here are some of the most prominent organizations and their contact information. Their Web sites often provide links to related organizations.

PROFESSIONAL AND INDUSTRY ASSOCIATIONS

Alliance for Innovative Manufacturing
Building 02-530, Room 225
Stanford, CA 94305-3036
650-723-9038
e-mail: cborn@stanford.edu
<www.stanford.edu/group/AIM/>

American Electronics Association
5201 Great America Parkway
Santa Clara, CA 95054
800-284-4232
<www.aeanet.org>

American Productivity and Quality Center
123 North Post Oak Lane, 3rd Floor
Houston, TX 77024
800-776-9676
e-mail: apqcinfo@apqc.org

ASME–American Society for Mechanical Engineers
Three Park Avenue
New York, NY 10016-5990
212-591-7722
<www.asme.org>

ASQ–American Society for Quality
600 N. Plankinton
Milwaukee, WI 53203
414-272-8575
<www.asq.org>

Association for Manufacturing Excellence
380 W. Palatine Road, Suite 7
Wheeling, IL 60090-5863
847-520-3282
<www.ame.org>

Association for Manufacturing Technology
7901 Westpark Drive
McLean, VA 22102
703-827-5288
e-mail: amt@mfgtech.org
<www.mfgtech.org>

ISA–The Instrumentation, Systems, and Automation Society
67 Alexander Drive
P.O. Box 12277
Research Triangle Park, NC 27709
919-549-8411
e-mail: info@isa.org
<www.isa.org>

Lean Enterprise Institute
P.O. Box 9
Brookline, MA 02446
617-713-2900

Manufacturers Alliance/MAPI
1525 Wilson Boulevard, Suite 900
Arlington, VA 22209-2411
703-841-9000
<www.mapi.net>

National Association of Industrial Technology
3300 Washtenaw Avenue, Suite 220
Ann Arbor, MI 48104-4200
734-677-0720
e-mail: nait@nait.org
<www.nait.org>

National Association of Manufacturers
1331 Pennsylvania Avenue, N.W.
Washington, DC 20004-1790
202-637-3000
e-mail: manufacturing@nam.org
<www.nam.org>

National Center for Manufacturing Sciences
3025 Boardwalk
Ann Arbor, MI 48108-3266
734-995-0300
<www.ncms.org>

Northeast Midwest Institute
218 D Street, S.E.
Washington, DC 20003
202-544-5200
<www.nemw.org>

SAE–Society of Automotive Engineers
400 Commonwealth Drive
Warrendale, PA 15096
724-776-4841

Society of Manufacturing Engineers
One SME Drive
Dearborn, MI 48121
800-733-4763
e-mail: assoc@sme.org
<www.sme.org>

EDUCATIONAL ORGANIZATIONS

Accreditation Board for Engineering and Technology
111 Market Place, Suite 1050
Baltimore, MD 21202
410-347-7700
e-mail: accreditation@abet.org
<www.abet.org>

Focus:HOPE
1355 Oakman Boulevard
Detroit, MI 48346
e-mail: manufacturing@focushope.edu
<www.focushope.edu>

GOVERNMENT ORGANIZATIONS

Manufacturing Extension Partnerships
100 Bureau Drive, Stop 3460
Gaithersburg, MD 20899-3460
800-637-4634
<www.mep.nist.gov>

Office of Science and Technology Policy
Executive Office of the President
Washington, DC 20502
202-395-7347
e-mail: ostinfo@ostp.eop.gov

U.S. Department of Commerce
1401 Constitution Avenue, N.W.
Washington, DC 20230
e-mail: devans@doc.gov
<www.doc.gov>

U.S. Department of Labor
Office of Public Affairs
200 Constitution Avenue, N.W.
Room S-1032
Washington, DC 20210
202-693-4650

Bibliography

BOOKS, ARTICLES, AND SPECIAL REPORTS

Chapter 1

Aeppel, Timothy. "Why Making Things Is out of Fashion." *Wall Street Journal*, 8 November 1999.

Bamberger, William, and Cathy Davidson. *Closing: The Life and Death of an American Factory*. New York: W.W. Norton/Center for Documentary Studies, 1998.

Bayard, Kimberly, and Kenneth Troske. "Examining the Employer Size-Wage Premium in Manufacturing, Retail Trade, and Service Industries." *American Economic Review*, May 1993.

Beal, Dave. "Making Manufacturing Work: Holding onto Factory Jobs." *St. Paul Pioneer Press*, 28 February 1999.

Boyd, Joseph A., "Manufacturing: Key to America's Future." *Business Forum* (summer 1990): 6–11.

Cohen, Stephen S., and John Zysman. *Manufacturing Matters: The Myth of the Post-Industrial Economy*. New York: Basic Books, 1987.

Cohn, Laura. "U.S. Factories Are the Stars." *Business Week,* 19 April 1999.

Dertouzos, Michael L., Richard K. Lester, Robert M. Solow, and the MIT Commission in Industrial Productivity. *Made in America: Regaining the Productive Edge*. Cambridge, Mass.: MIT Press, 1989.

Filardo, Andrew J., "Cyclical Implications of the Declining Manufacturing Employment Share." *Federal Reserve Bank of Kansas City; Economic Review* (second quarter 1997): 63–87.

Fingleton, Eamonn. *In Praise of Hard Industries*. New York: Houghton Mifflin, 1999.

"Harris Poll Shows Engineering Remains U.S. 'Stealth Profession.'" Press release, Institute of Electrical and Electronics Engineers, 4 September 1998.

Holland, Max. *When the Machine Stopped: A Cautionary Tale from Industrial America.* Boston: Harvard Business School Press, 1989.

Ip, Greg. "It's Official: Economy Is in a Recession." *Wall Street Journal,* 27 November 2001.

Jasinowski, Jerry. *Making It in America.* New York: Simon & Schuster, 1995.

Kessler, Andy. "CreativeAccounting.com." *Wall Street Journal,* 24 July 2001.

Lance, Bronwyn. "The Economic Impact of Immigration." *News World Communications,* May 2000.

McTeer, Robert. Remarks before the Board of the National Association of Manufacturers, 4 October 2000.

Madigan, Kathleen. "Keep Your Eye on the Factory Floor: Why the Manufacturing Data Are So Closely Watched." *Business Week,* 23 April 2001.

"Midwest Prospects and the New Economy." *Chicago Fed Letter.* Federal Reserve Bank of Chicago, October 2000.

Nothdurft, William. "A Railroad Runs Through It." Essay for Northwest Area Foundation, 1997.

Payne, Robert. *Report on America.* New York: John Day Co., 1949.

Rose, Robert. "Once the 'Rust Belt,' Midwest Now Boasts Revitalized Factories." *Wall Street Journal,* 3 January 1994.

Siekman, Philip. "The Big Myth about U.S. Manufacturing." *Fortune,* 2 October 1999.

"The Manufacturing Paradox." *Economist,* 3 November 2001.

U.S. Department of Commerce, Bureau of Economic Analysis, Regional Economic Analysis Division—June 2001.

Zajec, Andrew. "The New Manufacturing Machine." *Chicago Tribune,* 5 October 1998.

Chapter 2

Cassidy, John. "The Productivity Mirage." *New Yorker,* 27 November 2000.

Krugman, Paul. "Don't Count On It." *New York Times,* 5 September 2001.

"Measuring the New Economy: The Miracle of the Late-1990s Was Not Quite So Miraculous." *Economist,* 11 August 2001.

Popkin, Joel. "Producing Prosperity: Manufacturing Technology's Unmeasured Role in Economic Expansion." Study by Association for Manufacturing Technology, 2000.

"Productivity on Stilts." *Economist,* 10 June 2000.

Schlesinger, Jacob. "A Slide in Factory Jobs: The Pain of Progress." *Wall Street Journal,* 28 April 1997.

Chapter 3

Albert, Mark. "A Radically Different Production Plant." *Modern Machine Shop,* April 2000.

———. "The Radicals of Churubusco." *Modern Machine Shop,* December 1990.

Ashton, Patrick J., and Peter Iadicola. "Study of the Effects of Economic Displacement: The International Harvester Report." Project funded by International Harvester Corp. with assistance from the United Auto Workers, December 1985.

Economic Report to the Governor. Indiana Economic Development Council, 1997.

Ethridge, Mary, and John Russell. "Steel Company Adjusts to Difficult Times in Industry." *Akron Beacon Journal,* 13 January 2001.

Guthrie, Thomas L., and Valerie A. Richardson. "The Performance of the Northeast Indiana Economy Over the Past 30 Years." Community Research Institute, July 2000.

"Impact of General Motors on Allen County." Allen County Department of Planning, May 1999.

Ketzenberger, John. "Indiana's Man of Steel." *Indiana Business Magazine,* July 1995.

Marsh, Barbara. *A Corporate Tragedy: The Agony of International Harvester Company.* New York: Doubleday, 1985.

McKenna Frazier, Lynne. "Area Economy Still Linked to Detroit." *Fort Wayne News Sentinel,* 23 March 2000.

Nichols, David. "Busse: A Hot-Metal Man with Steel-Toed Shoes." *IPEW Alumni* magazine (fall 1997).

Preston, Richard. *American Steel.* New York: Prentice Hall Press, 1991.

Samways, Norman L. "Steel Dynamics: High Quality Flat-Rolled Products at Low Cost." *Iron and Steel Engineer,* April 1997.

Schrock, Lincoln. Various reports on manufacturing in Northeastern Indiana. 1982–2001.

Schroeder, Michael, and Walecia Konrad. "Nucor: Rolling Right Into Steel's Big Time." *Business Week,* 19 November 1990.

Stafford, John, and C. James Owen. "Land Use Impacts of an Industrial Plant Location: The Case of GM in Fort Wayne, Indiana." Report for 1988 annual meeting of Urban Affairs Association.

Chapter 4

Bukro, Casey. "Victims of Liability: Corporate America Is Fighting Back." *Chicago Tribune*, 11 September 1996.

County Business Patterns for 1977, 1979, 1986, 1988, 1995–1999. U.S. Census Bureau, 20 August 2001.

Crandall, Robert. *Manufacturing on the Move*. Washington, D.C.: Brookings Institution, 1993.

Economic Reports of the President for 1992, 1994, 1998–2001. U.S. Government Printing Office.

Harrison, Jack. "Jobs in Manufacturing Counties Tended to Pay More than in Nonmetro Counties as a Whole Through the Decade." Economic Research Service, 1997.

Manufacturers News, U.S. Manufacturers 1997–1998 and 1999–2000: Limited Data Fields for Research Purposes Prepared for University of St. Thomas.

Moody's Company Data, August 1994 and June 1995. New York: Moody's Investor Service, 1994 and 1995.

Olson, Walter K. *The Litigation Explosion: What Happened When America Unleashed the Lawsuit*. New York: Truman Talley Books-Dutton, 1991.

U.S. Census of Manufacturers, 1987, 1992.

Zimmerman, Fred. *The Relocation of Industry*. St. Paul, Minn.: University of St. Thomas Technology Press, 1998.

Chapter 5

Biomet Inc., annual reports, 1997–1998.

Dearlove, Des. "The Cluster Effect." *Strategy and Business* 24 (third quarter 2001): 54–65.

Kimball International, annual report, 1997

Quintanilla, Carl, and Robert Rose. "Some Tiny Towns Find a Way to Create Jobs, Attract Manufacturers." *Wall Street Journal*, 17 September 1996.

"The Facts about Modern Manufacturing." Manufacturing Institute, 1999.

"The Tufted Carpet Industry: History and Current Statistics, 1999." Carpet and Rug Institute.

Topolnicki, Denise M. "Great Towns with Great Jobs." *Money*, April 1996.

Chapter 6

Dennis, Lynn H., and Laura Herring. "Corporate Relocation Takes Its Toll on Society." *Workforce* (February 1999): 1–4.

Hammonds, Keith, and Ira Sager. "The Town IBM Left Behind." *Business Week*, 11 September 1995.

Harrison, Nick. "Leaving Soot and Slag Behind in Pittsburgh." *Urban Age* (summer 1999).

Lambert, Bruce. "From the Heights of Space to the Fall of an Industrial Empire." *New York Times*, 5 May 1996.

Chapter 7

Adams, Carolyn, et al. *Philadelphia: Neighborhoods, Division, and Conflict in a Postindustrial City.* Philadelphia: Temple University Press, 1991.

Binzen, Peter. "The Blue-Collar Job Drain." *Philadelphia Inquirer*, 10 May 1981.

Bissinger, Buzz. *A Prayer for the City.* New York: Vintage Books, 1997.

Bluestone, Barry, and Bennett Harrison. *The Deindustrialization of America.* New York: Basic Books, 1982.

Dilanian, Ken, and Susan Snyder. "A Mandate for Change." *Philadelphia Inquirer*, 22 July 2001.

Dorwart, Jeffery M., and Jean K. Wolf. *The Philadelphia Navy Yard.* Philadelphia: University of Pennsylvania Press, 2001.

Epstein, Jason. "The Tragical History of New York." *New York Review*, 9 April 1992.

Fernandez, Bob. "Precise and Scarce Skills Buoy Messinger Bearings." *Philadelphia Inquirer*, 12 February 1999.

Inman, Robert P. "Can Philadelphia Escape Its Fiscal Crisis with Another Tax Increase?" *Business Review*, Federal Reserve Bank of Philadelphia, September/October 1992.

Kershaw, Sarah. "Schools Turning from Teaching the Trades." *New York Times*, 21 June 2000.

Licht, Walter. *Getting Work: Philadelphia, 1840–1950*. Philadelphia: University of Pennsylvania Press, 1999.

Moss, Mitchell, Hugh O'Neill, and John Kedeshian. "Made in New York: The Future of Manufacturing in New York." Taub Urban Research Center, April 1996.

O'Connor, Matt. "Ex-Welder Gets 7 Years in Bank Fraud: Stoecker Faces Fine of $115 Million," *Chicago Tribune*, 31 October 1997.

Office of Philadelphia City Controller. "2001 Mid-Year Economic and Financial Report," January 2001.

Perez-Pena, Richard. "Bucking Trend, Debt in Albany Keeps Growing." *New York Times*, 15 July 1998.

"Philadelphia." *Fortune* magazine, June 1936.

Silcox, Harry C. *A Place to Live and Work*. University Park, Pa.: Pennsylvania State Press, 1994.

Snyder, Susan, and Dale Mezzacappa. "Deal Reached on Philadelphia Schools." *Philadelphia Inquirer*, 21 November 2001.

Starr, Roger. *The Rise and Fall of New York City*. New York: Basic Books, 1985.

Sugrue, Thomas J. *The Origins of the Urban Crisis: Race and Inequality in Postwar Detroit*. Princeton, N.J.: Princeton University Press, 1996.

"Workshop of the World." Special Report aired by WHYY-TV in Philadelphia, 13 March 2001.

Wilson, William Julius. *The Truly Disadvantaged*. Chicago: University of Chicago Press, 1987.

———. *When Work Disappears*. New York: Alfred A. Knopf, 1996.

Chapter 8

Adams, John S. "The Regional Service Economy—A Contemporary Mirage?" *The Journal of Applied Manufacturing Systems* 3, no. 1 (spring 1990): 3.

Bernstein, Jared with Lawrence Mishel and John Schmitt. *The State of Working America 2000-2001*. Economic Policy Institute, 2001.

Carson, Paul T. "The Loss of Manufacturing in America." Unpublished manuscript, 2001.

Economic Report of the President, United States Government Printing Office, Washington, 1992, 1994, 1998, 1999, 2000, and 2001.

U.S. Census of Manufacturers, 1992.

U.S. Department of State. "Country Reports." National Trade Data Bank, 1995.

U.S. Census of Manufacturers, 1987.

U.S. Department of Commerce International Trade Administration. "India - Aircraft Industry-IMI 940630." National Trade Data Bank, 1 March 1995.

U.S. Department of Commerce Bureau of Economic Analysis. U.S. International Transactions (Balance of Payments Basis). National Trade Data Bank, 1994.

U.S. Department of Commerce Economics and Statistics Administration. *USA Counties 1998.*

———. *Statistical Abstract of the United States 1999.*

———. *State and metropolitan Area Data Book 1997-1998.*

———. *USA Counties 1998.*

Chapter 9

"A Bunch of Cry-Babies? American Manufacturers and the Dollar." *Economist*, 18 August 2001.

Bloomquist, Lee. "A 'Home Run' for Steel." *Duluth News Tribune,* 6 July 2001.

Borjas, George J., and Valerie A. Ramey. "Time-Series Evidence on the Sources of Trends in Wage Inequality." *American Economic Review Papers and Proceedings,* May 1994.

Buckberg, Elaine, and Alun Thomas. "Wage Dispersion in the 1980s: Resurrecting the Role of Trade Through the Effects of Durable Employment Changes." *International Monetary Fund* (June 1996): 336–340.

Coughlin, Cletus C ., and Patricia S. Pollard. "Comparing Manufacturing Export Growth Across States: What Accounts for the Differences?" *Federal Reserve Bank of St. Louis Review* LXXXIII (January/February 2001): 25–40.

Coughlin, Cletus C. "Cross-Country Differences in the Industrial Composition and Location of Foreign-Owned Manufacturing in the United States." *Foreign Ownership and the Consequences of Direct Investment in the United States.* Ed. Douglas Woodward and Douglas Nigh. Westport, Conn.: Quorum Books, 1998, 97–118.

Dahl, Dick. "A Looming Battle: Winona Knitting." *Minnesota Business Journal,* 1986.

Economic Report of the President. Washington, D.C.: United States Government Printing Office, 1992, 1994, 1998, 1999, 2000, and 2001.

Edwards, John D. "Crude Oil and Alternative Energy Production Forecasts for the Twenty-First Century: The End of the Hydrocarbon Era." *American Association of Petroleum Geologists Bulletin* (August 1997): 1291–1305.

Goldberg, Linda S., and Keith Crockett. "The Dollar and U.S. Manufacturing." *Current Issues in Economics and Finance*, November 1998.

Holton, Richard, and Xia Yuan Lin. "China and the World Trade Association: Can the Assimilation Problems Be Overcome?" *Asian Survey*, August 1998.

Jasinowski, Jerry, Bob Stallman, and John Sweeney. Letters to President George W. Bush, 17 July 2001.

Matthews, Richard Guy. "Steel Smugglers Find Many Ways to Enter Lucrative U.S. Market." *Wall Street Journal*, 1 November 2001.

Office of the U.S. Trade Representative. "National Trade Estimate Report on Foreign Trade Barriers." National Trade Data Bank, 7 June 1994.

Orr, James. "Evolution of US trade with China." *Federal Reserve Bank of New York Quarterly Review* 16, no. 4 (winter 1991): 47–55.

Parry, Robert T. "U.S. Trade Deficits and International Competitiveness." *Vital Speeches* (1 December 1993): 98–100.

Romsaas, Jim. "Fight for Fairness." *Mesabi Daily News*, 6 July 2001.

U. S. Department of Commerce, U. S. Census Bureau. *U. S. Imports History Historical Summary, 1994–1998.*

Verespej, Michael. "Steel's Dilemma." *Industry Week*, 16 July 2001.

Viola, Tony. "LTV's Blunders Partially to Blame for Bankruptcy." *Crain's Cleveland Business*, 15 January 2001.

Von Sternberg, Bob. "Steel Imports Stir Range Ire." *Minneapolis Star Tribune*, 6 July 2001.

Welch, Jack. "A Matter of Exchange Rates." *Wall Street Journal*, 21 June 1994.

Chapter 10

Beal, Dave. "China's New Dynasty." Series in St. Paul Pioneer Press, September–December 1996.

Beaver, William. "Levi's is Leaving China." *Business Horizons*, 1 March 1995.

Bauer, Charles. *Boeing: The First Century.* Encumclaw, Wash.: TABA Publishing, 2001.

Chandler, Alfred D. Jr. *Scale and Scope, the Dynamics of Industrial Capitalism.* Cambridge, Mass.: Harvard Belknap Press, 1990.

Crown, Judith, and Glenn Coleman. *No Hands: The Rise and Fall of the Schwinn Bicycle Company, an American Institution.* New York: Henry Holt & Co., 1996.

"Fantastic Factories." *Johnson Journal,* February 2000.

Fine, Charles. *Clockspeed.* Reading, Mass.: Perseus Books, 1998.

Johnson, Jean M. "Human Resources for Science and Technology: The Asian Region." Technical paper, Atlanta, April 1993.

Lakenan, Bill, Darren Boyd, Ed Frey, and Keith Olive. "Why Cisco Fell: Outsourcing and Its Perils." *strategy+business* (third quarter 2001).

National Science Board. *Science and Engineering Indicators 2000.* Arlington, Va: National Science Foundation, 2000 (NSB-00-1).

National Science Board Committee on Industrial Support for R&D. *The Competitive Strength of U.S. Industrial Science and Technology; Strategic Issues.* Washington, D.C.: National Science Foundation, 1992.

Rose, Robert, and Carl Quintanilla. "Sara Lee's Plan to Contract Out Work Underscores a Trend Among U.S. Firms." *Wall Street Journal,* 17 September 1997.

Sequoia Fund annual meeting report. *Outstanding Investor Digest,* 2001 Patient Subscriber Bonus Edition.

Simpson, David. "Sharing the Wealth." *Appliance Magazine,* October 2000.

Solomon, Charlene M. "Moving Jobs to Offshore Markets: Why It's Done and How It Works." *Workforce,* July 1999.

Storch, Charles. "Schwinn Saga: Good Bikes, Bad Breaks." *Chicago Tribune,* 3 January 1993.

Thurm, Scott. "Solectron Becomes a Force in 'Stealth Manufacturing.'" *Wall Street Journal,* 8 August 1998.

Thurston, Charles W. "Branded Offshore Manufacturing Finds a Home in Ireland and Singapore." *Chemical Market Reporter,* June 1998.

Young, Jeffrey. *Cisco Unauthorized.* Roseville, Calif.: Prima Publishing, 2001.

Chapter 11

Markusen, Ann, Peter Hall, Scott Campbell, and Sabina Deitrick. *The Rise of the Gunbelt.* New York: Oxford University Press, 1991.

Markusen, Ann, and Sean Costigan. *Arming the Future.* New York: Council on Foreign Relations Press, 1999.

Marsh, Ann. "Creative Destruction." *Forbes*, 9 March 1998.

Matthews, Robert Guy. "Steelmakers Say They Are a Key Component of Security." *Wall Street Journal*, 19 September 2001.

National Research Council. *Defense Manufacturing in 2010 and Beyond: Historical Perspective on the U.S. Defense Industrial Base.* Washington, D.C.: National Academy Press, 1999.

Oden, Michael, and Ann Markusen, Dan Fleming, and Mark Drayse. "Post Cold War Frontiers: Defense Downsizing and Conversion in Los Angeles." Report for Center for Urban Policy Research, Rutgers University, 1996.

Oden, Michael, Catherine Hill, Elizabeth Mueller, Jonathan Feldman, and Ann Markusen. "Changing the Future: Converting the St. Louis Economy." Report for Center for Urban Policy Research, Rutgers University, 1993.

Pages, Erik. *Responding to Defense Dependence.* Westport, Conn.: Praeger, 1996.

Thomson, Allison. "Defense-Related Employment and Spending, 1996–2006." *Monthly Labor Review*, July 1998.

Chapter 12

Associated Press. "Honda Drives Resurgence in Central Ohio," *Chicago Tribune*, 26 June 1988.

Automotive News Market Data Book, May 1999.

Burstein, Melvin, and Arthur Rolnick. "Congress Should End the Economic War among the States." Region magazine of the Federal Reserve Bank of Minnneapolis, March 1995.

Culbreth, Andrea. "Toyota Comes to Princeton." *Princeton Daily Clarion*, 1 December 1995.

Glickman, Norman J., and Douglas P. Woodward. *The New Competitors: How Foreign Investors Are Changing the U.S. Economy.* New York: Basic Books, 1989.

Grace, Beth. "Wheels Spin Success for Ohio Town." *Chicago Tribune*, 26 June 1988.

Harbour Report: A Decade Later 1979-1989. Troy, Mich.: Harbour and Associates, 1990.

Harbour Reports for North America, 1996, 1998, 1999, 2000, and 2001. Troy, Mich.: Harbour and Associates.

Howenstine, Ned G. "Foreign Direct Investment in the United States: New Investment in 2000." *Survey of Current Business,* June 2001.

Jensen, Christopher. "Two of Honda's Ohio Assembly Plants among the Most Productive in the World." *Cleveland Plain Dealer,* 29 October 1998.

Klier, Thomas H. "Geographic Concentration in U.S. Manufacturing: Evidence from the U.S. Auto Supplier Industry." Federal Reserve Bank of Chicago, December 1998.

Segev, Eran, and Cletus C. Coughlin. "Location Determinants of New Foreign-Owned Manufacturing Plants." Federal Reserve Bank of St. Louis, 1997.

Treese, James, and John Huey. "Shaking Up Detroit: How Japanese Car Makers Are Beating the Big Three on Their Own Turf." *Business Week,* 14 August 1989.

Taylor, Alex. "The Man Who Put Honda Back on Track." *Fortune,* 9 September 1996.

White, Joseph B., Gregory L. White, and Norihiko Shirouzu. "Soon, the Big Three Won't Be, as Foreigners Make Inroads in U.S." *Wall Street Journal,* 13 August 2001.

Chapter 13

Bommer, Rolf. "Environmental Policy and Industrial Competitiveness: The Pollution-Haven Hypothesis Reconsidered." *Review of International Economics,* May 1999.

"Brown and Out in Beverly Hills." *Wall Street Journal,* 23 January 2001.

Coy, Peter, and Christopher Palmieri. "Gridlock on the Power Grid." *Business Week,* 28 August 2000.

Jones, Colin. "It Defies Logic to Reject Plans to Build a New South Bay Power Plant in Coyote Valley." *San Francisco Chronicle,* 2 January 2001.

Leavenworth, Stuart, and Dale Kasler. "Electricity Plants Gulping Fuel." *Sacramento Bee,* 11 February 2001.

National Science Board, Science and Engineering Indicators 2000. Arlington, Va.: National Science Foundation, 2000.

Palmieri, Christopher, Laura Cohn, and Wendy Zellner. "California's Power Failure." *Business Week,* 8 January 2001.

"Rival States Pitch Power to Woo California Firms." *Wall Street Journal,* 26 January 2001.

Schwartz, Nelson. "Pumping Out Profits," *Fortune,* 1 October 2001.

Shelley, Kristina J. "The Future of Jobs for College Graduates." *Monthly Labor Review*, July 1992.

Valles, Colleen. "Lack of Sites Plagues Plants." *Contra Costa Times*, 14 January 2001.

Chapter 14

"Collaboration & Jointness, the Fruit of Our Labor: Results at the Sartell Mill." Joint report from Champion International and Pace Local 7-274, 2000.

Coy, Peter. "Will AT&T Win 'The Baldrige Award for Quality in Mergers?'" *Business Week*, 6 May 1991.

Deogun, Nikhil, and Steven Lipin. "Cautionary Tales: When the Big Deals Turn Bad." *Wall Street Journal*, 8 December 1999.

Hambrick, Donald C., and Richard A. D'Aveni. "Large Corporate Failures as Downward Spirals." *Administrative Science Quarterly*, March 1988.

"How Mergers Go Wrong." *Economist*, 22 July 2000.

Kaplan, Steven N. *Mergers and Productivity*. National Bureau of Economic Research book. Chicago: University of Chicago Press, 2000.

KPMG Consulting. "Cross-border M&A Reaches All-time High." 1 February 2000.

Levy, Adam. "Promises Unfulfilled." *Bloomberg Markets*, April 2001.

"Merger Would Create Paper and Pulp Giant." *St. Paul Pioneer Press*, 18 February 2000.

Murray, Matt. "Why Jack Welch's Brand of Leadership Matters." *Wall Street Journal*, 5 September 2001.

Pfeffer, Jeffrey. *Competitive Advantage Through People: Unleashing the Power of the Workforce*. Boston: Harvard Business School Press, 1994.

Sirower, Mark L. *The Synergy Trap*. New York: Free Press, 1997.

Sobel, Robert. *The Rise and Fall of the Conglomerate Kings*. New York: Stein and Day, 1984.

Verity, John. "Is NCR Ready to Ring Up Some Cash? After Five Painful Years, AT&T Will Spin Off a Refurbished NCR." *Business Week*, 14 October 1996.

Vlasic, Bill, and Bradley Stertz. *Taken for a Ride: How Daimler-Benz Drove Off with Chrysler*. New York: William Morrow, 2000.

Zimmerman, Fred. *The Turnaround Experience: Real World Lessons in Revitalizing Corporations*. New York: McGraw-Hill, 1991.

Chapter 15

Barnard, Chester I. *The Functions of the Executive.* Cambridge, Mass.: Harvard University Press, 1968.

Byrne, John A. *Chainsaw: The Notorious Career of Al Dunlap in the Era of Profit-at-Any-Price.* New York: HarperCollins, 1999.

Collins, Jim. "Beware the Self-Promoting CEO." *Wall Street Journal,* 26 November 2001.

Dunlap, Albert J. *Mean Business.* New York: Times Books, 1997.

Follett, Mary Parker. *Dynamic Administration.* New York: Harper, 1941.

Gantt, Henry L. *Industrial Leadership.* New Haven, Conn.: Yale University Press, 1916.

Gantt, Henry L. "The Parting of the Ways" In *Classics in Management* Ed. Harwood F. Merrill. New York: American Management Association, 1960, 151–60.

Gertzen, Jason. "Harnischfeger Renamed Joy Global; Mining Equipment Company Seeks Fresh Start." *Milwaukee Journal Sentinel,* 13 July 2001.

Greenberg, Herb. "Short-Order Request: Sunbeam Is Toast." *Fortune,* 28 April 1997.

Hayes, Robert H., and William J. Abernathy. "Managing Our Way to Economic Decline." *Harvard Business Review,* July–August 1980.

Iverson, Ken. *Plain Talk.* New York: John Wiley & Sons, 1998.

Kohut, Andrew. Memo to staffers of Pew Research Center concerning "America's Place in the World" survey, 13 September 2001.

Laing, Jonathan R. "Grave Digger: How Harnischfeger's Flashy Chieftain Drove the Firm to Ruin." *Barron's,* 12 July 1999.

"New World Coming: American Security in the 21st Century." Report by The United States Commission on National Security/21st Century, 15 September 1999.

Norris, Floyd. "S.E.C. Accuses Former Sunbeam Official of Fraud." *New York Times,* 16 May 2001.

Norris, Floyd. "An Executive's Missing Years: Papering Over Past Problems." *New York Times,* 16 July 2001.

Sheldon, Oliver. "A Professional Creed for Management." In *Classics in Management* Ed. Merrill F. Harwood. New York: American Management Association, 1960.

Chapter 16

Bary, Andrew. "Down, But Not Out: America's Great Industrial Stocks May be Set for a Comeback." *Barron's,* 4 December 2000.

Berkshire Hathaway, annual report for 2000, 28 February 2001.

Berman, Harold. *The Great Myths of 1929 and the Lessons to be Learned.* New York: Greenwood Press, 1991.

"From Public to Private: Jason Incorporated." *Everest Advisor* newsletter, October 2000.

Brown, Ken. "Industrial Stocks' Early Rally Creates Investing Pitfalls." *Wall Street Journal,* 6 June 2001.

Burrows, Peter. "Leaving Wall Street—and Going Private." *Business Week,* 28 May 2001.

Chan, SuHan, George W. Gau, and Ko Wang. "Stock Market Reaction to Capital Investment Decisions: Evidence from Business Relocations." *Journal of Financial and Quantitative Analysis* (March 1995): 81–100.

Deutsch, Claudia. "Guevara to Reagan, and Beyond." *New York Times,* 17 September 2000.

Hahn, Avital Louria. "New Economy, Bad Math." *Investment Dealers Digest,* 23 October 2000.

Jason Inc. Various annual reports.

Leuthold Group. Study of manufacturers' valuations, June 2001.

Loomis, Carol, with Warren Buffett. "Mr. Buffett on the Stock Market." *Fortune,* 22 November 1999.

McClenahen, John. "Against the Grain: Some Investors Capitalize on Manufacturing." *Industry Week,* 10 January 2000.

Morgenson, Gretchen. "New Economy: Investors Finally Consider Internet Companies' Shaky Math." *New York Times,* 26 February 2001.

PaineWebber Index of Investor Optimism, monthly press releases, 1999–2001.

Panchek, Patricia. "Revenge of the Old Economy." *Industry Week,* 15 January 2001.

Perkins, Anthony, and Michael Perkins. *The Internet Bubble.* New York: HarperBusiness, 2001.

Picker, Ida. "The Buyout Kings of Washington." *Bloomberg Markets,* March 2001.

Revell, Janice. "Forget About Earnings: You Want Free Cash Flow—and Lots of It." *Fortune,* 11 June 2001.

Tice, David. "Analyzing the Analysts. Are Investors Getting Unbiased Research from Wall Street?" Testimony before House Capital Markets Committee, 14 June 2001.

U.S. Securities and Exchange Commission. SEC Filings and Forms (EDGAR), Financial Statements, Pro Forma Financial Information and Exhibits, several companies, 2000 and 2001.

Zehren, Charles. "Has Buffett Become a Casualty of the 'New Economy?'" *Seattle Times*, 10 March 2000.

Chapter 17

Amato, Ivan. "Fomenting a Revolution in Miniature." *Science*, 16 October 1998.

Caudle, Neil, and Elizabeth Zubritsky. "The Man Who Taught Carbon Dioxide to Clean." *Endeavors* magazine of the University of North Carolina at Chapel Hill (winter 1998).

Dyrness, Christine. "RTI's Latest Spinoff Could Be a Big Star." *Raleigh News and Observer*, 27 October 2000.

Hammer Siler George Associates. "The Research Triangle Park: The First 40 Years." Report prepared by Hammer Siler George for the Research Triangle Foundation, 19 February 1999.

Jones, Megan. "Weaving Fabric with Technology." *Cary News*, 1 April 2000.

Lane, Randall. "Involuntary Entrepreneurs." *Forbes*, 3 June 1996.

Larrabee, Charles X. *Many Missions: Research Triangle Institute's First 31 Years.* Durham, N.C.: Research Triangle Institute, 1991.

Norris, Jeannie Faris. "From Research to Reality." *NC State*, the alumni magazine of NC State University, autumn 1999.

Pearson, Daniel. "Nerves Fragile as Cisco Moves Ax for Job Cuts." *Triangle Business Journal*, 20 April 2001.

Rothacker, Rick. "Inside the Carolinas' Hottest High-Tech Address." *Charlotte Observer*, 25 September 2000.

Weisbecker, Lee. "Brawl Brews Over MCNC Cash." *Triangle Business Journal*, 9 June 2000.

Woestendiek, Kathyrn. "Profs and Profits." *North Carolina* magazine, July 1999.

Chapter 18

Blickley, George. "NIST Helps Small Firms Harvest New Technologies." *Control Engineering*, December 1996.

Carr, Kevin. "Manufacturing Extension Partnership: Helping America's Small Manufacturers." *Quality Digest,* September 1998.

"Growing Pains at Reitter & Schefenacker Ease." Focus on Manufacturing: Tennessee Manufacturing Extension Program, spring 1999.

"Manufacturing Extension Programs: Manufacturers' Views of Services." General Accounting Office, August 1995.

Chapter 19

Berner, Robert. "Wichita: Not So Far from Ground Zero." *Business Week,* 8 October 2001.

Leontief, Wassily. "The Ins and Outs of Input/Output Analysis." *Mechanical Engineering* 109, no. 1 (January 1987): 29.

Lerman, Robert I., and Hillard Pouncy. "The Compelling Case for Youth Apprenticeships." *The Public Interest.*

Oliver, Charles. "The Pensions Time Bomb." *Corporate Finance* (July 1994): 35–41.

Porter, Michael, and Debra van Opstal. "U.S. Competitiveness 2001: Strengths, Vulnerabilities, and Long-Term Priorities." *Report from Council on Competitiveness,* 14 February 2001.

Song, Kyung M., and Luke Timmerman. "Boeing Job Cuts Reach Deep as 5,000 Here Get Pink Slips." *Seattle Times,* 13 October 2001.

Taninecz, George. "America's Most Successful Small Manufacturers." *Industry Week,* 8 November 1999.

Index

Ada County, ID, 72
Age, of plants and companies, 60, 84, 90, 163
Agilent Technologies, 148–49
Agriculture, 27, 66
Airbus Industries, 29, 123
Aircraft industry, 28–29, 56, 233–34
    engine parts, 67
    trade deficits and, 123
Alcoa, 122, 230
Alcorn County, MS, 93
Allegheny County, PA, 87
Allen County, IN, 33–37
AlliedSignal, 178, 181, 188
Allis-Chalmers, 123, 183
American Association of Engineering Societies, 14
American Electronics Association, 15
American Optical, 240
American Steel (Preston), 39
AmeriSteel, 230
AMF, 182
Amp, 188
Andersen Corp., 172
Anderson, Wendell, 137–38
Androscoggin County, ME, 93
Anheuser-Busch, 180
Apparel industry, 19, 91
Armstrong, 84
Armstrong, Michael, 197
Ashton, Pat, 34
Asia Pulp & Paper, 196
Asian financial crisis, 8, 134–35
Asp, Bill, 67
Associations, 261–64
AT&T, 180, 183, 197

Atlanta, GA, 244
Auburn Cord Duesenberg Co., 33
Austin, TX, 72
Auto and truck industry, 11, 12, 21, 22, 56, 80, 98, 243
    auto parts manufacturing, 145, 226
    capital spending, 29
    foreign competition and, 29–30
    foreign-owned vehicle factories, 158–64
    globalizers and, 78
    imports, 120
    Indiana and, 34–35, 44
    Mexico and, 139
    relocation and, 53
    South America and, 30
    trade deficits and, 123
Automation equipment, 14

Barnard, Chester, 193
Barry, David, 218
Baseball, major league, 85, 87
Bauer, Eugene, 140
Bayh, Evan, 161
Becton-Dickinson, 66
Beecher, William, 240
Behlen, Walter, 66
Behlen Manufacturing, 66
"Beige wallpaper managers," 194
Benefits, 19–20
Benton County, AR, 75
Benton County, OR, 67, 80–81
Berdan, Frank, 80
Berkshire Hathaway, 202–3
Bermo, 144

Bernstein, Jared, 116
Bethlehem Steel, 39, 193
Binghamton, NY, 90
Biomet, 66
Bissinger, Buzz, 97, 99
Bloomberg Markets, 178, 181
Blystone, John, 188
BMW, 160
Boeing, 28–29, 72, 87, 155, 157, 233–34
    Asian subcontractors and, 141
Boeing: The First Century (Bauer), 140
Bolt, Beranek and Newman, 152
Bond ratings, 108
Brazil, engineering degrees in, 140
Breed Technologies, 43
Bregi, Jim, 231
Bremer Commission, 191
Bronx County, NY, 91
Broome County, NY, 90
Buffalo, NY, 83
Buffett, Warren, 202–3
Building codes, 57
Burns, Katie, 213
Burroughs-Sperry, 180
Burroughs Wellcome, 218
Busse, Keith, 32, 37, 38–41, 44, 45
Byrne, John, 195

C&A Tool, 31–32, 41–42
Cabell County, WV, 93
California, energy costs and, 170
Calpine Corp., 170
Campbell Taggert, 180
Capital equipment, 14
Capital spending, auto industry, 29
Carbon dioxide, uses of, 222–24
Carnegie Steel, 182
Carpeting, 77, 203
Carson, Paul T., 116
Carson, Terri, 223
Cass County, ND, 11, 72
Caterpillar, 93, 121
Census Bureau, 249
Cerf, Vinton, 152
Champion Paper, 184–87
Charitable giving, 9
Chemical production, 17, 93, 123
Chicago, IL, 98, 106

China
    engineering degrees in, 140
    trade deficit, 125, 127–28
China Bicycles Company, 146
Chrysler, 13, 139, 180–81
Cincinnati Milicron, 12
Cisco Systems, 170, 212, 215–16
    outsourcing and, 147
Cisco Unauthorized (Young), 147
Citizens Bank, 9
Civera, Mario, 97
Clockspeed (Fine), 146
Cluster counties, 76–78
Coal industry, 19, 83
Coca-Cola, 160
Coffee County, GA, 67
Coffey, Matt, 147–48
Cohen, Stephen, 201
Cole, Mike, 223
Coleman, Glenn, 146
Collins, Jim, 197
Colorado Gas, 187
Community Research Institute, 42
Compact Strip Production, 38
Compensation
    changes and poverty rate, 113
    disparity, and manufacturing,
        115–16
    manufacturing vs. retail, 17
    wage levels in northeast Indiana,
        42–43
Competition, foreign, 11–13, 28–30, 41
Composite materials, 78
Computer manufacturing, 17, 56, 80,
    136–38
    components, foreign manufacture
        of, 28
    computer-aided design, 152
    hardware, 24–25
    trade deficits and, 122
Connecticut, defense systems and, 83
Conrow, Dick, 31–32, 41–42
Construction, 111
    incentives, 35–36
Consumer appliances, 123
Contract manufacturers, 145
Control Data Corporation, 136–38
Convergence, 224

Cook County, IL, 87. *See also* Chicago, IL

Corporate Tragedy, A: The Agony of International Harvester Company (Marsh), 34

Cost-driven mergers, 184

Council for Entrepreneurial Development, 219

Council on Competitiveness, 235, 238

Counties, manufacturing analysis of, 10–11. *See also specific county*; Counties gaining momentum; Counties losing momentum

Counties gaining momentum, 64–81
    cluster counties, 76–78
    decentralization policies and, 79–80
    freeway flyers, 55, 68–70, 248
    globalizers, 78
    gradual growers, 55, 73–76, 225, 248
    hinterland highspots, 50, 55, 64–68, 248
    innovators, 78–79
    methodology for choosing, 247–48
    metro movers, 55, 70–73, 248
    near misses, 79

Counties losing momentum, 82–94
    methodology for choosing, 248–49
    midrange sliders, 248
    sliding Goliaths, 248
    smaller sliders, 248

Crawfordsville Project, 38–39

Cray, Seymour, 137

Cray Research, 137, 138

"Creative destruction" theory, 240

Crone, Ted, 105

Cronos Integrated Microsystems, 218, 219–20

Crouch, Mark, 43

Crown, Judith, 146

Cummings, AL, 9

Cummings Research Park, 79, 213

Cummins Engine, 188

Currency values, trade deficit and, 133–35

Cusciotta, Tom, 185, 186

Customers, shifting locations of, 60

Cuyahoga County, OH, 87

Czech Technical University, 139

Daimler-Benz, 13

DaimlerChrysler, 30, 162, 163, 178–79, 181

Dalton, GA, 77

Dalton State College, 77

Dana Corp., 66

Dane County, WI, 76, 245

Daugherty, Dick, 215

De Puy Inc., 66

Decentralization policies, 79–80

Deere & Co., 121, 129, 182

Defense-aerospace industry, 10, 87, 88, 90, 150–57

Defense-industrial base, shifting of, 150–57

Delaware Valley Industrial Resource Center, 109

Denso, 158

DeSimone, Joe, 211–12, 222–24

Detroit, MI, 98, 243

Dickenson, Larry, 140

Digital Equipment, 76

Digital technology, 5

Dillon, John, 185–86

Divergence, 224

Dollar value, 133

Donnelley & Sons, 66

Doppler Gear, 231

Douglas, Michael, 150

Downsizing, 91

Dubois County, IN, 69, 77

Dunigan, Shelia, 220–21, 232

Dunlap, Albert J. ("Chainsaw Al"), 14, 194–95

DuPont, 84, 93, 212, 222

Durable goods, 6, 26

Durham County, NC, 72

Dutchess County, NY, 90

Dynamic Administration (Follett), 194

Eaker Air Force Base, 69

Economic incentives, 61

Economies of scale, 143–44, 179

Economist Intelligence Unit study, 162

Economist, The, 25

Education
engineering degrees, 139–40, 169, 173–74, 236
manufacturing and, 167, 239
technical, 30, 140
U.S. decline in, 235

Efficiency, 54

Electronics industry, 72, 87
foreign suppliers and, 141

Elion, Gertrude, 216

Elkhart County, IN, 77, 234

E-mail, 152

Emotionalism, 62–63

Employment
changes by major sector, 111–12
trends, 19
manufacturing, 7

Endicott, NY, 90

Endicott-Johnson, 90

Engineering, 12
degrees, 139–40, 169, 173–74, 236
perception of, 14

Engineering Research Associates, 137

Engler, John, 36

Enron, 210, 241

Ephlin, Don, 53

Epson, 72

Epstein, Jason, 106–7

Ericsson, 212

Erie County, NY, 87

Essex County, NJ, 87

Eurodollar, 179

European Commission, 181

Exports, 8–10, 120

Exxon, 178

Fabricated metal products, 17, 22

Factories, 167, 169–77
aging industrial professionals, 176
engineering and, 169, 173–74
jobs, 9, 177
management and, 192
opposition to location of (NIMBYism), 13, 170–72

Fairfield County, CT, 87

Falling Down, 150, 154

Farris, Bill, 59

Federal Reserve index of manufacturing production, 7

Ferguson, Gillum, 105

Finance, 26, 27, 111

Financial crisis, Asian, 8

Fine, Charles, 146

Fiorina, Carly, 197

Fitch, Robert, 107

Follett, Mary Parker, 194

Food industry, 17, 19, 22

Ford, 30, 139, 151, 162–63, 177, 194, 212, 244

Foreign competition, 28–30, 41, 93, 234

Foreign investment, 158–65

Foreign trade, 8–10

Fort Wayne, IN, 32–36

Fortune magazine, 99

Foxcon, 231

Frazier, Lynne McKenna, 44

Freeway flyers, 55, 68–70, 78, 248
employment changes by sector, 112
government expenditures per capita, 114
household income changes, 113
manufacturing employment history, 252–53

Frigidaire, 7

Fringe benefits, 19–20

Fruehauf, 101, 105

Fulton County, GA, 244

Functions of the Executive, The (Barnard), 193

Furniture industry, 93

Gateley, Gary, 227

Gates, Bill and Melinda, 9

General Electric, 33, 90, 93, 123, 133, 181, 188–89

General Motors Corp., 30, 35, 52, 160, 163, 212
mergers and, 182
plants in Mexico, 139
Toyota and, 160, 162, 163

General Signal, 187
Geographic location, assessment of, 80
Germany
    auto and truck manufacturers, 12, 160
    power tool production, 227
Giant Manufacturing, 146
Gibelhaus, Gary, 66
Gibson County, IN, 78
Giddings and Lewis, 12
Giuliani, Rudolph, 108
Glass container manufacturing, 93
GlaxoSmithKline, 212, 216–18
Globalization, 11, 136–49
    economies of scale, 143–44
    foreign-owned U.S. companies, 159
    outsourcing, 144–49
    suppliers, 140–43
    trade deficit and, 138–40
Globalizers, 78
GM. *See* General Motors Corp.
Goldfarb, Bob, 127
Good to Great (Collins), 197
Gordon, Robert, 24–25
Grabill Corp., 105
Grade, Jeffrey T., 196
Gradual growers, 55, 73–76, 225, 248
    employment changes by sector, 112
    household income changes, 113
    manufacturing employment history, 253–54
Greenback Fan Corp., 75
Greenberg, Herb, 195
Greenspan, Alan, 25
Grippe, Samantha, 119
Grumman Corp., 87
Guidant, 137
Guilds, 76
Guthrie, Thomas, 36, 42

H.S. Die and Mold, 177
Hamilton, IN, 37
Hammer Siler George Associates, 214
Hangers, 211–12, 223, 224
Harbour, James, 139

Harbour Report, 139, 163, 165
Hardis, Stephen, 10, 169, 173
Harney, Dennis, 77
Harnischfeger Industries, 196
Harrison County, MS, 93
Hart & Cooley, 228, 230
Hayes, Rutherford B., 96
Hayes, Samuel, 190
Haynes, Victoria Franchetti, 218
Health care industry, 111, 112
Health insurance, 21
Hedonic price index, 25
Henry County, VA, 93
Henry Disston Saw Works, 96
Hewlett-Packard, 67, 76, 80–81, 148–49, 197
Hidalgo County, TX, 76
Hinterland highspots, 50, 55, 64–68, 248
    employment changes by sector, 112
    government expenditures per capita, 114
    household income changes, 113
    manufacturing employment history, 250
Hitchings, George, 216
Hodges, Luther, 214
Hohlmaier, Karl, 142
Holifield, Cecil, 69
"Hollow Corporation, The," 144–45
Holton, Richard, 127
Homeland security, 156–57
Honda Motor Co., 12, 30, 78, 158, 160, 161–62
Honeywell, 137, 138, 178, 181
Hook, Ed, 109, 232
Houldin, Joe, 109
Household income, 113
Howard, Robert, 37
Hudson County, NJ, 87, 91
Hutchinson Technology, 67, 81
Hutchinson, MN, 67

Iadicola, Peter, 34
IBM, 90, 91, 137, 138, 160, 212, 215, 216
    outsourcing and, 146

Idaho, 53
Immigrants, factory jobs and, 9
Impact, 36
Imports, trade deficit and, 12, 120, 133
Inco, 93
Income
    changes and poverty rate, 113
    disparity, and manufacturing,
        115–16
    manufacturing vs. retail, 17
    wage levels in northeast Indiana,
        42–43
Index of Investor Optimism, 202
Indiana, 32–45
    auto industry and, 34–35, 44, 45
    C&A Tool, 31–32, 41–42
    foreign-owned facilities in, 158
    Fort Wayne, 32–36
    International Harvester, 22, 33–34
    Kosciusko County, 66
    manufacturing in, 234
    move to Mexico from, 43
    Steel Dynamics Inc., 32, 37, 40
    wage levels, 42–43
    see also specific counties
Indiana Economic Development
    Commission, 44
Indiana Northeast Development, 34
Industrial classification system, 19, 23
Industrial machinery, 87
Industrial swarming, 61, 76
Information technology, 72, 216
Infrastructure, inadequacy of, 57
Ingersoll Milling, 12
Inman, Robert, 106
Innovation, 199, 212, 224, 235, 236
Innovators, 78–79
Insley, Susan, 161
Institute of Electrical and Electronics
    Engineers, 14
Instruments, 19, 87
Insurance, 21, 26, 27, 111
Intel, 72, 212, 220
Intermet, 228, 230
International Harvester, 22, 33–34, 182
International Monetary Fund, 16
International Paper, 185–86
International Science Yearbook, The, 212

Internet, 152, 204
    auctioning, 148
    -driven technologies,
        productivity and, 24–25
    infatuation with, 5, 210
Internet Bubble, The (Perkins and
    Perkins), 204
Investment-driven mergers, 184
Investments, 201–10
    foreign, 158–65, 239
    manufacturers and, 8–9
Isothermal forging, 151
Iverson, Ken, 191

Jackson Utility, 229–30
Jackson, MI, 36
Jackson, TN, 225–26, 228–31
Japan
    auto and truck manufacturers,
        12, 158
    engineering degrees in, 139–40
    investment in U.S., 164–65
    power tools, 227
    production and, 6
Jasinowski, Jerry, 134
Jason Inc., 208–9
Javonovich and MacDonald, 207
JDS Uniphase, 220
Joel Popkin and Co., 26–27
John Deere, 84
Johnson Controls, 231
Johnson, Bob, 176
Johnson, NY, 90
Joint Strike Fighter contract, 157
Jones, Colin, 171
Joseph, Gene, 161
Joy Global, 196

Kaglie, Richard, 15
Kahn, Bob, 152
Kaiser Industries, 151
Kanawha County, WV, 93
Kaplan family, 187
Kawamoto, Nobuhiko, 162
Kearney & Trecker, 12
Keck, Damon, 40
Kellogg Foundation, 9
Kelsey-Hayes, 100–102, 105

Kennedy, Randy, 228
Kessel, Richard, 171
Kessler, Andy, 5
Ketchum, Ralph David, 102
Khurana, Rakesh, 197
Kimball International, 69
Kimberly-Clark, 195
Kings County, NY, 113
Kohut, Andrew, 192
Kolakowski, Manfred, 38–39
Kolbe & Kolbe, 75
Korea, auto manufacturing and, 30
Kosciusko County, IN, 66
KPMG International, 178, 190
Krugman, Paul, 25
Kuban, Bill, 141
Kurt Manufacturing, 141

Labor
    high cost of, 58
    insufficient supply of, 57
    -management systems, 164
    relations, 239
Lake County, IN, 242–43
Lance, Bronwyn, 9
Land shortages, 57
Langone, Ken, 211
Larimer County, CO, 72
La Salle County, IL, 93
Lash, William H., 128
Lead Award, 30
Leadership, 167, 191–98, 236, 238
Leather industry, 19
Lee County, FL, 76
Lefkovich, Tobias, 196
Leland, Henry, 194
Leuthold Group, 203
Levi Strauss, 84
Levin, Jerry, 195–96
Levine, Lawrence T., 145
Lewandowski, Tom, 43
Lienhart, Brad, 3–4, 222
Lilly Foundation, 9
Link, 90
Lionel, 182
Liquidation, 58
Litigation, 58–59
Litton Industries, 182

Lockheed Martin, 29, 155, 157
Logan County, OH, 78
Los Angeles County, CA, 154
"Loss of Manufacturing in America,
    The," 116
Lowenstein, Roger, 195
LTV, 119, 129, 182, 183, 193
Lucent Technologies, 183, 212, 213
Luger, Michael, 214, 215
Lutz, Bob, 194

McClain, Jim, 222–24
McCoy, Alan, 129
McDonnell Douglas, 28–29, 87, 154–55
McGill Bearing Corp., 39
McGillivary, Peter, 143
McKnight Foundation, 9
McLean County, IN, 78
McLeod County, MN, 67, 81
McTeer, Bob, 4
McWherter Center of Advanced
    Industrial Technologies, 226, 229
Machine tool industry, 11–12
Machinery, 17, 19, 22
Madison County, TN, 75, 225–29
Maguire, Frank, 100–105
Mahoning County, OH, 244–45
Maine, Susan, 14–15
Management, 58. See also Leadership
Manatee County, FL, 73
Manhattan, NYC, 87
Mansour, Mohamed, 221–22
Manufacturing
    American attitude toward, 167,
        175
    boosting, 237–40
    defense-related jobs, 150
    employee shortage, 15
    employment history, detailed
        statistics, 250–60
    fringe benefits, 19–20
    importance of, 241–46
    income disparity and, 115–16
    jobs, 242
    organizations. See Manufacturing
        organizations
    outsourcing and, 15
    payroll, by major industry, 17–19

Manufacturing, *continued*
    productivity, 6–7
    prosperity and, 111–16
    relocation. *See* Relocation
    subsectors, 203
    taxes and, 114–15
    U.S./world comparisons, 6
Manufacturing Extension Partnership,
    225–26
Manufacturing Matters (Cohen and
    Zysman), 201
Manufacturing News Database, 84
Manufacturing organizations, 261–65
    educational, 264
    government, 264–65
    professional/industry, 261–64
Marathon County, WI, 75
Maricopa County, AZ, 79
Marion County, IA, 67
Markus, Karen, 219–20
Markusen, Ann, 153, 154, 155
Marquip, 233
Marsh, Barbara, 34
Marshall County, IN, 79
Martin, Vince, 208–9
Marz, Sam, 67
Massachusetts, defense systems and,
    83
Massachusetts Institute for a New
    Commonwealth, 9
Mathews, Robert, 109
Mattison Technologies, 59
Maura County, TN, 69
Maxwell, Bill, 112
Maytag, 75
Mazda, 36, 164
Mean Business (Dunlap), 195
Medical devices, 66, 76, 77–78, 123
Medical research firms, 72
Medieval guilds, 76
Mediocrity, 91
Medtronic, 76, 77–78, 137, 184, 192–93
Meiland, Nico, 146
Menke, Robert Sr., 69
Mercedes-Benz, 160, 164
Merchant, M. Eugene, 176
Mergers and acquisitions, 13, 43, 58,
    167, 178–90, 235, 239

cost reductions and, 183
foreign investment and, 159
magnitude of, 178
managerial model, search for,
    188–90
regulatory changes and, 179
types of, 184
Messinger Bearings, 109, 232
Metro movers, 55, 70–73, 248
    employment changes by sector,
        112
    government expenditures per
        capita, 114
    household income changes, 113
    manufacturing employment
        history, 251–52
Mexico, auto manufacturing in, 139
Micell Technologies, 211, 222–24
Michelin, 158
Michigan Economic Development
    Corporation, 15
Midrange sliders, 82, 88–91, 248
    employment changes by sector,
        112
    household income changes, 113
    manufacturing employment
        history, 256–58
Midwest manufacturing, 11, 14–15
Miller, Dane, 66
Millet, Mark, 40
Minimills, 38, 242
Mining, 27
    productivity reports and, 26
    trade deficit and, 119, 128
Minnesota Iron Range, 119
Mishel, Lawrence, 116
Mississippi County, AR, 69
Mitsubishi, 162, 164
Mobil, 178
Modern Machine Shop, 32
Mohamed, Mansour, 3–4
Money magazine, 67
Monroe County, MS, 93
Motor home industry, 77, 146
Motor-vehicle components, 66
Mraz, Dan, 67
Mueller, Everett, 132
Mueller, Franz, 116

Multifactor productivity, 26–27
Murray, Inc., 230–31

NAFTA, 44
Napa County, CA, 77
NASA, 109
Nasdaq, 201, 202
Nash, Jim, 131, 232
Nassau County, NY, 87
National Association of
    Manufacturers (NAM), 4, 5–6
National Institutes of Health, 216
National Research Council, 151, 152
National Science Foundation, 8, 175,
    212
National security, 150
NCR, 180, 183
Near misses, 79
Nebraska, 53
NEC, 72
Netscape, 152
Network Systems, 137, 138
Nevada, 53
New economy, 4, 24
New England factory jobs, 9
New Mexico, 53
New York, 53
New York City, NY, 106–8
New York Power Authority, 171
Newport County, RI, 93
Newton, Harry, 202
Nichols, Robert, 129
NIMBY, 13, 167, 170–72, 236
Nissan, 160, 162, 163
No Hands (Crown and Coleman), 146
Nocera, Joe, 195
Nonyang University (Singapore), 30,
    139
Norfolk Southern Railroad, 35
Nortel Networks, 212, 213, 216
North American Free Trade
    Agreement, 44
North American Industry
    Classification System (NAICS), 249
North Carolina State University, 3
North Carolina, Research Triangle
    Park and, 213
North Dakota, 11, 53

Northeast Buffalo Highway, 83
Northeast Indiana Innovation Center,
    44
Northeast Midwest Institute, 84
Northeast Power Coordinating
    Council, 171
Northrup, 87, 154
Northumberland County, PA, 93
Nothdurft, William, 10
"Not in my backyard" (NIMBY), 13,
    167, 170–72, 236
Nucor Corp., 38–39, 122, 177, 189, 193
Nummi, 164

Oden, Michael, 155
Office equipment, trade deficits and,
    122
Offload/offtake agreements, 140–41
Ohio, auto production in, 161–62, 164
Oil embargo, 116
Oil refineries, 172
Okuda, Hiroshi, 161
Onan, 188
Optical instruments, foreign
    manufacture of, 28
Oracle, 205
Origins of the Urban Crisis (Sugrue), 98
Orr, James, 127
Osteoporosis treatment, 216–18
Outagamie County, WI, 76
Outsourcing, 25, 144–49
Overcapacity, 13
Owatonna Tool Co., 187
Owens Corning Fiberglass, 75
Ownership changes, manufacturing
    relocation and, 61

Pacific Rim countries, 127–28
Pages, Erik, 153, 155
Paker-Hannifin, 189
Paper industry, 76, 184–87
Partnerships, 199, 225–31, 237
Payne, Robert, 11
Payroll, 9
    growth trends, 53–54, 64
    relocation factors and, 61
    wage levels in northeast Indiana,
        42–43

Pennsylvania
  coal and, 83
  defense systems and, 83
  steel industry and, 78
  textile industry and, 91
  see also Philadelphia, PA;
    Pittsburgh, PA; specific counties
Pentagon terrorist attack, 191
Pentair Corp., 75, 184, 225, 227–28
Peoria County, IL, 245
Perkins, Anthony, 204
Perkins, Michael, 204
Peterbilt, 72
Petroleum industry, 19, 21
Pew Research Center, 191–92
Pfeffer, Jeffrey, 175
Pfister & Vogel, 130
Pfizer, 178
Pharmaceuticals, 72, 205
Philadelphia, PA, 11, 95–106, 109–10
  bond rating, 96–97
  manufacturing history, 95, 98–100
  loss of industrial base, 96–97, 98,
    101–4
  population decline, 97
  strengths of, 96
  textile industry, 105
  wage tax, 105–6
Philadelphia: Neighborhoods, Division
  and Conflict in a Postindustrial City,
  100
Philadelphia County, PA, 96
Pickens County, SC, 91, 93
Pima County, AZ, 76
Pittsburgh, PA, 243
Plain Talk (Iverson), 191
Plastics industry, 17, 19
Platte County, NE, 66
Polluted sites, 57, 83
Pontopoc County, MS, 67
Porter-Cable, 225–28
Postindustrialism, 100, 239, 240
Poughkeepsie, NY, 90–91
Poultry slaughtering, 67
Poverty, 113–14
  household income changes
    1989–1997, 113
Power generation machinery, 123

Power tools, 227
Prayer for the City, A (Bissinger), 97
Preston, Richard, 39
Price County, WI, 233
Price-cutting, 13
Price-to-sales ratios, 204–5
PricewaterhouseCoopers Money Tree
  Survey, 219
Primary metals industry, 19, 21, 22, 122
Pringles factory, 228
Printing industry, 87
Procter & Gamble, 228–29, 230
Product liability judgments, 58–59
Production, 6–7, 8
Productivity, 24–27
  gains, 10, 26
  Internet and, 24–25
  measurements of, 26
  multifactor, 26–27
  reports, 26
  unit labor costs, 26
Profits, by industry, 21–22
Prosperity, 1
  employment/payroll by industry,
    17–19
  income disparity, and
    manufacturing, 115–16
  productivity, and economic
    benefits, 24–27
  profits, by industry, 21–22
  value, rewards of adding, 22–24
Public services, 58
Public subsidies, 238–39
Publishing, 87
Purodenso, 228, 230
Pushes, Glenn, 40

Quaker Oats, 180
Qualcomm, 205
Quality of companies, 73, 234
Quinn, David, 43

Raleigh-Durham, NC, 213, 215
RAND Corp., 152
Raytheon Systems, 72, 155
Real estate, 26, 27, 111
Real gross domestic product per
  employee, 27

Recreational vehicle industry, 77, 146
Red Wing Shoe, 130–31, 232
Regulations, 58, 238
Reinert, John R., 14
Reitter & Schefenacker, 226
Relocation, 49–63
    attracting forces, 60–62
    changes in market tastes and, 53
    classifications, 49–50, 55
    company issues, 62–63
    by county, 51
    database, 49
    emotionalism and, 62–63
    management quality and, 52
    reasons for, 56–62
    repelling forces, 57–60, 95
Remington Rand, 137
Remmele Engineering, 177
Renault, 30
Rendell, Ed, 109
Republic Steel, 183
Research and development, 8–9,
    211–12
    corporate spending on, 213
    decline in spending on, 235
    industry classifications, 214
Research Triangle Institute, 218–19
Research Triangle Park, 8–9, 72,
    211–24, 245
Responding to Defense Dependence
    (Pages), 153
Restructurings, 90
Retail trade, 17
Rhone-Poulenc, 93
Richmond County, NC, 93
Ridgewater College, 67
Riley, Frank, 13, 14
Rise and Fall of Conglomerate Kings, The
    (Sobel), 182
Rise and Fall of New York City, The
    (Starr), 107
Rise of the Gunbelt, The (Markusen), 153
Robert Bosch, 158
Roberts, Edward O. Jr., 36
Rockingham County, VA, 69
Rockwell International, 227
Romack, Tim, 222
Rubber industry, 19

Rule of 70, 24
Russia, engineering degrees in, 140
Rutherford County, TN, 78

S.B. Foot Tannery, 130
S.C. Johnson, 145–46
Saltillo, Mexico, 139
Satellite facilities, 90
Saturn Corp., 69, 226
Schenectady County, NY, 93
Schmale, Gary, 66–67
Schmitt, John, 116
Schrock, Lincoln, 34, 35, 42, 43, 44–45
Schumpeter, Joseph, 196, 240
Schwinn Bicycle Company, 146–47
Scott County, KY, 78
Scott Paper, 195
Seagate, 138, 208
Sealed Power Piston Ring Co., 187
Sedgwick County, KS, 233–34
Sekora, Michael, 153
Semiconductors, 156
Seppa, Tapani, 172
Services, 7, 27, 111, 242
    productivity reports, 26
Shadell, Arthur, 99
Shanghai, 235
Shaw Industries, 203
Shelby County, OH, 78
Shipbuilding, 93
Shoes, foreign competition and, 93
Sikorsky Aircraft, 87
Singapore, 235
Sirower, Mark, 179–80
Skelton, Richard, 226
Skill transfers, 142, 234
Slater, Samuel, 83
Sliding Goliaths, 82, 85–87, 95, 248
    employment changes by sector,
    112
    government expenditures per
    capita, 114
    household income changes, 113
    manufacturing employment
    history, 258–60
Smaller sliders, 82, 91–94, 248
    employment changes by sector,
    112

Smaller sliders, *continued*
    household income changes, 113
    manufacturing employment
        history, 255–56
SMS Compact Strip Production
    machine, 45
SMSSchloemann-Siemag A.G., 38
Snafu, 224
Snapple, 180
SNE, 75
Snohomish County, WA, 72
Sobel, Robert, 182
Society of Manufacturing Engineers,
    30, 176
Solectron, 216
Sonoma, 77
Soros, George, 211
Souder, Mark, 44
South America, auto manufacturing
    and, 30
South Dakota, 53
Southeast Asia, auto manufacturing
    and, 30
Space race, 151
Spartanburg County, SC, 78
Spectrum Acquisitions, 226
"Spin-on," 153
Springfield, OH, 34
SPX Corp., 187–88, 189
St. Joseph County, IN, 93, 234
St. Paul's Port Authority, 83
Stafford, John, 35
Standard Industry Classification
    (SIC), 23, 249
Stanford, 9
Stanford Research Park, 213
State of Working America 2000–2001, The
    (Bernstein, Mishel, and Schmitt), 116
Stearns County, MN, 76
Steel Dynamics Inc., 32, 37, 40, 43,
    44–45
Steel industry, 37–40, 78, 80, 119, 234,
    242–43
    foreign suppliers, 141
    leadership and, 193
    minimills, 38, 242
    stock market and, 207
    trade deficits and, 122, 128–29

Stewardship, 197–98
Stillwell, Jerry, 161
Stock market, 201–10
    technical stocks, 201–2, 204–8,
        210
Stoecker, William, 101–2, 105
Stora Enso, 186
Stover, John, 207
Studebaker, 79
Styline Industries, 69
Subaru-Isuzu, 160, 164
Sugrue, Thomas, 98
Sunbeam Corp., 14, 195–96
Sunlaw Energy Corp., 171
"Supplier of the Year," 227
Suppliers, 234
    foreign, 138, 140–43
    shifting locations of, 60
Supply chain management, 145
Sweazy, Bill, 130, 131
Sweeney, John, 134
Synergy Trap, The (Sirower), 179–80

Talladega County, AL, 93
Taub Urban Research Center, 108
Taxes, 238
    manufacturing intensity and,
        114–15
    relocation and, 58, 61
Tazewell County, IL, 93, 245
Technical stocks, 201–2, 204–8, 210
Teets, Richard, 40
Teflon, 222
Tektronics, 72
Tennessee, 11
    employee training and, 229
    energy costs, 170
    see also specific counties
Tennessee Valley Authority (TVA),
    229–30
Terrorist attacks, 150–51, 156, 191–92
Testa, William, 15
Texas, 53
Textile industry, 83, 91, 105
    foreign competition and, 93
Thinsulate, 236
Thomas, Jeff, 229
Thornton, Jim, 137

3M, 67, 79–80, 137, 160, 236
3Tex, 4, 220–22, 232
Tice, David, 206–7, 208
Timken, 139
Timken, W.R. Jr., 5–6
Tippecanoe County, IN, 78
Tire industry, 207–8
Tool makers, foreign, 41, 241
Tool Products, 228
Toone, Russell, 226
Toyota, 30, 160, 161, 164, 210, 231
Trade deficit, 28, 119–35, 138–40, 142,
    234, 238
    balance slipping in key
        industries, 120–22
    China and the Pacific Rim,
        127–28
    larger deficits in key industries,
        122–25
    machine tools and, 12
    non-oil, 120–21
    Red Wing Shoe, 130–31
    rubber and plastic molds, 142
    U.S. dollar value and, 133
    U.S. imports/exports by country
        in 2000, 125–26
Train, Mark, 209
Transplants, 78, 158–65
Transportation
    equipment industry, 17, 19, 93
    manufacturing relocation and, 58,
        61
Travis County, TX, 72, 245
Triangle Pharmaceuticals, 218
Tropicana, 73
Troxler, William Jr., 220
Troxler Electronic Laboratories, 220
Truck manufacturers. See Auto and
    truck industry
TRW, 154
Tuscaloosa County, AL, 75, 78
Tyco International, 188, 189

U.S. Bureau of the Census, 249
U.S. Steel, 182, 242
UBS PaineWebber-Gallup, 202
Union Carbide, 93
Union County, NJ, 87

Union County, OH, 78
Unisys, 137, 180
Unit labor costs, 26
United Auto Workers, 52
United Nations Industrial
    Development Organization, 6
United States Commission on
    National Security/21st Century, 191
Univac, 138
Unova, 12
UPM-Kymmene, 185
Utah, 53

Valero Energy, 172
Value-added, 22–24
    foreign competition and, 28
Van de Ven, Andrew, 224
Vance County, NC, 93
Vermeer Manufacturing, 67
Vestil Manufacturing, 35
Volkswagen, 30, 160

Walden, Mike, 214
Wall Street, 201–10
War, defense spending and, 151
Warner & Swasey, 12
Warner-Lambert, 178, 240
Washington County, MN, 75
Washington County, OR, 72
Washoe County, NV, 76
Wayne County, MI, 87, 243
Weather, manufacturing relocation
    and, 61
Welch, Jack, 133–34, 188, 189
Westinghouse, 123
Whitfield County, GA, 77
Wholesale trade, 26, 27, 111
"Why Cisco Fell: Outsourcing and Its
    Perils," 147
Will, Chris, 181
Williams, Ted Sr., 224
Wilma (dry cleaning system), 211–12,
    223
Wilson, William Julius, 98
Winnebago, 146, 189
Winona County, MN, 78
Winona Knitting Mills, 132
Woodward, George, 77

Woodward, Pete, 132
Woodworking, 77
Work ethic, 60
"Workshop of the World" (WHYY documentary), 98, 110
World Health Organization, 217
World Trade Center attack, 191
World Trade Organization, 44, 127
World Wide Web, 152
Wyoming, 53

Xia Yuan Lin, 127

Young, Jeffrey, 147
Youngstown, OH, 244

Ziebarth, Todd, 97
Zimmer, J.O., 66
Ziptronix, 218–19
Zysman, John, 201

About the Authors

Fred Zimmerman is a professor of manufacturing systems engineering and international management at the University of St. Thomas in St. Paul, Minnesota. In 1985, he started the school's program in manufacturing engineering. He holds a Ph.D. in management from the University of Minnesota, and has taught at Universidad Catolica in Montevideo, Uruguay, and the Czech Management Center in Celevice, Czech Republic.

Zimmerman has spent more than 25 years in industry as an engineer, manager, vice president, and president, and has served on the boards of 14 corporations. He currently serves on the corporate boards of two of the companies mentioned in this book: Winnebago Industries and Bermo. He has written numerous professional and technical articles and two books, *The Turnaround Experience: Real-World Lessons in Revitalizing Corporations* and *The Relocation of Industry*. He resides in Minnetonka, Minnesota, with his wife, Joanell. The Zimmermans have five children and have hosted many foster children.

Dave Beal is a business columnist at the St. Paul Pioneer Press. Earlier, he was executive business editor at the paper and, before that, business editor at the Milwaukee Journal. He has a graduate degree in journalism from Syracuse University, and has been an adjunct instructor in the MBA program at the University of St. Thomas.

Beal has won numerous awards for his business reporting, including the INGAA-University of Missouri, John Hancock, and Overseas Press Club national competitions. Early in 1998, he received his newspaper's Special Achievement Award. He is a former president of the Society of American Business Editors and Writers. He resides in Roseville, Minnesota, with his wife, Caroline. The Beals have six children.

MANUFACURING WORKS

FOR SPECIAL DISCOUNTS on 20 or more copies of *Manufacturing Works: The Vital Link Between Production and Prosperity,* please contact Dearborn Trade Special Sales at 800-621-9621, extension 4410.

Dearborn™
Trade Publishing
A **Kaplan Professional** Company